# A NEW KIND OF NORMAL

**Alison Keenan**

ISBN: 978-1-9164953-0-2

Hope is the thing with feathers
That perches in the soul
And sings the tune without the words
And never stops at all


– Emily Dickinson

# ACKNOWLEDGEMENTS

I have to begin with my husband Colin, who believed in me sufficiently to buy me a computer, a desk and chair, and give me the impetus to write what until then, had only been in my head. Thank you for all that you are to me. To Justine Taylor my copy-editor who heard 'my voice', and taught me how to use emotion and words to bring my story to life. Huge gratitude to Veronica Strain who spent an inordinate amount of time working with me to make this book the best I could make it - V your insight and encouragement have been invaluable. My nephew Paul Tumber who designed this beautiful cover for me, but also in memory of his mother who died of breast cancer. To Caz Jones for proof reading my writing, and for Yvonne Betancourt, for turning my manuscript into a book with her fabulous formatting. I must also thank my colleagues Julia Roberts and Debbie Flint for all their help and advice in making the whole process of self-publishing so much simpler. And finally to all those of you who created the support network that is Ali's Army – forever in your debt.

# Introduction

The Great Room of The Grosvenor House Hotel was alive with colour, a predominantly pink hue bathing the backdrops and staging. The enormous crystal chandeliers cast their twinkling light over the vast number of designer clad diners, accentuating the fine fabrics and fabulous jewellery they were wearing. The atmosphere was electric and the sense of anticipation tangible at this, the fifteenth Breast Cancer Care Fashion Show.

Our table was right next to the catwalk and I'd already spotted Lisa Snowdon, Geri Halliwell and Vanessa Feltz amongst the equally glamorous but unknown individuals seated near to me. Shifting slightly in my seat I looked sideways at their faces, all fixated on Arlene Philips who was introducing the patron of the charity, Cherie Blair. My nerves were getting the better of me, and I felt an overwhelmingly strong desire to empty the glass of red wine I'd been nursing. I tried to focus my attention on Ms Blair instead, noticing, as I scanned the room before turning back to the stage, a number of women sitting unnaturally upright in their chairs, their immaculately coiffured hair just a little too perfect, their smiles a little too fragile. As I watched them, I reached up and ran my fingers through the fine tendrils of hair that had escaped from my up-do before curling my hands into my lap. Cherie finished her speech, and as the applause subsided, Arlene introduced me by name. I took a deep breath, stood up, and walked slowly towards the stage.

I'd been fine during the read through, and was hugely impressed with the hotel's amazing autocue system. It consisted of two completely clear glass-like screens which were visible only to the speaker and not to the audience, but as Cherie Blair left the podium, and walked gingerly down the short flight of steps, her right buttock whacked this elaborately placed piece of technology and left me with a one-sided view of the next six minutes! Undeterred – well, hoping to appear that way – I launched into my introduction, explaining that my employer, QVC, had been the official broadcaster of the Breast Cancer Care Fashion Show for the previous fifteen years and was very proud to support the Charity. As I spoke, I could hear the chinking of glasses and buzz of conversation and feeling ever so slightly distracted, I looked up and away from my script for a moment. For a split second my mind travelled. I'd been here just two years before – different dress, same remit – but somehow not. I took a deep breath and continued.

'We can all *try* and imagine what it's like to live

with cancer and its treatment, but until – God forbid – it happens to you, you don't really know.

'Of course tonight, wearing their finery and having had a complete makeover, our models will once again prove that this wretched disease won't beat them. And I have to be honest and tell you that if it weren't for a wig, false eyelashes, painted brows and a bit of padding I'd be standing here, looking more like Yoda in a dress!

'I was diagnosed with breast cancer on the eighteenth of January this year. Invasive lobular breast cancer, and it's a devious one. Doesn't show on a mammogram, ultrasound or MRI – a biopsy's the only way to detect it. Following a lumpectomy, mastectomy, total lymph clearance, six months of chemotherapy and fifteen radiotherapy sessions – my final one was last Friday – I can't quite believe I'm here tonight!'

There was an almost imperceptible ripple of applause and then silence, which I broke.

'So how has cancer changed my life over the last nine months? Well, I haven't been able to work since January, and that's been hard. I have missed my friends and that sense of purpose and belonging. I have however, saved a fortune on shampoos, conditioners, make-up and epilation – because girls *nothing* will ever be as effective as chemotherapy when it comes to hair removal! I've had to swap my lacy lingerie for sports bras to accommodate the rugby-ball-shaped expander that I have in place of my right breast. Reconstruction is planned for the spring when I'll lose my left breast too – and

that's on medical recommendation. I have found
it is *impossible* to fasten buttons or jewellery with
numb fingers, and yet *entirely possible* to feel hung
over and jetlagged without drinking any alcohol or
stepping on to a plane – the joys of chemo.'

The sound of loud laughter and applause filled
the room as I continued.

'I'd be lost in bed without my hat – it's bloody
freezing with no hair – I don't know how you bald
guys manage! Oh, except when you're having a hot
flush and then it's a godsend. That said I have yet to
find a double-sided tape that stays sticky and holds
your wig in place when you're sweating buckets!
I have discovered that pineapple is really good for
mouth ulcers, although it doesn't help nosebleeds.
There is a knack to applying false eyelashes, and it's
a knack I clearly don't have.

The rather fetching sleeve and glove I'm wearing is
to contain the Popeye-like proportions of my right
arm and hand, thanks to lymphedema. And I have
lost almost *all* of my once beautiful fingernails, and
both my big toenails. It's all part of the curative
treatment I've been given, and most of it will
improve... but it's crap when you're going through
it.'

'But I have got through it, and I feel lucky—'
I felt my voice start to waver, but was once again
interrupted by the sounds of stamping, whistling,
and cheering. Looking out at the sea of faces, I felt
tears prick my eyes. Reaching for the tissue I'd

hidden in my compression sleeve, I blew my nose rather loudly as the audience settled, and having apologised I continued, my words clear in the now silent room.

'I feel lucky because I'm still here. I have been loved, supported and carried through this seemingly never-ending tunnel by the medical professionals, my family, and my wonderful friends. We all understand there are no promises at the end of the treatment, and I'll be on Tamoxifen for the next five years, but my daughter Lucy told me I had to get better forever... and so I'll keep praying that one day they will find something to make us *all* better, forever.'

The audience erupted into a frenzy of whoops and applause, and gave me my first-ever standing ovation and the only one the charity had seen in their fifteen-year history! I stood for a moment in disbelief, before looking over to the table where I could see my then partner, now husband Colin, my daughter Lucy and a number of my closest friends. And that's when the tears came. The sense of relief overwhelmed me. Not just that I'd got through the speech, but that I'd got through the previous ten months. And yet that's what anyone finding themselves in this situation has to do: there is no other option.

That moment was over seven years ago. It's been a long haul, but I'm still here to tell the tale, and over those years I have been asked so many times by so many people to write it all down. Everything. From my finding the first lump, through my diagnosis, my treatment, my reconstructive surgery, and most importantly my recovery. And so finally, after an inordinate number of false starts, I have. I'd be lying if I said I hadn't written it for myself, because it's been an incredibly cathartic thing to do, but I've also written it for all those of you who may receive a diagnosis of breast cancer one day; all those of you who already have; all those of you who know and love someone who is living with this disease, and for all those of you who have lost someone to it.

No two experiences are the same and I can only tell you of my own. However, as I said in my speech, I have been lucky, and I want to assure anyone who treads the same path I have, or anyone supporting those who do, that there is *always* hope. You can get through it, and I pray you will, as I have done. I hope that this book may be a comfort and support to you.

Stay strong, lean on those who love you, and never forget to look for the silver linings… they're always there.

# CHAPTER ONE

It's Sod's law when you get to bed late, there's invariably something that'll wake you far earlier than you'd choose. I was on my own that morning when my mobile rang at 7.30am, and as I'd worked a late shift and not got into bed until 3am, I was in a deep sleep. The irritating ring tone pierced my subconscious, and as I fumbled around in the dark trying to find the phone, I was already worrying that it might be one of my children, or maybe my mum.

'Hello?' I mumbled, trying to focus on my phone in the gloom. I was very surprised to hear my breast consultant introduce himself, apologising for calling so early.

'I did try you twice last night, but couldn't get through. I have the biopsy results and I have to tell you that they've come back as indeterminate. Therefore we will need to do a tissue biopsy to make a definitive diagnosis.'

I was tangled up in my duvet when he said this, and having lost my balance, I fell off the bed in a rather untidy heap. I didn't have time to disentangle myself before he went on to explain that I'd have to come back to the hospital as a day patient because I'd need a general anaesthetic for the biopsy. He was hoping to find space for me in theatre the following Wednesday.

'Please try not to worry, Alison. It is only precautionary because the fine-needle biopsy wasn't all that clear.'

'So when you say indeterminate, what exactly do you mean?' I asked, propping myself up against the divan.

'I can't really say until we have actually look at the tissue itself, and I promise I'll be back to you as soon as I can with an appointment.'


I guess we all react differently when hearing something we'd rather not know, but this wasn't the first abnormal result I'd had. With a history of lumpy breasts, and endless ultrasounds and biopsies, I'd had several, but always, on further examination, they'd turned out to be nothing. And so, having thanked my consultant, although in truth I wasn't remotely grateful for the news he'd given me, I unravelled myself from the bed linen and told myself not to be daft, as it was unlikely to be anything this time either. I rubbed my thumb over the ridge on my right breast and tried not to allow myself to think of the unthinkable, but I was tired and that always makes me a bit antsy. Under normal circumstances I would have called Colin, my partner of the last three years, but as we were – to coin that very American phrase – 'on a break,'

I thought it might look as though I was trying to get a sympathy vote, especially if it turned out to be nothing. I knew I wouldn't get back to sleep again with all that buzzing around in my head, and so I decided to get up and shower instead. After prepping online for my shift, I sorted out my emails, then my bedroom, and headed off to meet two of my good friends from work, Kathy and Debbie. I work as a presenter for QVC the Shopping Channel and had started there in the year 2000, which is where I'd met them. We all had similar working backgrounds, and had joined the presentation team within six months of each other.

I think it's really important at this juncture for me to mention my friends, although in truth they probably deserve a chapter all to themselves! I've been very lucky and blessed all my life to have been surrounded by a group of incredible people – men and women – who have been more like family than friends to me. Yo and Roz appear regularly in this book because they were right by my side throughout the following months and have remained there. Yo's real name is Jo, but I've called her Yo since we met at secondary school when we were eleven years old and the nickname has stuck. I'd initially addressed her as Yohannasburg Edgewise, God knows why, but realising it was far too long to be practical, I'd shortened it to Yo. She was invariably one of the first people I'd call when there was an issue, but I was hesitant this time. I'd 'cried wolf' in the past and caused her to worry unnecessarily, and knowing that she'd be just as concerned this time, I decided to keep it to myself until I was given the all clear. Roz and I had also been at the same school, but it wasn't until we were in our thirties that we became friends, and because of her nursing background, I'd confided in her about the initial needle biopsy. She'd been very supportive, but confident that it would be nothing – I didn't quite know how to tell her either.

The previous ten years had seen myself, Kathy and Debbie working a four day week at QVC, and so it was a rare occurrence for all of us to be free at the same time. Lunches together were few and far between, but one thing you could never accuse a QVC presenter of being, is lost for words. We had a great time; chatting, catching up on things and putting the world to rights, but as we gathered up our belongings ready to leave, Debbie turned and asked me if I'd heard anything after the needle biopsy I'd had on Tuesday. I had completely forgotten that I'd told her about it, and the protracted pause that followed caused them both to stop what they were doing and look at me.

I sat back down on the chair with a somewhat dramatic thud, not that I have a particularly huge backside, you understand, it was just that the weight of not saying anything had worn heavily on me.

'Look, I'm sure it's nothing, but they think they've found something in the biopsy. The consultant called me this morning and said the result was "indeterminate", whatever that means.'

Kathy sat down next to me and put her hand on mine. 'It probably means just that, Ali. I bet it's nothing. You've been here before.'

'You're right. Anyway, he wants to take a tissue sample or some sort of biopsy just to make sure, and he said he's going to try and squeeze me in next Wednesday.'

'I think I'm on shift, but I'm sure I could wangle a day off if you need me to take you?' said Debbie.

'No, honestly it's fine. As Kathy says, it'll be nothing, and I'm not working that day anyway. Seriously, I feel better for having told you both. Don't worry, or you'll make me worry!'

As soon as I got back to work I decided I would call Yo. Having explained the situation to the girls, it didn't feel right not to tell her. Besides, their positive comments had bolstered me. As always she was measured yet supportive.

'Oh sweetie I'm sorry, I'm sure you're right and it's nothing, but I know you're worried. Look, I reckon I could get cover for the school run on Wednesday, so why don't I come over the night before? I could take you into hospital then?'

'Are you sure? That'd be great. I could make you something for dinner and we could share a bottle of something nice!'

'That sounds like a plan! Have you told Colin?'.

'No, I don't want to. It won't be anything, and I really want to try and stick with this whole thing of not being in touch at the moment. I think this would sound like an excuse.'

"Probably best" she said, confirming that she'd be with me at seven on Tuesday.

As agreed, Yo stayed with me, and all things

considered, I slept pretty well that night – though perhaps the bottle of wine helped! We were up early that morning, and arrived at the hospital in plenty of time to be taken to my own little private room. I had continued with my private health care when I moved to Bedfordshire, and the wait time was almost non-existent. Hospital rooms all look the same to me, very neat and orderly, comfortable and clean, but sometimes a little daunting. Not that day though, as Yo had me laughing out loud in the car on the way to the hospital, regaling me with stories of highly improbable medical intervention while under anaesthetic, and so my mood was light. We were welcomed to the hospital and chaperoned to the allocated room where the nurse showed us where the various call buttons and light switches were. I was given a gown and the obligatory pair of paper pants to wear, plus a form to fill in. Having made sure I had a pen to carry out the latter, the nurse left the room.

The first question on the form requiring an answer was 'General description of appearance on admission to hospital?' We couldn't work this one out at all and became quite ridiculous suggesting things like 'dishevelled, lost, could've made more of an effort, and clearly unwell...!' I have since learned from Roz, who was a nurse for many years that this question is always asked, just in case somebody is found wandering around the hospital and doesn't remember who they are or why they are there. The staff would then have a description of how they looked and what they were wearing when they were admitted, which of course makes absolute sense. However, as we weren't in possession of this nugget of information, we continued working our way through the form inventing all kinds of ludicrous answers.

'Any notable scars or birthmarks?'

'You could always mention your episiotomy?' suggested Yo with a smirk.

'It's hardly notable or even noticeable!' I said.

'It depends where they're looking!'

'My paper pants will be my protector!'

'One fart and you'd be through those!' she said with authority.

Laughing, I moved on to the next question. 'It says here I've got to mention anything I'm allergic to.'

'That's easy: the colour beige and men with facial hair.'

'Not you, me! It's all about me!'

We were snorting with laughter at this point. Heaven only knows what the patients in the adjoining rooms were thinking! This hysteria made it very difficult for me to get out of my clothes, and into my surgical gown and paper pants! I'm never very sure which way round you're supposed to wear either of them, so I had some tapes tied and some not, and one leg in and one out of my drawers when the door opened and my consultant walked in.

Without raising his head from the file of notes that he was holding, he said 'Good morning' and then proceeded to tell me that cancer was graded in numbers – from one to number five, and that the result from the cells he had taken was "currently a number three." He was standing in front of me with his head bowed over the notes.

I looked over his shoulder at Yo and mouthed the words, 'What the...?'

'It's okay pet, it's okay,' she mouthed back at me, but I felt butterflies begin to move in my tummy.

Raising his head the surgeon focused his eyes on mine.

'I'm planning to take just a small sample from one of the lumps, making the margins as wide as possible. I am hopeful there won't be anything sinister in the there.'

'Wouldn't it make more sense to take the whole lot? I mean if it is cancerous, wouldn't it be better to take it all?'

'If I do that, you'd probably be left with a fairly large dent on that part of your breast.'

'Seriously, I'd rather have a dent than something left behind that might cause a problem.'

'Well if you're happy with that, that is what I will do' he said and kindly patted my hand. Having told me that the anaesthetist would be in to talk to me shortly, he left the room. I felt my legs buckle underneath me and I sat down with a thump on the side of the bed.

Yo came straight over and put her arm around me. 'Well done, poppet. No point in fannying around and only take a bit of it. Once it's gone, you'll feel better. Think of all the biopsies you've already had?'

'I know, but they've never actually said cancer

before.'

'They just want to be certain, Ali. Everything's going to be fine, girly-wirly. I really believe that.'

'Thanks, Yo.' I said, looking directly at her, and holding on to her words while taking comfort from them, as I always have done.

When I came round from the anaesthetic, I had a huge sticking plaster across my breast. The morphine made it pretty much impossible for me to have any serious thoughts, but while I was in recovery my consultant came to see me and said he'd taken all three lumps and I wasn't to worry as they had all looked the same. I didn't know what to make of his comment, but was just glad that, although I felt a little uncomfortable, the worst was over. Yo and I made light work of the substantial sandwiches that were brought to the room, and then she drove me home, telling me to call her *whenever* I needed to.

I went back to work the next day and had to choose clothes that would hide my rather large dressing. I still have the black satin blouse I wore that day to present my jewellery hour, complete with the safety pin I'd used to make the material cover my plaster. I hadn't realised until that day, just how much of my working wardrobe consisted of low-necked tops! I sold a great deal of jewellery on QVC, and necklaces and pendants look far better next to the skin rather than against material. On a lighter note, there are literally thousands of photographs and short videos of my cleavage, on a website called TV Babes! I thought it was a bit creepy initially, although maybe a tad flattering now, but I haven't had the courage to look at them since my surgery.

Of course it wasn't just my friends who knew about the lumpectomy. I had told my mum and my children about the tissue biopsy, although I'd assured them it was nothing to worry about, reminding them *all* of the situation five years previously, when I'd had a multiple biopsy that had turned out to be nothing. I have three children, Lucy being the eldest. At that time she was twenty-five years old, my son Sam had just turned twenty-one, and Jack my youngest child, almost eighteen. I didn't tell them that the consultant had said it was cancer. I was still half hoping that he would have been able to take it all when he'd carried out the biopsy. However, I did promise them that as soon as I had any news, I would call. I decided to go back on my decision and rang Colin.

'Hi there, how are you?'

'I'm okay. Plodding along.'

'I know we said we wouldn't call each other, but I've had a bit of bad news.'

'What's the matter?'

'Well, you know that lump on my boob, the one I had checked out last summer? They've done a tissue biopsy, and they think it may be cancer.'

I heard him take a breath in.

'Oh God. Ali, I'm so sorry. Is there anything I can do?'

I didn't know what to say. There was a part of me that would have given anything to see him, to have him hold me and make me feel better in the way only he knew how, but I didn't want him to think I was using this as an excuse. I tried to stay strong in my resolve.

'No it's fine. I'm fine.'

'You've had scares before though, like last summer. I'm sure this will be okay. When will they have the results?'

'They said a week.'

'Promise me you'll let me know. Please.'

'I will, I promise.' I said.

Neither of us spoke. I missed him. I wished I could tell him I loved him and that I was scared, and that I wanted him with me.

'Take care, Babygirl.'

'And you. You too my Bear.'

As the surgery had taken place on the Wednesday my consultant assured me that he should have the results within a week. And so began what felt like the longest wait of my life.

# CHAPTER TWO

The seven days rolled into eight, then nine, and although I did everything I could to distract myself from thinking about the possible outcome, it was damned near impossible. While I was waiting for news, I went to a previously planned get together with five girlfriends of mine who still lived in the village I'd moved to when Jack was just three years old. Suzanne, Sue, Diane, Deb and Julie are about as good a bunch of friends anyone could ever ask for. We have shared so much over the last twenty odd years or so, and between us have eighteen children!

We'd planned the afternoon at a local spa months before, but I now wouldn't be able to have a back massage or get into the hot tub with my friends because of my blasted procedure and the plaster that covered the stitches. I was highly pissed off about it! Most of our girlie gatherings were fuelled by a fair amount of alcohol and this was no different. Of course the more I drank, the more maudlin I became. I hadn't wanted to bang on about it all, but I think I pretty much monopolised the conversation. The girls were very sweet and very positive, and raised my spirits somewhat, but I have to admit that my mood was lifted completely when I made the decision to have my eyebrows tinted. Sounds rather random I know, but it was one of the treatments that had been planned for the day, and as I have very light brows I decided to go a tad darker... Think Groucho Marx! I was absolutely horrified, then hysterical with laughter, and the complete look of surprise I had on my face because of my brows, made most folk who saw me over the next three days continually ask 'What?' ... I still have the photo I took of myself to send to my sister, which always makes me laugh.

That was the last real laugh I had for a while, because on Tuesday the 18th January, I was finally given my results.


I'd expected to hear from the nurse on the Monday, but by four in the afternoon there was still no phone call so I rang the hospital and managed to get through to her. She apologised profusely and said they'd been running more tests, which could only be carried out by a senior radiographer. She said that the results would be in the following day, and asked me to come to the evening clinic where my consultant would go through them with me. I thanked her and hung up, feeling instantly annoyed that I hadn't suggested he just tell me over the phone tomorrow night instead of me having to head all the way into the hospital. However, my annoyance was almost immediately replaced with a sick feeling in my stomach. Why did he want to tell me in person? Should I fear the worst?

I was glad that I was working, and a late shift too, so I was pretty knackered when I got home but I didn't sleep well that night. The day itself dragged interminably with me playing stupid mind games along the lines of 'what if?' and 'nah, not a chance.' My usual gambit of believing it's never bad news until you're told it's bad news wasn't working so, perched on a dining room chair I decided to write a text on my phone saying everything was fine, which I planned to send to my family and friends who were waiting on the result. I saved it in my drafts folder and put my phone away.

As I've already mentioned, my partner Colin and I were living separately at the time and although in contact occasionally, we were still struggling through our issues. Lucy had said she would take me to the hospital to get the results, but I really didn't want her to. If it was cancer, I didn't think I could bear to have one of my children with me when I was told. I didn't know how I would react if it was bad news – none of us do really do we? What I did know though, was that if my girl was with me, then I wouldn't want to fall apart in front of her – my instinct to protect would come to the fore and I'd want to hold it together, but I didn't know if I'd be able to. I asked Colin to take me instead.

Of course, the very fact I had thought it through at all, meant that deep down was the very real fear that after all the years of dodging this disease, it had finally caught up with me.

I hadn't seen Colin for over a fortnight when he arrived at the cottage. From the window I watched him walk down the path, his jaw set, his eyes focused resolutely on the front door. When I opened it, his large frame filled the doorway and he immediately put his arms around me. Listening to his heart through the soft wool of his jumper, I allowed myself for a split second to believe it was going to be all right. He gently put his hand on the side of my face and I looked up at him.

'Hello my Bear.'

'Hello, Babygirl. Are you okay?'

'Not really.' I admitted. 'We'd best get it over with eh?'

He hugged me tightly. 'It's going to be all right Ali.'

I so wished I believed him, but my heart was playing hopscotch and my head was in mess. It is what it is, I told myself, but what if that meant cancer??

I carried on playing these mind games for pretty much our entire journey to the hospital, planning to sit on the blue seats rather than the grey in the waiting room, because they were lucky. Thinking about my shift that evening, because of course it would be good news and I could go straight on to work. Believing that if we found a parking space straight away in the busy car park, then all would be well. Hoping that I wouldn't need to change into a gown, because the consultant wouldn't need to examine me, as there was nothing to worry about.

Well, we found a parking space straight away, and once inside the hospital, I made my way towards a blue seat in the waiting room; Colin had to sit on the grey one. Our bottoms had barely had chance to warm the upholstery before the nurse came through the door.

'Alison Keenan?'

I looked up into the face of a woman young enough to be my daughter, her turquoise uniform clashing a little with the thick black opaque tights she wore. I remember thinking it odd she had to ask my name as Colin and I were the only ones in the waiting room. 'That'll be me,' I said, sitting bolt upright and reaching out for Colin's hand, which felt unusually cold. I suddenly had an overwhelming urge to wee, but thought I'd better wait.

'The consultant's ready for you, if you'd like to come with me? Both of you?' she asked as Colin and I stood up.

'Yes, if that's okay?' I replied, looking sideways at Colin, who was nodding in agreement.

'Of course,' the nurse replied, in a slightly jollier way than I felt was necessary.

Awkwardly, as though we were in a three-legged

race, we walked together behind the nurse into a little consulting room on the right, where my consultant greeted me. All I could think of as she gestured for us to sit was that I hadn't been asked to change into a gown! Yay!

I could draw you a picture of the consultant's room right now, with the exact position of the clock on the wall, and the time at 5:40 p.m. There was a green plastic frog sitting on his desk, possibly a present from one of his children or there to distract someone if they were upset. There was also a box of tissues, which weren't Kleenex, but some thin and scratchy-looking alternative. Bit cheap, I thought, considering this was a private hospital...

'I am really sorry that it has taken us so long to get back to you, but we needed to be absolutely certain. As you have probably gathered by now, the results are not good.'

I took a deep breath and looked directly into the dark brown eyes of the consultant. They held my gaze, as he leaned slightly forwards, the expression on his handsome and now familiar face almost sad. 'You have invasive lobular carcinoma of the right breast, and we will need to perform a mastectomy...'

There was silence.

'Do you understand what I have told you?' he asked gently.

I exhaled, nodded slowly, and my world tilted.

I felt Colin's arm, warm and heavy, around my shoulder but I shifted my gaze to the consultant's immaculately tailored suit and matching tie.

'We will need to carry out an ultrasound of your lymph nodes, although I don't believe we will find anything there, and then I'd like you to have an MRI scan to make sure this is the only tumour. I am truly sorry.'

Only then did I bury my face in Colin's chest while fighting back the tears. This couldn't be right? Surely? I wanted to howl, but felt I couldn't. Not there, not then, not in front of them all. All my prayers, all of my hopes, all my positive thoughts had been worthless. I had cancer.

The consultant handed me a tissue and I wiped my eyes, swallowing awkwardly before asking him how soon he'd need to carry out the surgery. He explained that there were other scans he would have to carry out first, as if the cancer was only in *one* part of the breast, then I may only need a partial mastectomy, but they wanted to be certain. The breast care nurse smiled kindly at me, and Colin tightened his grip on my shoulder. No one spoke.

In that instant I had the crazy idea that perhaps I could make a run for it. I could get out of this scenario that I'd had played so many times over in my head during the last fourteen days. I shifted in my chair but just as I felt I had enough energy to get the hell out of there, I was told that they'd like to do the ultrasound of the lymph nodes under my arm *now*, before I left. They would then be in touch with dates and times for the other tests. I suddenly felt unbelievably weary and looked up at Colin, who, with his thumb, gently wiped away the tears that were trickling unwittingly down my face. He helped me to my feet and then held my hand tightly as we followed the nurse out of the room and along the corridor towards the Imaging Department of the hospital.

Having left Colin outside in a separate waiting room, I found myself in a small and chilly little room that was occupied by the radiographer. Lying on the narrow bed with my right arm above my head, I tried not to shiver as she ran the transducer around and up into my armpit. It wasn't just fear that was making me feel cold, but also the fact I was naked from the waist up, and had a large amount of conductive gel squeezed on to my chest, that I swear she must have taken out of a fridge! I craned my neck to see if I could look at the screen.

'What are you looking for?' I asked her. I sounded completely different, my voice harsh and flat.

'We just want to make sure that none of the lymph nodes are enlarged.'

I lay my head back on the pillow 'You mean if they're enlarged they're cancerous?'

'Not necessarily,' she said 'but it's useful to be made aware of any changes.'

I didn't want to ask any more questions, so while she applied a gentle pressure, I just closed my eyes and prayed.

# CHAPTER THREE

Of course, as you've probably worked out by now, this bombshell came after almost fifteen years of regular breast check-ups, mammograms, ultrasounds, fine-needle aspirations and biopsies, *all* of them negative. The most recent had been just six months before and yet I had managed to dodge this cruel and crafty cancer all that time.

Like my mother, I've always had lumpy breasts, but the first time I'd ever felt concerned, was when I was in my mid-thirties. I found a lump that felt like a pea on my left breast, just a little way round from my armpit. I spent several weeks fiddling with it, before speaking to my then husband Tommy and deciding to head off to the One Stop Breast Clinic in Shrewsbury, close to where I lived at the time. I remember we had to drop the children off at my mum's and then get to the clinic. There, I was given a mammogram, and after that was read, I was told I would need a fine-needle aspiration of the lump so that they could take some tissue for analysis. Having been ushered into a little side room, a heavy-handed nurse proceeded to push a large needle into the lump and then pump away at it many times to draw the tissue out. It hurt like hell, although I didn't say anything. After getting dressed somewhat shakily, I headed out to reception where my husband was waiting. We were told it would be at least an hour before they would have the results and so, while I cried quietly, he drove me to a petrol station where we bought some paracetamol and a bottle of water.

'It won't be anything,' I insisted.

'I know,' he replied.

But of course deep down, I didn't really believe that. I hadn't thought for one moment they would need to take any tissue for a biopsy, and had truly believed they'd do the mammogram and then give me the all clear. My youngest child was just a year old and I had a fabulous job working for the BBC. My marriage was strong and happy, but this had the potential to change everything.

When I'm nervous I tend to focus on as many different things as possible, so that my mind can't allow itself the luxury of concentrating on just the one terrifying thought. I remember the chairs in that particular consultant's office were grey while the carpet was navy blue, and the very faded green and yellow curtains had clearly been overlooked in the recent refurbishment.

'Well, I'm delighted to tell you that there are no abnormalities in this tissue sample so nothing to worry about at all. You do though have very lumpy breasts and mild fibro-cystic disease in both, so check them regularly, and if you find anything else, do come and see us.' I could have kissed him, but instead gave him one of my biggest smiles and, reaching for my husband's hand, we both stood up and left the room.

Some years later, I found another lump on same breast, in the upper quadrant just above the nipple. The fact that the nipple had become inverted was actually what had alerted me to the lump. It felt quite large – in fact more like two lumps – but I knew that it might well disappear or reduce over my twenty-eight-day cycle. To be honest, I was more distressed about the nipple that stubbornly refused to react normally, and had become noticeable – by its absence – through my clothing. I was at that time, still working in radio, but also appearing regularly with my husband on *This Morning*. We had been taken on to present the Granada TV daytime show while Richard Madeley and Judy Finnigan were away. Because I could, I spoke to Dr Chris Steele, their resident doctor about my concerns, and he suggested I get it checked out. 'Better to be told it's nothing than leave it,' he said, and of course he was right.

Our local GP in the Bedfordshire village we'd moved to, was absolutely charming, and having looked at my nipple – it took him a while to find it – he said he would happily refer me to a surgeon at the Stoke Mandeville Hospital who could put a running stitch around the edge of it, and then it should just pop out! Relieved, although a little embarrassed, I was then asked to jump up on to the couch so that he could examine the lumps. This doctor was a true gent, but I have to admit to being somewhat confused when he knelt on the floor by the side of me before reaching up and over me to gently examine my right breast... I thought I was going to laugh and had to ask him why was he on the floor. He looked up at me from his kneeling position and explained that this way he applied less pressure and would easily feel anything suspect. Yes, he could feel the lumpy area, but then he could feel several, and felt sure they were all part of the fibro-cystic disease that had been noted all those years before. Mightily relieved, I hopped off the couch, and headed to the local supermarket to get something special for tea to celebrate.

I think I was in the freezer aisle when my mobile phone started ringing. The doctor I had just left twenty minutes earlier was calling to explain apologetically that an inverted nipple could well be the sign of something sinister, and he really should have realised this. He told me he had made an appointment for me at the One Stop Breast Clinic at Harpenden, and I must head there immediately to get it checked. I immediately thought of my three children who were then aged four, seven and eleven. They remained in the front of my mind throughout the following week, when following an ultrasound, I was subsequently referred to the local hospital for a multiple core biopsy. This was to be done under general anaesthetic as it's quite an invasive and painful procedure, and I was told I would have a week to wait before the results were through. My girlfriends from the village took me into hospital that day, and waited with me until I was taken to theatre. My husband – who was very involved with his radio career at that time – then picked me up and took me home, and so began the waiting game...

Apart from the obvious side effects of the anaesthetic, my only other visible symptoms were an enormously swollen right breast, which was so bruised it looked far more like an aubergine than a boob! Three large plasters were stuck over the incisions and God was it sore.

Of course the less noticeable, but far more exhausting, psychological side effect was the worry, constantly there, gnawing away at me in the wee small hours, and breaking my concentration during the daytime. I would fall asleep dreaming of the kind of music I should like to have played at my funeral, what the children would wear to the ceremony and who would look after them if my husband couldn't cope. Our lives were busier and his work took precedence over most things – he didn't manage well when I wasn't firing on all cylinders. I was asked to present *This Morning* on my own during that week long wait, but had to decline as I didn't feel I would be able to concentrate sufficiently to carry a two-hour live show. The editor said she thought I was 'stoic' and as my addled brain wouldn't allow me to remember the meaning of this I had to look it up in the dictionary! This was my dream job and had literally changed the course of my career, but the fear of cancer overrode everything, seeping into my psyche like a fog.

After seven days of hell, and a half hour wait to see the breast specialist, my husband and I were ushered into a large and airy consulting room where we were told that I was absolutely fine; the multiple biopsies had been completely clear and, although I should continue with my regular breast checks, there was no need for a follow up. I could also go ahead and have the nipple inversion rectified.

Relieved? I have never known a feeling like it. And when I picked my children up from school that day and hugged them so tightly they complained, I thanked God for having given me this chance.

# Chapter Four

I'm a great list maker, and slightly fanatical about prioritising events, but these last two weeks had made a mockery of my once orderly life. The breast surgeon's words kept playing over in my mind, and although what he'd said was pretty much what I'd feared, I'd just kept on hoping and believing, until the word 'cancer' was uttered.

Being the bearer of bad tidings is never easy. There is an innate sense of guilt attached to imparting that kind of news to others. Your truth will become their truth, and the ripple effect is far reaching. Ironically, it's the ones who you least want to tell who you have to speak to first.

When my father died very suddenly aged just fifty-four, I had to tell my grandparents the devastating news that their only child had died of a heart attack. There had been no warning, no previous illness or symptoms, and I had spent the best part of the entire day with him before his death.

Lucy was just eighteen months old, and while she slept we put *our* world to rights. He talked a little about how leaving home and the three of us children had been incredibly hard, and although

he hadn't seen us that often, he had never stopped
thinking about us. I had been just nine years
old that Christmas when he'd packed his bag
on Boxing Day and moved out of our lives. My
dad was enigmatic, charismatic, charming and
handsome, well that's how I always saw him. When
I was sixteen I learned of the numerous affairs
he'd had and how he'd broken my mum's heart;
I just couldn't see how this was the same man.
To me, he was kind and funny; he'd always been
complimentary and encouraging and had seen the
good in me. He enjoyed my company and I his.
The last day we spent together was no exception.
'There's life in the old dog yet,' he said as he kissed
me goodbye that afternoon. He died just five hours
later.

Several weeks after his death, when his wife
was clearing the house they had shared, she gave
me a large shoebox. Inside it were all the letters,
postcards, birthday and Father's Day cards I'd sent
to him over the previous eighteen years. He'd kept
every one of them.

Telling my grandparents that their only child
had died was possibly one of the hardest things
I've ever done in my entire life. Their despair was
devastating. My grandfather passed away just a
year later, followed shortly by my grandmother; I
firmly believe they both lost the will to live. I felt
hollow, exactly as I had done all those years before
when Dad had left home, except this time I had
lost him forever. My own feelings of sorrow were
overshadowed because of the pain I had caused my

grandparents. It is something I have never been at peace with.

There is never anywhere really private in a hospital or clinic, with most walkways and waiting rooms full of patients and people. So I waited until Colin and I were back in the car before I called Lucy. I heard the sharp intake of breath when I told her my diagnosis, and then fought back my tears as she did her best to cover her own. I asked if she would pick Sam and Jack up and bring them back home to me where I would explain everything. The next person I called was my mum who cried, saying she felt terribly guilty. I didn't really understand what she meant, telling her that there was nothing to be guilty of. I really couldn't deal with such a thought at that moment, so when she asked if I would like her to call my sister Jenny, I told her that I felt I should let her know, and explained that I had a long list and was working my through it. The falsely cheery text I'd written several hours earlier stayed in the drafts section of my phone as I rang each member of my family and friends individually. Before I could dial Roz's number, she'd called me from the hospice where she worked as a palliative nurse. I told her it wasn't good news, and I remember her soft reassuring voice telling me that we would sort it. Years later she admitted that once she knew, although she accepted it was my diagnosis, for those who loved me, the abject fear that they might lose me was terrifying. Speaking with her reminded me that I had to call work as well, because I'd expected to go in and do my shift that night. Once again, my news was greeted with noticeable concern and sadness, but complete understanding.

I felt like a parrot going over and over the same thing, and each time I explained that it was indeed cancer, the tears came. My poor sister was devastated, this being the second time she'd been told that another close family member had cancer. She had been for a check-up when our mum was diagnosed just six months earlier, but I could tell she was genuinely shocked and scared. She said she'd get over to see me just as soon as she could, and told me to try not to worry. I ended the call, apologising several times to Colin who was driving, as we'd barely spoken to each other since we got into the car. He just reached across and put his hand on my leg, telling me not to worry.

As we drove down the bumpy road that led back to the cottage, I felt sick. I really didn't want to have to tell my sons, although I knew that the very fact their sister had driven them both to the cottage meant they had probably guessed. Our headlights caught the back of Lucy's car as we swung on to the kerb to park, and I choked back a sob. I had assumed Colin would come in with me, but he felt very strongly that my children, particularly my boys, might try and put a brave face on it if he was there. It wasn't going to be easy, he knew that, but he would be right outside if I needed him. He was correct of course, but I felt at a complete loss. I clung on to him for just a moment before getting out of the car. My legs were like lead weights but mentally, I felt like a piece of cotton in the wind as I walked towards the little gate and moved down the garden path towards the front door.

Lucy must have heard the car as she opened the door before I'd even got my hand on the latch. 'It's going to be all right, Mum,' she whispered into my neck as she wrapped her arms around me, and I leaned into her, the rough texture of her coat scraping my face. I screwed my eyes up tightly to stop the tears. 'I love you,' she said as she let go of me gently, and whispering the same sentiment back to her, I squeezed her hand.

Not trusting myself to speak, I took a deep breath. My boys, Sam and Jack, were sitting on the sofa. They didn't get up, both looking straight at me, their faces the colour of putty. I put my handbag down on the floor, and walked towards them, and perching on the edge of the coffee table, I leaned forwards so that I could have some form of contact with them.

'I don't know what to say really, or how to say it, and you've probably guessed, but they've told me it's cancer and I'm going to need a mastectomy. Quite probably chemotherapy too. But hopefully now they know, they can make me better.'

'Mum…' Jack's voice broke as he started to cry.

'It's all right, pet, I'm going to be all right, I promise,' I said, my arms around them both; willing myself to believe it.

Sam sniffed loudly.

'Please don't worry.' My voice was muffled by

his jumper. 'They're really nice at the hospital and they're going to get things moving as soon as they can, so we don't have too long to wait.'

I sat back slightly, but kept my hands on their knees, although I wanted to dry my tears.

'When have you got to go in?' Sam asked, wiping his eyes roughly with his sleeve.

'I'm not sure really, they've got a few more tests to do.'

'It's not anywhere else is it?' asked Jack.

'Don't be daft, Jack, why would it be?' Sam said abruptly.

Why not? I thought, but responded reassuringly.

'I doubt it, Jack, I think it's something I've had for a while, but we didn't realise.'

Again, the silence sat significantly between us. I've wondered sometimes since then, if it's harder for sons to hear their mother has a diagnosis of breast cancer as opposed to say lung or bowel cancer? Purely because of the connotation and the obvious physical changes after surgery? Maybe because it's a part of a woman's body that takes on a different meaning to boys once they're older, and is awkward when associated with their mother. I'm not sure, but I know they struggled.

'Is there anything else I can tell you, or you want to know?'

'It's more than I wanted to know.' Sam said in a small voice.

I caught his gaze.

'I'm so sorry, Mum,' he said, his eyes dark with tears. 'For all of it.'

I shook my head slowly and softly told him it was okay.

'Me too. I'm sorry too Mum,' added Jack, reaching for my hand with his cold fingers and squeezing it. I looked at my sons, men now, but always my boys to me. I used to be able to kiss them and make it better, but not this time.

Lucy was standing next to me. 'I know they haven't confirmed the date yet, Mum, but do you know if they'll be using implants or your own tissue for the reconstruction? Will they do it at the same time as the mastectomy? And what about your nipple? I know it's not always necessary to take it, but we need to find out before you agree to the surgery. I don't think we've got a lot of time, so would you like me order a couple of books about it?'

Without warning, a vision of my mother's flat and iodine-stained chest flashed into my mind, and I fought back the tears. Christ! This was real. It was going to happen, like it had done for her, and soon. I felt beaten, exhausted and empty.

'Lu, I really think we should talk about this another time,' interjected Sam. 'Mum's got more than enough to think about right now—'

'I know! But this is something I can get on with so she doesn't have to worry about it!'

'Whatever,' Sam said, moving so that my hand slid off his knee.

'Sammo, it's okay, love, and Looma, you're right, it is something I need to think about, so maybe you could come with me next time and we can both speak to the breast nurse? I'm rubbish at remembering anything, so that would be a real help. Honestly, Sam, I'll be okay. I'm sure I'll feel better about it all in the morning. It's just been a shock... For us all... Can I get you anything? Have you eaten?' I patted Jack's hand and stood up.

I was the one who was hurting them, but I had to be brave for them. Introducing my fear into their lives, where it would gnaw away at them, leaving them with an innate sense of unease... I wanted to crawl into the corner and weep.

'You're not going to die, are you?' Jack whispered, as he stood up and put his arms tightly round me.

'No love, I'm not.' I whispered back. 'I'm going to be fine, honestly. I love you. All of you.'

I could feel his ribcage through his jumper, and felt a wave of despair. What if I wasn't there to cajole, nag, provide or love? Had I brought them up to be able to cope with whatever life threw at them? I seriously doubted it. I sniffed loudly.

'You must promise me that you'll tell me if you're worried, and ask me anything you need to?' I unravelled myself from Jack's arms, and looked at each of them. My little family. I still saw them as that; little people who needed me. Not responsible adults with their own lives to lead. Each nodded silently as I reached into my handbag for more tissues.

I texted Colin to ask if he'd join us but he felt it would be better to give everyone a little time. Lucy poured me a large glass of wine and then she and the boys stayed with me for an hour or so. We talked about nothing very much really, it was just comforting to have them there but, as Lucy was working the next day, and I was flagging, she suggested I had an early night. The boys were in agreement, and I told them I'd be fine as Colin was on his way back. After hugging each of them very tightly, I opened my front door and watched them walk up the garden path to the car.

Once they had driven off, I decided to go up to bed rather than waiting up for Colin and still clutching my glass of wine I tried to carefully negotiate the very narrow and winding staircase that had made this cottage so endearing to me when I first viewed it. With each step my panic increased, and once in my bedroom at the top of the landing, I didn't bother to turn the light on, but put my glass down, and sat on the edge of the mattress in the darkness, sobbing uncontrollably. 'Oh my God,' I said out loud. 'Please, no. I can't do this. What if it's everywhere?' Grabbing my mobile, I called my sister. Poor Jenny. She has always been the voice of reason and, although she is younger than me, she has been protective of me throughout my adult life.

'Why are you on your own? Where are the children?'

'It's all right; they've gone. I told them to go,' I sniffed. 'I don't want them to see me like this. Colin said he'd come back, but I think I might have upset him, so—'

'I'll call him now,' Jenny said decisively. 'He loves you! In spite of everything that's going on between you two at the moment, he loves you. He'll want to be with you, and you mustn't be on your own tonight. Promise me? I'll get him to call you, but if you've not heard within five minutes call me back, and I'll come over myself.'

It was a very generous offer, as Jenny lives two hours away in Hampshire, but luckily she didn't have to. Colin did come back, and he stayed with me that night, and it was him who held me and stroked my hair and told me loved me and would always love me no matter what…

# CHAPTER FIVE

It wasn't God but the NHS I had to thank for making me book the appointment for the mammogram that originally flagged the fact I had an abnormality. When you are fifty years old – which I was in March 2010 – the NHS automatically invite you to visit your local hospital or GP surgery for a couple of health checks. My first invitation was for a smear test, and it dropped through the letterbox literally days after my fiftieth birthday. The second invite complete with a date for my mammogram, arrived the following week. The thoughts of both these procedures didn't appeal to me, and so I put the invitations behind my collection of birthday cards, and promptly forgot about it.

Because of my propensity to lumpy breasts, I'd had a number of mammograms over the previous fourteen years. Although it had been a long while since I'd had any cause for concern, I had noticed a slightly ridged area a couple of months earlier, similar in size to the top part of my thumb, on the top quadrant of my right breast. It hadn't gone away, and hadn't changed shape, and so I decided that perhaps a mammogram would be sensible. However, the date they suggested coincided with work and so I had to call and promise that I would rearrange it. I was working as a freelance presenter for QVC in those days, and to say my schedule was irregular was an understatement! With my days and hours changing on a weekly basis, it wasn't always that easy planning ahead.

It must have been mid-June when I found both of the NHS invites stuffed into the back of my bureau, and although occasionally when showering or at the gym I'd felt the lumps, I hadn't done anything about them. However, the ridged area now felt slightly more prominent and so I gave the local screening service a call and arranged to see them for a mammogram on 1st July. Roz, who'd been a constant in my life over the previous fifteen years, was marrying Chris the following day, and I was thrilled for the pair of them. She'd gone through her own marriage breakdown not long before my seventeen year relationship dissolved and we'd been through some tough times together. I was delighted when she'd met Chris, and was so excited about the wedding that I wasn't really thinking about much else as I arrived for my appointment.

I stood in front of the nurse and undid my gown.

'Anything we should know about?' she asked, and so I showed her the ridged area and she told me she would flag it on the X-ray for the breast consultant. The results would be posted to me within two weeks. I left the clinic to get packed for our celebratory weekend, and didn't even think of it again until a week later. I don't really know what it was that troubled me, but I just had a bad feeling. I called the screening service and they repeated that they wouldn't have any results for me until the end of the following week, and so panicking somewhat uncharacteristically, I decided I'd book in privately to the One Stop Breast Clinic at Harpenden, where I'd been all those years before.

I managed to get an appointment for the following day and explained my concerns to the very charming breast consultant. I hadn't been able to get the mammogram sent across to his clinic, but I was examined, and then sent for an ultrasound, which he assured me would show up any abnormalities. The radiographer spent some time going over the lumpy area, but told me I had nothing to worry about, and this is what she would tell the consultant. Again, he was very reassuring and confident, saying that if the lumps were still there in six months' time, I was to go back and he would re-scan the area. I left feeling relieved, and even managed a wry smile when three days later I received a letter from the local NHS Breast Screening Service, telling me that they had made a follow-up appointment for me that week as they had found something on the mammogram. I called them and told them I had already been for an ultrasound, which had proved to be normal, and so I didn't want to waste their time. The nurse thanked me and I got on with my life... until the end of that week.

Colin answered the phone to my mum, but as we were rushing to leave the house for a dinner date I mouthed at him that I would call her back. He shook his head and gently told me that she needed to speak to me now.

Ironically my mum had been to have a mammogram a few weeks before me, and had been recalled, which wasn't a surprise, considering the symptoms she told me about. For months I'd been nagging her to go and see someone, as the inverted nipple she'd had for years had become inflamed and itchy. Her GP had initially given her antihistamine cream which I thought was crazy – and not surprisingly didn't help – and so on my insistence, she had reluctantly gone back. The second time she was prescribed a fungal cream that she duly applied, but again, it made no difference. Eventually – and I did have to be firm with her – she arranged to have a mammogram. Like me just two weeks earlier, hers had shown something irregular and so they had given her a fine-needle aspiration of the area. We had been waiting on the results.

'Alison, I'm really sorry love, but the test has come back and I've got Invasive Lobular Cancer. They are going to give me a mastectomy, but the surgeons said I can have the summer to myself and it will be done in September. They feel it's safe to leave it for now as nothing's going to change over the next month or so…'

I have rarely felt as helpless as I did at that moment – not knowing what to say or do for the right thing. Desperately wanting to comfort her, but fighting with my worst fears – was it okay to leave her with the cancer in her body for another eight weeks or more? What if she didn't survive the surgery? How would she cope if she had to have chemotherapy? What if her cancer was incurable? What if she were to die?

Because this is what cancer does to you: forget the brave fundraising campaigns that boast *'Cancer, we're out to get you.'* They're wrong. IT'S out to get YOU, and it does. And like dropping a pebble into water, the ripples that move from its centre affect everything in its wake, and somehow we are never quite the same…

# CHAPTER SIX

In the week following my diagnosis I spent at least four days at the hospital. The ultrasound under my arm had shown several enlarged lymph nodes and so my breast surgeon had suggested I had what they called a sentinel node biopsy. He explained that the sentinel node is the first lymph node to which cancer cells are most likely to spread from a primary tumour. A negative result would suggest that the cancer didn't have the ability to spread, but a positive result would mean that it could be present in other lymph nodes and possibly other organs. As the test involved a radioactive dye being injected into the breast it would need to take place at the much larger General Hospital in Bedfordshire, where they had the correct equipment to carry out this specific test. He was very clear that this was purely to reassure us both that the cancer hadn't spread, and he genuinely wasn't expecting a bad result. That said, he did want me to have an MRI of my breasts to see if there were any further tumours on the right side, and whether there were any hidden problems in the left breast.

I'd only ever had one MRI scan prior to this and that was some four years earlier when I'd been struggling with chronic sciatic pain. All I remembered of the experience was having to lie perfectly still inside a tunnel-like machine, while the incredibly loud banging noise made by the imaging process made the whole bed vibrate! I'll be honest I wasn't looking forward to this scan at all. Colin had said he would take me to the hospital, which in one respect was a huge comfort, but because we still hadn't resolved the issues that had caused us to separate, I felt confused. Too much had been said to enable us to leave it all behind and move forwards. The situation I now found myself in somehow heightened our differences, and made the love between us although still evident, feel fragile.

There really wasn't room in my head though to make sense of it that day, and so I held his hand tightly as the technician ran through the procedure. What I hadn't realised was if you're having your chest scanned, you need to lie on your front with your breasts unceremoniously dropped inside two apertures that look very like two empty flowerpots! As I still had the rather large bandage on my right breast, I was a little concerned that it might not fit inside the opening, but with some gentle wriggling and jiggling, the nurse and I managed it.

I hoped that Colin would be able to come in and sit with me while I was having the scan, but he'd been involved in an accident years before which had unfortunately left tiny fragments of metal in one of his eyes. Because MRI is a magnetic resonance imaging system, they couldn't take the risk.

It was quite claustrophobic being manoeuvred face down into the narrow tunnel where the ceiling was just above my head. Of course, once you're in position it's imperative you stay still as any movement can ruin the imaging process, and they may well have to start again. I had been given a sort of rubber ball that was an alarm, and I was told to squeeze if I was panicked or couldn't cope. As an aside: if you find yourself facing one of these scans and feel really concerned, you can ask for a mild sedative, which will help. It wasn't so much the scan, more the fact that now I had been diagnosed with cancer, I was convinced that the MRI would discover further disease in my second breast, and that was my only thought.

Having made sure I was as comfortable as I could be lying prone on the very hard rigid bed, with my boobs inside these two little pots, the machine automatically moved me into the tunnel.

I was given the option of listening to music through the ear-defending headphones that are offered to each patient. My artist of choice was Michael Bublé as I'm a huge fan. However, I realised within the first ten seconds that I wouldn't hear his dulcet tones at all, as the machine was extraordinarily loud! What began with something akin to heavy breathing or a heartbeat was followed with various sounds like alarms or sirens, all at different levels, and fighting for supremacy! It felt like I'd been in there for an eternity, but in truth it was only about twenty-five minutes before the machine stopped, and the bed moved backwards and out into the brightly lit room. I'd be lying if I said I'd been thinking about anything other than what they might discover when they looked at the images they had produced, but I was on the rollercoaster, heading down a very steep hill, and dreading the upturn before another drop.

And the drop came a little sooner than I expected as I had a call the following morning saying I would have to return to the hospital for another MRI that afternoon. Apparently the technician had carried out the wrong kind of imaging, and they needed to do it again. I was absolutely convinced that they had found something untoward, and this was just a ruse to get me back to the hospital to have a second look. That might sound irrational, but my sense of reasoning was shot.

Roz met me at the hospital and sat with me while the technician explained what would happen this time. I have known Roz since I was eleven years old, and it was her wedding I'd been to following my mammogram the previous summer. Although we went our separate ways after we'd left school, she got in touch with me many years later, when she saw me presenting *This Morning*. We met up and have been incredibly close ever since. Roz's background and entire career has been in the caring and nursing profession. She was working at a hospice as a palliative nurse when I was diagnosed, and from that day onwards, she was always my point of reference if ever I was concerned about anything.

I know my nerves didn't help me on that day, believing as I did that the staff weren't being entirely honest with me, but of course they were, and I was mistaken. It *was* to be a different scan, and this time around, I would need to have something called Gadolinium – a contrast agent that allows abnormalities in the breast to be seen on the MRI – injected into my bloodstream to highlight both breasts during the imaging process. Unfortunately I come from a family of folk whose veins are very difficult to locate, and on this particular occasion, mine had taken a nosedive! Add to the mix, my genuine fear and concern as to what they were looking for, meant the nurse didn't have a hope in hell of getting that line in. I could feel the sweat running down my back, as she tried first one arm, and then the other, and then the back of my hands. She became more and more distressed by the situation and her inability to carry out her job, and I was feeling distinctly sick and sore when she finally conceded and called for the doctor. I don't remember much about him except his name was Tom and he suggested that I lay flat on a gurney with my arm hanging down as it would help the veins, which it did and enabled him to get a line in. They gave me a few minutes to gather myself.

Sitting up, I started to cry. 'If I can't get through this, how on earth am I going to get through surgery and chemo?'

Roz held me really tight. 'You're going to be absolutely fine. You're far stronger than you be-lieve, and I'll be with you whenever you need me.'

And she was. While the scanner banged away she kept her hand on my ankle the entire forty-five minutes it took for the imaging to take place. And she kept me company on my drive home, while her lovely husband Chris, who'd driven up separately to meet us, followed us in their car. They waited with me until Colin arrived, and then they headed back to the hospital to get Roz's car. It had been a very long day for us all.

# CHAPTER SEVEN

Along with requests for a pair of roller skates, or to dream of the Batman actor Adam West, at seven years old you'd find me most nights asking God for breasts. Nothing too big mind, just something that would heave up and down in my vest when I was feeling dramatic, which according to my family was quite often! Breasts were the epitome of femininity to me, but luckily I had no idea at that point I'd have to wait another eight years before my prayers would be answered. I would pore over the Littlewoods catalogues my mum received, choosing which bra shape and cup size I would prefer, and working out what I could possibly afford on just one shilling a week pocket money. I didn't really have much idea what real breasts looked like, as my mother was always properly covered and I had never seen her without underwear. I loved all the old black-and-white films where the heroine was corseted into a gorgeous gown, her heaving bosom taking central stage, and I firmly believed that someone like Errol Flynn wouldn't be drawn, in quite the same way, to a smaller breasted gal!

The women on both sides of my family tended

to have large breasts. My maternal grandmother before she'd suffered ill health and my dad's far more statuesque mother also. My own mum too was very curvy as were both her sisters, and so I felt it was my divine right to follow suit. I cannot begin to describe to you my feelings of fury when my sister – twenty months younger than me – started busting out all over at just eleven years old. In fact, there had been a few girls in my junior school with pretty impressive bust lines at just ten years old. Ironically, my sibling could not have been more upset by the appearance of her twin peaks as she was a tomboy and more than happy to remain that way. I was, however, by this time in the third year at the same secondary school, and was so flat-chested I was almost inverted. Life was terribly unfair.

A great deal of my early youth was spent staring enviously at my peers and willing my chest to start expanding as theirs had, but to no avail. I remember a particularly hot summer's day in the early seventies when my friend Valentina and I cycled to our local open-air swimming pool. She was already in a B-cup, but was desperately self-conscious about her nipples. In fact, if ever we left her house – even for a bike ride – she insisted on sticking Elastoplast over them both! Almost apoplectic with envy and irritation, I'd been doing some thinking, and had decided on desperate measures. Stuffed away in the bottom of our toy cupboard at home was a small amount of Plasticine, and so before Valentina and I headed off to The Upper Deck open-air swimming pool that day, I spent some time modelling for

myself a pair of small but pert breasts. These
were secreted in my rucksack, and while she
was preoccupied with her plasters, I popped the
Plasticine inside my bikini top. Result! As we strode
out poolside, I walked just a little taller, and a tad
more carefully than usual, trying to catch the eye of
the many completely disinterested boys there. We
found a sunny spot, and settled down for the day.

Of course it was all good while I sat up – which
I did for a very long time admiring my silhouette
in the afternoon sunshine – but lying down was a
different matter. Worried that the rather vivid blue
Plasticine breasts might slip out of my bikini top
if I lay on my back, I decided to lie on my tummy
instead. The large grey paving slabs were hot, hard
and incredibly uncomfortable, and as my towel was
tiny, I decided it would be far more effective as a
pillow than a rug. I sort of wiggled into position,
grazing my hips and knees on the concrete and then
lay completely still, with the sun beating down on
my back.

With a face full of cotton fibres and no sun cream
on my back – remember, this was the seventies and
SPFs were a thing of the future – I remained prone,
sweating profusely, and probably burning. But far
worse than that, was the effect this compression had
on my cunningly created cleavage! As I lay there
on the hot slabs, not only did the Plasticine squash
down and bulge out under my arms, but it began
to melt and leak through the side of my lime-green
bikini! Of course I was blissfully unaware of this
until I sat up. Oh the shame...Trying to cover my

embarrassment with my tiny towel wasn't easy,
and Valentina was far too preoccupied with loss
of adhesion to her plasters to be of assistance. I
think the blue Plasticine stains remained, indelibly
marking the spot until the good old upper deck was
flattened some years later to make way for an old
people's home.

# CHAPTER EIGHT

One of the questions you will always be asked when attending a breast clinic or having a mammogram is 'Do you have a history of breast cancer in the family?' Up until the summer of 2010 I didn't, but that changed following my mum's diagnosis. She had remained remarkably calm and strong on the phone and insisted that I wasn't to visit her, but to wait until she'd had the procedure when she would need my help. However, Colin and I cobbled together a story about a weekend away on the South Coast, so we could pop in for a cup of tea on our way. I just had to see her. Squeezing her tight, I felt her pillow-like softness pressing into me, and I tried to erase the terrifying thought of her impending surgery. Childish to think I'd never considered her not being in my life, especially as I was now in my fifties and had lost my dad when I was just twenty-seven years old. Time had suddenly become remarkably precious because I was consumed with an inherent fear that it was running out...

Mum's surgery two months later was a success, and although her permanently flat right side with its livid scars was hard for her to cope with at first, she put on a brave face – as she always has done – and got on with her life. I came to stay with her just as soon as she was home from hospital and remember helping her to wash herself. I honestly didn't know what to expect as I gently pulled her nightie off over her head. Where her right breast had been, there was a very large clear plastic plaster adhered to her chest. Beneath it her skin looked flat, ludicrously tanned because of the iodine, but with large stark incisions.

Mum's surgeon had chosen not to rebuild her breast, and at seventy-five years old, Mum was happy with this decision. She's been incredibly stalwart and strong, but I know deep down the loss of her breast has upset her. And sadly this is what breast cancer does to a woman. The surgery is brutal, and the mental recovery difficult. It robs you of your femininity, but this procedure gives your best chance of survival; it's just hard to accept when your body is changed in such a devastating way.

Years ago I had seen a film called *Soldier Blue* starring Peter Strauss and Candice Bergen and directed by Ralph Nelson. It had been criticised for its graphic brutality that I hasten to add, I had been *completely* unaware of when I entered the cinema. I abhor violence and indeed my children even now will tell me to avoid certain TV shows or films as 'You wouldn't like them, Mum, they're too violent'. In this film there is scene depicting a notorious massacre where several Native American women are tied to a post and then have their breasts cut off.

That image haunted me for years…

As a result of my mum's diagnosis, she got in touch with her consultant who suggested that I go back to the hospital I had been to just a few weeks before, to tell them of her diagnosis. Even though I have been given the all clear, he felt it best to check it out. I did as my mother suggested, and turned up at the hospital where I saw a different consultant who seemed very surprised to see me. He had my notes in front of him.

'I see that you came to see my colleague a couple of weeks ago concerned about an area of nodularity on your right breast.'

'Yes, that's right.'

'You had an examination and ultrasound scan that showed a lot of benign changes, but he assured you there was nothing suspicious or worrying? I believe he also reviewed your mammogram with our consultant radiologist and was happy with that too, suggesting that you come back in six months for a follow up?'

'Yes, he did. It's just that when I saw him there was no history of breast cancer in our family, but my mum was diagnosed last week, and her consultant felt I should come back and see you.'

'What kind of breast cancer has your mother been diagnosed with?'

'Invasive lobular carcinoma and they've told her she'll need a mastectomy.'

'That is not a familial cancer' he said abruptly.

'I didn't know that,' I said politely.

He reiterated that the results of the mammogram

and subsequent ultrasound had proven that yes I had a 'busy breast' with a significant number of benign cysts but that there was nothing sinister, and so I shouldn't worry.

'Well, if you're sure…' I heard myself say, to which he replied he was, but added that he'd be more than happy to see me in six months' time for another check- up if I was still concerned.

Which of course is what I did, and the rest as they say, is history.

# CHAPTER NINE

I had a couple of days' grace before the surgeon would have the result of the MRI, and as he wanted to present the findings at the multidisciplinary meeting, he promised he would have news for me late Friday morning after he'd spoken to the other consultants. Colin had cancelled his day's work and had planned to stay with me, but I hadn't remembered, and decided to go and get my hair cut. My thinking was that if I was going to have to have chemotherapy it would be better to have it shorter so there was less to lose. He didn't argue with me, but just looked defeated as I left the house.

I settled myself into the high-backed padded chair in the salon and watched the young stylist cut several inches off my highlighted locks, occasionally glancing nervously at my phone that was on the shelf in front of me. My consultant had said he would be in touch with me by 11 a.m. and the minutes were ticking away. I didn't genuinely believe he would call me. I thought it would be a repeat of what had happened the week before, and I would need to get in touch with him. Fighting to make conversation over the sound of the turbo-charged hairdryer I almost missed my mobile bursting into life and vibrating dangerously towards the edge of the shelf. The stylist turned off the dryer and gestured towards my phone. I grabbed it, and with a suddenly dry mouth confirmed that I was indeed Alison Keenan and yes this was a good time. Bless him, the lovely lad looking after me discreetly handed me a lined pad and a pencil, and gestured to me to go into the back room of the salon.

I still have the piece of paper I made my notes on. It says 'MRI not showing carcinoma – may not be visible with this form of imaging. Unanimous decision to proceed with sentinel node biopsy. Disease occult on all imaging tests. Need to assess axillary lymph node status. Isotype – blue dye. Luton and Dunstable Hospital.'

There was an overwhelming smell of peroxide in the back room, and the vase of dusty silk flowers did nothing to lift my mood. Having ended the call, I couldn't quite believe what I'd just been told, and sighing deeply I walked back into the salon. I don't remember much about leaving, except that I gave the young lad a hefty tip. Sitting in my car with the sun shining through the windscreen, I realised this was it. It wasn't going away, it had got me, and I leaned my head on the steering wheel and sobbed.

Colin wasn't there when I got home, and although a part of me was relieved as I didn't want to pretend to be positive about this latest development, there was an even larger part of me that needed him to be positive for me. I looked around the sitting room, realising that the overnight bag he'd left at the bottom of the stairs was no longer there. Neither was his coat. A half empty mug of tea sat on the coffee table. I pulled my phone out of my bag and dialled his number. It rang and rang before eventually going to automatic answer. 'Please leave a message after the tone.'

I took a deep breath. 'It's only me. I'm sorry about this morning, I should have told you. I should have asked you to come with me or something. They want to run another scan thing to see if it's spread anywhere else. I don't know what to think, really…' I paused. 'Are you coming here this weekend? Perhaps we could—' A loud beeping noise severed my suggestion.

'This voicemail box is full and cannot receive any more messages,' I was told before the call ended automatically.

'I'm sorry,' I whispered.

It was only a matter of days before I had my appointment at the Luton and Dunstable Hospital for my sentinel node biopsy. The mighty medical machine was now in motion, and on this occasion it was Debbie who was able to stay with me the night before and then take me to the hospital in the wee small hours of the morning. To be fair it had been pretty much the wee small hours of the morning when we'd gone to bed, a couple of bottles of wine down, so we were feeling a tad jaded! Having found a parking space, we didn't have a clue where we were going, but after about fifteen minutes of walking purposefully through endless corridors, we finally found someone in uniform, and they pointed us in the right direction.

Debbie is another one of those wonderful women who always sees the funny side to life. Maybe it's her Liverpudlian upbringing, or just a corking sense of humour, but she was great company and once we'd settled ourselves in the waiting room she kept me entertained while I waited for the nurse to call me.

The procedure I was to have determines if the cancer has spread beyond a primary tumour into the lymphatic system. A sentinel node biopsy is used most commonly in evaluating breast cancer and melanoma. The sentinel nodes are the first few nodes into which the tumour drains, and the biopsy involves injecting a tracer material that helps the surgeon locate the sentinel node during surgery. The sentinel nodes are then removed and analysed in a laboratory. If they are free of cancer, then it's unlikely the cancer has spread anywhere else, and so removing additional lymph nodes is unnecessary. If though, the sentinel node reveals cancer, then it is likely to be present in additional lymph nodes, and possibly other organs. This information can help the surgeon or doctor determine the stage of the cancer, that is, the extent of the disease within the body, and develop an appropriate treatment plan.

A radioactive substance – known as a tracer – is injected into the breast and is allowed to work its way around the area for a couple of hours. After only a few minutes wait, I was called into a little side room to have this done. It was a completely painless procedure and took literally a moment, so before we knew it, Debbie and I were directed to the private wing of the hospital, where once again a pristine room awaited us. I knew I wasn't allowed anything to eat or drink before the procedure, and as we had at least a couple of hours to kill, I told Debbie that if she wanted breakfast to feel free. Bless her; she declined, saying she wasn't hungry, although I could hear her tummy rumbling as the time ticked by. Why is it that when you are told you can't have something you desperately want it! That time in the morning I would never normally even have had breakfast! But watching the hands move incredibly slowly round the face of the clock in my room I was absolutely parched and starving! Debbie kept me occupied, regaling me with stories of her time at BBC Radio 2, and the various celebrities she had met and interviewed. First class entertainment!

At around about 10 a.m. a distinguished-looking gentleman with a bow tie came to see me, and introduced himself as my anaesthetist. He was charm personified, and as with all medical professionals prior to a procedure, he took time to ask questions and make notes, before describing what his role as my anaesthetist would involve. His description of what was going to happen made it sound quite inviting!

'What you will feel first of all is something akin to drinking a large gin and tonic. If you like that feeling, I can increase it so it feels like several gin and tonics, but if you don't like it, I can make you sleep.' I'm sure you can imagine mine and Debbie's response to this statement! Even after he'd left the room we were still chatting about our alcoholic preferences!

It wasn't long afterwards that my surgeon came to talk through the actual procedure, adding that he felt it would be very unlikely and unlucky if indeed the sentinel node was involved, but that this was a very accurate way of finding out. I have to admit that having talked to my mother just the night before, I knew that this test was very rarely carried out in most general hospitals as they didn't have the right equipment. I was very fortunate that my local hospital did indeed have the right equipment and had managed to put it all in place so swiftly for me. Apart from the fact I was starving and gagging for a glass of water, I did feel in quite good spirits and realising it wouldn't be much longer before I was needed in theatre, I changed into my gown.

I still hadn't mastered the art of which tape went where, but was giving it my best attention when Yo turned up. She was relieving Debbie, who needed to get back to work, and had very kindly offered to drive me home. It only seemed a matter of moments before a nurse appeared in the doorway to tell me that they were now ready for me. I slipped my feet into my slippers, hugged Debbie and thanked her for looking after me; then Yo, who said she'd be there when I came back to the room. I took a deep breath, crossed the fingers on both my hands and, smiling and waving at my friends in a jazz hands fashion, I followed the nurse out into the corridor.

I'll never know what it was that changed my mood that day, but when I came round after the anaesthetic, I felt deep in the heart of me that something was seriously wrong. All these tests, and each time being told it would be fine when it wasn't. You have to admire the nursing profession, for their endless patience, kindness and understanding. I didn't feel able to talk to any of them although they continued to try, and I kept my head stubbornly turned to the left, looking at the wall in silence as they wheeled me along the corridor back to my room. This was real. I knew I had cancer, but I now believed that the likelihood was it had spread throughout my body. This was the lowest point for me, and I couldn't speak to Yo or Debbie – who was still there – when I was brought back into the room. I just lay there with my face turned away from them crying quietly.

Yo came and sat on the bed and put her arm around me, asking me what was wrong, but I had nothing to say. Everything was moving too fast and I didn't feel able to cope. I lay there for a long while, Yo sitting with me, until I thought I heard the sound of someone crying in the corridor. A long time afterwards I found out that it was Deb. She told me that up until that point she'd always believed me when I'd said I was going to be fine, and doubted that I would even need a full mastectomy, that it was highly unlikely I'd even have to have chemotherapy! But having seen me so upset after this latest procedure, she was as frightened for me as I was for myself.

Something I have realised over the years is that it's often just as hard to be on the outside looking in, as it is to be right in the thick of it.

I was still on that roller coaster, but with a fair few steep hills to climb...

# CHAPTER TEN

When you're young, life stretches ahead of you like a skipping rope. Full of untold excitement, experiences and, hopefully, love! I, however, felt that love was a long way off for me as the boys in my class didn't give me a second glance. I was convinced it was because of my vest-wearing status, as all my girlfriends' bust lines blossomed but my chest remained stubbornly flat until the summer of 1973, when I was rewarded with two little peaks. I spent weeks imploring my mum to take me to Kingston- Upon -Thames to buy a bra, and to this day the memory of a pale lilac creation with pink rose buds from M&S – size 32AA – is an incredibly fond one. Mum thought that a white bra would be more appropriate for going underneath my school blouse, but I wanted to make sure the boys in my class knew I was wearing one, and on this occasion I got my own way. Whether it was the mix of manmade fibres, or the particularly warm summer were blessed with, some six months later, I was rewarded for all my years of longing with a fabulous pair of breasts that looked like small Ogen melons, and were situated just under my chin. Marvellous!

Finally I was interesting to the opposite sex, and although my selection of bras consisted mainly of rather severe white cotton designs, the bri-nylon blouses we all wore then were pretty transparent. No more did I have to sit with my arms crossed over me to hide my flatness. In truth I didn't need a bra and could have got away with wearing just a vest, as unfettered, my boobs weren't going anywhere!

So you can imagine how thrilled I was when asked to the cinema by one of my brother's friends, two years older than me, and in the fifth year at my school. He was a regular visitor to our family home, and I'd been cycling to school with his sister for years, so I was more excited than nervous as we sat down on our red velvet seats at the Esher Embassy Picture House.

*Raid on Entebbe* is not one of the most romantic films I've ever seen, and I have to admit to finding it very hard to concentrate on the somewhat weak plot, as this chap spent the entire ninety minutes with his arm around my shoulder, twiddling my left nipple as if he was trying to find Radio 1! We didn't ever find out what would happen if he twiddled the right nipple, as he didn't ask me out again. From then on, aside from a few furtive fumbles, I kept my orbs to myself, until I was sixteen years old and headed off to Somerset for a long-awaited holiday with my best friend Yo.

It was the summer of '76. The sun shone from May until September without a break, and we were continuously warned of the hideous drought that would follow. It was also the year I finished secondary school, having taken my CSEs and O' Levels during May and June. Revision for these exams had taken place outdoors – either in the garden or at the infamous Upper Deck Swimming Pool. I was already nut brown, and thoroughly looking forward to showing off my tan, and as we boarded the coach at Victoria Station, I loosened my shoulder straps and tried to calculate which side we should sit to gain the optimum saturation of rays through the window!

We were lucky enough to be staying with friends of Yo's family, who had won the Football Pools a few years back. They lived in an unbelievably enormous house, with acres of land, and you could have slept eight people side by side in the bed we had. As the house was quite a way out of the local village, and so we thought it would be an adventure to borrow a couple of bikes and cycle to Hinkley Point on the Bristol Channel. We were unaware of the nuclear power station there – to be fair, it had only been completed in February that year –but you would have thought that the enormous reactors would have given us a clue. However, it was hot, we wanted to swim, and were not at all deterred by the many fences we had to negotiate or heave our bikes over to get to the sea. Finally, we found a small area of shore, abandoned our bikes, and ran into the water, which was incredibly warm. After faffing around for an hour or so, we thought we'd better head back. As we hadn't brought towels with us, and didn't want to get our clothes wet, we decided we'd make the journey home wearing nothing more than our bikinis... rather small bikinis if my memory serves me correctly.

Not only was it very hot that summer, it was also a dreadful time for those of us who suffered from hay fever. Whatever the type of pollen in the air over Somerset that year, my medication didn't touch it. As it got worse and I became more frantic with itching eyes and throat, Yo decided we needed to ask for help. Having battled our way back over the fences, and cycled miles along the country lanes, we weren't too far from 'home' in a very pretty village, the name of which escapes me. Looking back I'm surprised it's not a name forever embossed on my brain, because unbelievably and unashamedly, wearing just our tiny bikinis, we knocked on the door of a total stranger in the hope they would give us some water to drink, and cotton wool for my eyes, which were half closed and streaming. What I do remember very clearly, in spite of my impaired eyesight, is the incredibly good-looking, tall and fit young man who, having listened to our plight, invited us into the welcoming coolness of his little cottage. He gave us cold water to drink, and tissues for my eyes, and even offered to search out some antihistamines. I also remember equally clearly, my eyes refocusing, as the front door opened and an attractive twenty-something female walked into the front room where we were standing.

'What the hell is going on here?' she demanded.

'Well, these two were in a spot of bother and so I've just given them a glass of water and—'

We didn't wait to hear the rest, putting down our glasses with a thump, we pushed rather rudely and breasts first, past the bewildered woman, out into the sunshine, where we leapt on to our bikes and pedalled like billy-ho, wheezing with laughter all the way home.

It wasn't long after that I met my first husband, and although he was always very complimentary about my shape, he wasn't really a 'boob' man. Neither was my second husband, and so the interest in my late twenties and thirties was purely maternal, when I successfully breast fed all three of my children. I say successfully, but that was down to an enormous amount of effort on my part. In the same way a midwife will have you believe that giving birth is perfectly natural, and yet it feels like trying to pass a watermelon through your right nostril, breast-feeding is almost as awkward! Not only did my breasts almost double in size, but they were so hard, it was impossible for any of my babies to be pressed up against them for very long!

That said, I did persevere, as my midwife told me that 'Breast is Best', and along with nipple shields, maternity bras and a breast pump, Rotersept Spray became my best friend. Once I got the hang of it, I loved being able to bond with each of my children this way, but it wasn't ever that easy for me. I coped with cracked nipples, and struggled with mastitis, which is incredibly painful – akin only to having your breasts bound - as I did, with crepe bandage. Why, I hear you ask? This was the recommended method to help prevent the milk coming in once you'd decided to stop breast-feeding. After such punishment, my once magnificent orbs were slightly softer and less round, and probably several inches closer to my navel than they had been before, but they still looked pretty good in a bra.

In my mid-forties, following my second divorce, I started dating a man who loved every inch of me, including my breasts, and made me feel like a teenager, but with experience! I was his 'adventure playground' and on my fiftieth birthday he baked me an enormous birthday cake and told me that I had a body most twenty-year-olds would be proud of... I am sure you can sense the irony when nine months later, I was told gently by the breast consultant that I did indeed have breast cancer, invasive lobular cancer, and I would need a mastectomy. My world tilted.

# CHAPTER ELEVEN

My consultant called me a few days after the sentinel node biopsy, and in a defeated tone said that unfortunately yet again it was bad news. The cancer was indeed in my sentinel node and therefore potentially in other nodes and possibly other organs. He would now want to do a complete axillary clearance, which to you and me means taking all the lymph nodes from under my arm, in case there was further spread. Based on this latest result, I would now be facing a complete mastectomy followed by chemotherapy, and then the possibility of radiotherapy. He also added that it might well be necessary in the future to perform a second risk-reducing mastectomy of the left breast too, as the cancer had been so difficult to find. I was standing in the dining room of the little cottage I rented, and felt the tears begin to prickle in my eyes.

Yo was with me as she had been all morning, and I put the phone on speaker so she could hear everything that was being said. Up to this point it had been purely conjecture as to whether a plastic surgeon would be needed, but now it was a priority.

My surgery would require both consultants in theatre – my breast surgeon said he would perform the mastectomy and the plastic surgeon would carry out the reconstruction. He was suggesting a skin-sparing mastectomy, involving an expander, but might as well have been talking in a foreign language, as neither meant anything to me. He told me that as there were at least three plastic surgeons at the hospital, I could choose between any of them, but that the gentleman he normally worked with was free to see me on Monday to talk through the procedure. He realised that it had been almost a month since my initial appointment, and wanted to get on with everything and so he had booked the theatre for that Wednesday, the 2nd of February. 'Is that date okay for you?' he asked politely. I took a deep breath and told him that I guessed it would have to be okay, although it was my son Jack's eighteenth birthday…

'I am sorry…truly. It is a bummer.'

It seemed such an odd phrase to use, although we've laughed about it since, but he was right. He concluded our conversation by saying at least now we knew what we were dealing with, and everything could be put in place. I thanked him and ended the call.

I could sense the sunshine warming my back as it streamed through the dining room window, but I felt cold inside. I had an overwhelming feeling of complete defeat.

'I don't want to do this.' I said to Yo.

'I know' she said in a somewhat muffled manner,

her face in my hair as she hugged me tightly, 'but it's going to be all right, Ali, I promise.'

I hung on to those words, like a drowning man to a life raft...

On the 2nd of February, eighteen years earlier, I had been struggling through a somewhat protracted labour with Jack, my third child. He'd been born at five minutes to midnight, weighing a massive ten pounds, two and half ounces. Things hadn't gone according to plan and after seventeen hours he'd eventually been delivered by emergency caesarean section. In spite of the panic, and the scary dash to theatre, he had been born safely, and my beautiful baby boy represented a new life for all of us to love. Now, at a time when we should all have been celebrating this milestone with him, I would once more be in a surgical theatre, facing the first step of what I felt was going to a be a very long road to recovery.

# CHAPTER TWELVE

As I have mentioned, my long-term relationship with Colin had been under pressure, and we were living separately at the time of my diagnosis. It wasn't what either of us wanted, but we were floundering. Although we were still seeing each other, we had decided there were certain things we needed to sort out before we could move forward. No one could have predicted what was going to happen, and in *any* situation this would not have been easy to deal with. When I told Colin about the lumpectomy, neither of us knew where we were headed, but once I had my diagnosis, he knew exactly where he wanted to be, and I knew where I needed him to be. We had loved each other for very long time, and although certain things had made our relationship difficult for a while, I really wanted to believe that what we had was a solid foundation. Something that I could hopefully rely on, when the rest of my life seemed to be set on shifting sands.

Lucy, Jack and I had spent the weekend before

my planned surgery, in Milton Keynes, shopping. Not only for Jack's birthday present, but also for things I'd need to take to hospital, which included pyjamas, slippers, a dressing gown, and a few sports bras. I'd been told by the plastic surgeon that I would need to wear these after my surgery, to support the expander and help me to heal. Although I work in retail, I don't enjoy shopping, unless I'm buying things for other people. It's mainly because I have a lousy track record of finding what I set out to buy! Feeling the need to bring something back with me, I inevitably buy a totally inappropriate garment and never wear it! Lucy was the best person to keep tabs on things, as she's always been particularly diligent at sticking to a list. So having found the perfect present for Jack, the memory of which now sadly eludes me, we decided to head into John Lewis for my essentials.

The lingerie department of John Lewis in Milton Keynes is enormous. Spanning almost the entire first floor, it encompasses all forms of underwear from tights and thongs, socks and stockings, corsetry and cami knickers, to row upon row of bras. It's not just these beautiful, lacy, strappy, satin and silk creations that catch the eye, but the notably larger-than-life posters and billboards showing beautiful women wearing them, their softly rounded and perfectly positioned breasts on display for all to see. Up until two weeks ago, I had spent many a happy hour sifting through all sorts of gorgeous garments, imagining myself in them, and imagining Colin's reaction to seeing me in them. In truth, I rarely bought underwear for myself, as he was very much in tune with what I liked, and always spoilt me with his choices. I had a fabulous collection of all kinds of lacy lovelies.

I don't know how long I stood staring at the bras, or which particular design it was that made me cry, but Jack came and put his arms round me and then led me over to where Lucy was standing, right next to the sports bras. We didn't speak, there wasn't anything to say, but once again I felt the roles reverse, and my children, bless them, pulled together to support me.

Having been told that my mastectomy would be on Jack's eighteenth birthday, all previous plans for a meal out, had to be changed to the night before, and although Jack said he was perfectly happy with this arrangement, I felt yet again that the cancer was screwing with my life. I met with the children on the first of February and we had dinner at Nando's, which was then – and still is – Jack's favourite place to eat. At thirteen years old, he'd decided he didn't like birthday cake, and so I'd stopped making them for him. Previous years had seen him requesting cheesecake or a shop bought chocolate tart, which I had thought sad, as I found a certain satisfaction from baking something special for my children. Ever since Lucy was born I had made a dedicated birthday cake for her, followed by Sam and of course Jack. I was then asked by my friends and other members of the family if I could create something for their children too. Someone once paid me to make a cake in the shape of a horse which took me ten hours to finish and looked more like a wolf!

I wouldn't describe myself as being particularly artistic, but over the years I became more adventurous and had some fairly impressive results when creating things as abstract as a pair of training shoes, a barbeque, a Monster Truck and a fire engine, all out of Victoria Sandwich and ready to roll icing! When Jack was younger I had made him a Sonic the Hedgehog cake, and a Pikachu cake, which were both very well received, but now he was all grown up… And so, on that particular day I hadn't thought about baking anything, and hadn't bought anything either. Thank heavens for Lucy, who in her wisdom and thoughtfulness, had purchased muffins and even remembered candles!

Having finished our meal, we headed back to Sam's flat. Lucy had kept her purchases in the car, and managed to conceal them from Jack as we made our way into Sam's front room. Not the largest of spaces, it was dominated by a large and circular love seat made for two. I'd bought it several years before, but when I moved to the cottage I no longer had room for it. Sam flopped down on to it, while Jack balanced next to me, on the edge of the small sofa. As no one spoke, I broke the silence.

'Of course, this day eighteen years ago I was in the Royal Shrewsbury awaiting your arrival, Jack.'

'I know, Mum,' he said softly.

I remembered the room, and the little cot, and

my beautiful baby…

'Well they'd started my labour off the day before, but you weren't going anywhere, you were more than happy where you were. You were almost born on the fourth! Of course, if it hadn't have been for that lovely Australian doctor—'

'You might still be in labour now!' Lucy interjected from the kitchen where she was sorting out the cakes.

I laughed and looked sideways at Jack, his long fringe obscuring his eyes. I noticed a few whiskers growing on his chin.

'You'll have to start shaving soon.' I said touching his face gently with my finger.

'I've got more hairs up my nose than he's got on his face.' Sam said loudly.

Before Jack could respond, Lucy appeared carrying the plate full of muffins, each one illuminated with its own candle.

'Ta da! Happy Birthday, Jack!'

'Yes, happy birthday, my dove boy.' I said, using my pet name for him as I put my arm around his bony shoulders and kissed him on the cheek.

'Happy birthday, mate.' Sam said.

'You'd better blow these out before they set fire to the muffins!' Lucy said, moving to put the plate down.

'Before you do that, can I get a photo of the three of you?' I said, scrabbling in my handbag for my phone.

'God, Mum! Hurry up then!'

I took out my phone and got them to stand

together before taking the picture. The lit candles created a weird shadow across their faces before Jack blew them all out, and Lucy plonked the plate down. I looked across at the three of them and felt the tears well up. I remembered the sense of despair I'd felt following my mum's diagnosis, and before her surgery. The overwhelmingly sick sense of fear. Was this how they were feeling? I hated the thought.

'Did you get it, Mum?' Sam came over to me. I nodded trying to blink my tears away. 'It's going to be okay.' He said quietly, and hugged me to him. At six feet three, I could almost stand under his chin, and leaning into him, I could hear his heart beating through his T-shirt. Those words had been my mantra for him when he'd been so ill following his motorbike accident, and I had willed him and myself to believe it. That night I lacked the conviction, finding it hard to believe that I would be there with them for Jack's nineteenth birthday the following year.

It may seem odd, but I never talked to any of my children on any of these occasions about how they felt. 'Least said, soonest mended,' was one of my nanny Timm's favourite sayings, and something I firmly believed in. I sensed that they had been steeped in stress ever since I told them I had cancer, and I didn't believe talking about it would help any of us. However, when I kissed each of them goodbye and left Sam's flat to head home, it was with a heavy heart and more than a few tears.

Cancer manages to put an unspeakable spin on any situation. Nothing is straightforward, or as you would expect, and everything seems fractured with fear. For me, it was primarily the thought of the disease within my body that filled me with dread, but there was also my pending surgery and the treatment that lay ahead. I imagined my children were possibly feeling much the same way, but I really wasn't too sure. However, unlike all the years before when it had been my job to cocoon them and keep them safe from danger, I couldn't protect them from this… and I couldn't protect myself.

Colin was waiting at the cottage when I got back. He had been invited to Jack's birthday celebrations, but had made the decision to stay away, convincing me that this was a special time, and one where the children needed to be with just me. We made love that night. It was beautiful but bittersweet, and there were tears from both of us, but I did sleep, safe in his arms, until morning.

We agreed that Yo should take me to the hospital, and Colin would be there for me when I came out of theatre. She arrived around 9:30 a.m. just after he'd left and as I knew she wouldn't have had breakfast, I was pottering about in the kitchen making toast. Although I'd showered and washed my hair I was still in my pyjamas, reluctant to get dressed. With my bag packed the night before, all I had to do was

decide what I would wear to hospital. It needed
to be something I could also wear home after the
operation. It may sound odd, but it wasn't so much
the outfit itself that I had been deliberating over, but
the underwear. The new sports bras I'd bought at
the weekend were in the bottom of my packed bag.
The sensible side of me said to wear one of those, as
they were the surgeon's recommendation, but I felt
more emotional than sensible, and decided to sift
through my underwear and find something pretty to
wear.

I chose a stunning black lace Simone Perele
creation and considering the time of the year, a
ridiculously thin T-shirt. I looked at my reflection
in the mirror and was transported back to my senior
school years, when we had a name for girls who
wore black underwear that you could see through
their school blouse! Was I too old to be a tart? 'Sod
it,' I said under my breath, and reached for my coat
before heading down the stairs.

We had been told to arrive at the hospital just
an hour before the operation, as it meant less time
sitting around thinking about things – although in
truth I had thought of little else for the past four
weeks… Yo and I were just unpacking my things
when the breast surgeon came through, and having
gone over the formalities as always, he said he
would see me in theatre. Next was the anaesthetist,
and I was pleased to see it was the same dapper gent
who had created his 'gin and tonic' analogy the last
time I had been in theatre. He was a little less jolly
this time, more measured, and patted me kindly on

the hand before leaving to join the breast surgeon. The nurse, who was also in attendance, asked me to get undressed and put my gown on, as it wouldn't be much longer now. She then smiled at me and Yo and left the room.

I took a deep breath in, and was about to take my T-shirt off when the door opened one more time. I had forgotten that there were to be two surgeons operating at the same time. The plastic surgeon, whom I'd briefly met two days earlier, strode into the room with a very large camera slung around his neck. He was accompanied by his secretary who smiled across at me, while he confirmed who I was, reminded me of his name and his role that day in theatre, and then told me unceremoniously to take my off my T-shirt and bra as he needed to take photographs of me. If I had felt self-conscious before I was acutely embarrassed now. He walked to the window while I was undressing and closed the curtains, before asking me to stand in front of them, facing him. After taking several pictures, he told me to turn to the side so he could take a few more. No words were spoken. I have rarely felt as vulnerable. 'I will come and see you after the surgery,' he said, as he strode out of the room. Yo muttered under her breath to his secretary, 'We don't like him...'

This was the only occasion in my entire time at this particular hospital where I had been upset by someone. In hindsight, I thought that this was possibly the surgeon's way of dealing with a difficult situation, but I know I should have told him how he had made me feel, so that he wouldn't treat anyone else that way.

I felt stupid as I looked at my lace lingerie on the bedcover. Stupid because I had wanted to hang on to the feeling it gave me when I wore it. Stupid because I was unlikely to experience that emotion again, and scared because I had no idea how I would feel after the surgery. Unbidden, the scene from the film *Soldier Blue* flooded my mind, and I put my arm protectively across myself while reaching for the hospital gown with my free hand. Yo folded my T-shirt and picked up my bra. 'I'll put it somewhere safe for you,' she said.

It was only a short distance to the operating theatre, but it seemed like a long way. Once there, all I could feel was despair, and as I lay on the trolley being prepped for my surgery I started to shake uncontrollably. You know that almost convulsive shaking that sets your teeth chattering and your limbs twitching?

'Are you okay?' asked the nurse who was checking my details.

'Sorry. I feel cold.' I replied.

From where I was lying I saw a man I assumed to be another member of the surgical team walking towards me. 'I have just the thing,' he said in a soft voice. Disappearing out of my line of vision, he reappeared a few moments later with a heated blanket that he laid over me. 'It's going to be fine,' he said as he hooked the blanket under my feet, and then left as swiftly as he'd arrived. I never knew who he was, but I will remember him always.

The warmth slowed my heartbeat and my shaking, and I closed my eyes. I didn't have long to wait before the anaesthetist arrived and within moments had the cannula in position, and was ready to send me to sleep. 'You weren't too keen on the gin and tonic were you?' he asked me. I shook my head slowly, but didn't feel able to speak. 'It'll all be over soon, try not to worry,' he said kindly, but how could I *not* worry? I had cancer, I was about to lose my right breast, and all the lymph nodes remaining under my right arm. I knew the cancer had already spread there, and so now I had to pray that this damned disease hadn't set up somewhere else in my body. The thought of the chemotherapy terrified me, but I'd had to accept it was going to be the most effective treatment for me. It was with a sense of defeat I closed my eyes again, all these thoughts muddying my mind as the anaesthetic crept coldly through my veins. As the room started to spin, it *was* the terror of waking up once it was over that consumed me.

# Chapter Thirteen

I was in surgery for just on six hours, but have a very little memory of coming round in recovery or even being taken back to my room. I do though remember crying as soon as I saw Colin, who was waiting there, as he had promised he would be. He looked drawn and tired, but came straight over to comfort me.

'It's okay Ali. It's over. You'll feel better now.' He kissed my free hand.

Yo was also there, standing on the other side of the bed next to the nurse who was busy attaching a fluid filled bag to a stand. She leaned over and kissed me on the cheek. 'Well done, poppet,' she said. 'What are these for?' she asked the nurse, gesturing to the various drips, bags and monitors. 'Did it all go according to plan?'

'Yes, the surgeons are happy, but we want to make sure that Alison isn't in any pain so we've rigged her up to this PCA, which will help her to manage her own pain relief.'

'How does that work then?'

'It's an electronically controlled infusion pump, and it's programmed to deliver a specific amount of morphine. We use all kinds of analgesics, but this is most effective. Alison?' I looked up at her. 'You just need to press this button and a pre-prescribed dose will be administered automatically. You can't overdo it, but it should keep on top of things.'

'Thank you.'

'What's the rest of it for?' asked Colin who'd come around to the other side of the bed and was standing next to Yo.

'Well, this line in the back of her hand is attached to the glucose drip as she was a little longer in theatre than we thought she'd be. She has a catheter so she doesn't need to get out of bed for a wee, and the two lines coming out of the side of her chest are drains. See these bottles here? Well, any excess or build-up of fluid will drain off into them.'

'Liking the sound of self-administered morphine!' said Yo with a smile.

'So am I.' I moved awkwardly, trying to avoid the bandages across my chest and wincing as I caught the cannula in the back of my hand.

'Take it easy, Ali.' Colin's hand rested gently on the blanket over my thigh. I looked into his eyes and felt a sense of defeat.

It was by now nearly 8 p.m., and the nurse came to change me out of my theatre gown and dress me in my pyjamas. I looked away so I wouldn't need to see the bandages covering the place where my breast had been, and pressed my PCA. I had absolutely no feeling across my chest, but my right shoulder and arm felt very stiff and sore. The nurse explained that this was normal because I had been given a full axillary node clearance – the technical term for the removal of all the lymph nodes from the armpit area. Not everyone having a mastectomy needs to have all their lymph nodes taken, but as there isn't currently a test available to ascertain accurately whether there's cancer in the nodes or not, removing some or all of them, is considered the safest option. As we already knew I had cancer in the sentinel node and several others, it was for me, the only decision.

I drifted in and out of consciousness but was awake when Colin said that he would leave me to get some sleep, and would be back the following day. He kissed me gently and stroked my hair, and I held on to his warm hands. It's usually at this point in a film that something profound or monumentally moving is said, but neither of us had the words, and I was crying again anyway. Yo, bless her, had decided she would stay the night, and as I was in a private room, the night staff allowed her to set up a blow-up bed next to mine. It was a long night for both of us, punctuated by regular visits from the nurse who came in to check my blood pressure, temperature and pain levels. Something else that kept us awake was my incessant scratching, because although the morphine was great at keeping the pain at bay it made me itch all over! Both my mother and my son Sam had struggled with this side effect when given morphine for pain, and so I was in two minds about whether to continue with it or not. By morning, my shoulder and arm felt even more stiff and sore, which concerned me, but the nurse again reassured me that it was normal following this kind of surgery, and that a physio would be popping in to see me, as I would need to begin an exercise regime to help with the pain. The thought of exercising made me sweat, as propped up in bed I could only just about manage to eat my breakfast! Of course it didn't help that my left hand was still attached to the drip and the PCA, and my right arm was restricted because of the two drains, the dressing across my chest, and the stiffness in my shoulder. I had something that looked like a mini trapeze suspended above the bed, but hadn't yet worked out how to use it.

Yo, having had her breakfast, let the air bed down and then sat next to me on the bed. I pointed to the trapeze.

'What do you suppose that's for?'

'Ali you're slacking! A little imagination needed here!'

'Such as?'

'Well, you could launch yourself at the next unsuspecting male who enters the room, and catch him unawares!' she smirked.

'I'd knock him for six! Don't think he'd be that happy.'

'I doubt he'd be able to complain with his mouth full!' She made me laugh for the first time in quite a few days.

The physiotherapist arrived not long after that and, armed with several illustrative leaflets, she told me that although my arm and shoulder were sore, and the drains were still in, I would need to begin exercising immediately.

'And there you were thinking you could just relax, watch daytime TV and eat grapes,' Yo said. 'Come on honeybun, if anyone can do it, you can.'

You wouldn't believe how ridiculously difficult it was for me to put my hands on my shoulders and then raise my elbows forwards and down, after this kind of surgery! That, and having to clasp my hands behind my neck while keeping my head upright tested my patience to the limit. I looked over at Yo who, realising I was struggling, got up from the chair and stood by the bed, her hand gently on my arm. 'It's okay Ali, it'll get easier.'

'I bloody hope so! This is impossible!'

However, it was trying to put my hand behind my back and reach up towards my neck that broke me, although my profanity was immediately replaced with an apology to the poor physio who was of course there to help me.

'Please, don't apologise,' she said. 'That's mild compared to most!'

Yo came and sat next to me on the bed. 'Does she really have to do these?' she asked, visibly upset.

'I'm sorry but yes, and I know it's hard, and it's going to hurt, but you've got to stick with it. If you don't, the fluid may well build up and there could possibly be cording in the arm.'

'Cording?' Yo and I asked in unison.

'It's a tightening down the upper arm and into the elbow and occasionally it'll extend into the forearm. If it happens you'll know within the first week. You'll get a kind of strong pulling sensation in your arm, which will make it sore to move.'

'So what do I do if that happens?'

'You get in touch with me, and we'll have to work out another exercise regime to sort it.'

Yo and I looked at one another, and then at the physio.

'Well I'd better crack on then!'

'One other thing. When they remove your drains, you'll be less restricted so I can give you a different set of exercises then.'

'Will she need to come back into the hospital and see you for those?' Yo asked.

'Yes. Ali, you'll need an outpatient's appointment, and once we're up to date, I can give you specific exercises you can do at home.'

'Will she need the trapeze?' I shot a look at Yo 'Only asking,' she said winking at me.

'No trapeze required, but you will need to keep up with the exercising for at least four to six weeks.'

I genuinely hadn't any idea that this was part of my recovery, and I think because everything moved so quickly no one had the chance to run through it with me. I hadn't even wanted to think about what would happen after the surgery, preferring just to get my head down and get on with what I knew. Looking back though, I wish I'd been told, or better yet, had had the gumption to ask! If you find yourself in this position following surgery, my advice to you is to try not to worry unduly about the discomfort and the issues surrounding movement of your arm. Like everything, if you manage to keep up with what your physiotherapist suggests, in time it will pass.

# CHAPTER FOURTEEN

Being in hospital for any length of time can be difficult for some, I know, but I felt safe there, and very well cared for. It was a haven to me, in spite of the pain and discomfort, and stopped me from looking too far into the future. I had plenty of visitors, which was lovely and helped keep my spirits up. Roz and Chris were the first to arrive the morning after my surgery, and as always their compassion and kindness were a huge comfort. I know their presence helped Colin and my children immensely, particularly Jack who was very upset after his initial visit. Roz spent some time with him, and her love and support helped enormously. Sadly, Chris was no stranger to this scenario. His first wife had lost her seven-year battle to breast cancer some years earlier, and when he was just fifteen years old he had lost his own mother to lung cancer. In spite of this, and my genuine sadness for his loss, he never made me feel awkward, uncomfortable or thoughtless if I talked about myself or how I felt. In fact he actively encouraged it, which I have always thought was very brave and selfless of him.

My girlfriends from the village popped in that week, as did Colette and David, and my Aunty

Edna came all the way from Sussex by train to see me. She's not actually my aunt, but she married my dad's best friend Ian the week after I was born. She and Ian socialised regularly with Mum and Dad, and had even lived with us for a while before emigrating to New Zealand for a short time. They'd been back in England when Dad left home, and had been particularly supportive of my mum and we three children. They were ever present during my teenage years, and it was Edna who advised me on where best to get my hair highlighted, and what not to put up with from my first boyfriend! She was also single-handedly responsible for bringing about my life long obsession with the sun, having returned from the island of Kos, looking absolutely gorgeous with her skin a fabulous nut brown. Life took us in different directions until the early nineties when we were reunited, and from that point forward the strong bond that had been made when I was a child was strengthened. Ian and Edna never had children of their own, yet her understanding and intuition of how relationships work was remarkable. I was able to support her through her four-year battle of caring for Ian after he was diagnosed with Alzheimer's, and she supported me through my very difficult divorce. When I was diagnosed with cancer she heard what I was unable to say, and without me ever needing to ask, was right by my side when I needed her.

Charlie, Kathy and Debbie all came to visit too, and I was inundated with cards and flowers from the QVC viewers, which left me feeling incredibly cared for.

Although I wasn't in pain, the itching from the morphine had become increasingly worse, and the ability to sleep or relax eluded me. Because of this I decided on the second day, while my children were with me, to tell the nurse that I really didn't think I needed it anymore and I'd be happy for them to take the PCA away. Not one of my better ideas! As the afternoon wore on, I began to experience a strong pain down my right side, which clearly the morphine had been masking very effectively. The last thing I wanted to do was to make a fuss in front of the children, but I could already feel the sweat beading on my top lip with the effort, so having made the excuse of being incredibly tired, I asked if they'd mind leaving a tad earlier? As soon as I thought they would be far enough down the corridor not to see my call light come on, I immediately rang for the nurse. Mercifully, the Oramorph she prescribed, which is a liquid morphine to be taken orally, did the trick and stopped the itching, which was a mighty relief!

Once the PCA had gone, I didn't need the catheter, which I rather missed! There is something liberating about being able to wee in bed, and not even having to consider using the toilet! I'd only ever had a catheter once before, and that was after the emergency C-section to deliver Jack. The following morning as I fed my son, I thanked the nurse for providing me with the hot water bottle I was warming my feet on. Her face was a picture as she rushed over and whipped back the sheet to reveal not the aforementioned cosy comforter, but a clear cushion-like bag filled with my own urine!

Each day in between visitors, I did my exercises with the physio, and each day the nurse came in and checked under my dressings while I kept my head turned away. The breast nurse who had been supporting me ever since my diagnosis, came to see me too, and tried to coax me gently into accepting that the surgery was the only way they could get rid of the cancer in my breast, and it was a necessary part of my recovery. I knew that following my skin-sparing mastectomy, the plastic surgeon had placed a rugby-ball-shaped expander in my chest, complete with a small valve that was just under the skin below my armpit. It felt tight and uncomfortable which was weird, as I basically had no feeling across the right side of my chest. I guess it was more of a sense of discomfort, and alien to me. I'd already been told that I would need to come back to the hospital in a few weeks to see the plastic surgeon, as he planned to inject saline through the valve, and increase the size of the expander. This would gently stretch the skin in readiness for a permanent silicone implant after I'd had my chemo and radiotherapy. I knew my chest wasn't completely flat like my mum's, because I could see a slight bump through my pyjamas, but any more than that I didn't really feel ready to face at this point.

I think it was on my third day that I had the first

of my drains taken out. Their job had been to keep the chest area clear of fluids, using fine tubes that carried any liquids out and into a couple of vacuum-sealed clear containers so that none of it could get back into the body. These tubes were inserted while I was under anaesthetic, and I had no idea how long they were, but I did know that I'd be fully conscious when they were removed. I tried hard not to think about that part of it.

Luckily for me I had the same nurses each day, and felt very comfortable with all of them. The nurse who came to take the drain out got me to lean against three pillows, so I was propped almost upright but facing away from her. She then put her hand on my back, and told me that once she was ready, I would need to take a deep breath and let it out slowly so she could pull the drain out through a small hole in the side of my chest. It was the strangest feeling – not really painful– but an incredible pressure and pulling sensation that built up within the chest. It was pretty heavy going for the nurse though, and the drain itself was a lot longer than I had anticipated, so she had to heave pretty hard to get the thing to come out. Because I was breathing out rather loudly, I wasn't able to make any other sound, which was probably a good thing, but I do remember feeling childishly pleased when the nurse told me I'd had been very brave, as it hadn't been a pleasant experience for either of us!

They came to remove the second drain on the fifth day, and told me that once it was out, not only could I finally have a bath, but I'd also be able to go home the following day. Lucy had come to see me that evening, and was thrilled when I told her. I wanted to share her enthusiasm, but in truth I felt very scared about leaving. Hospital had become a sanctuary to me. I hadn't even had the courage to look at myself since my surgery, and so when I told Lucy how I felt, she said she would stay the night with me, and we could talk it through.

I must have done something very good in my life to have been blessed with such a kind and thoughtful daughter, and talk we did, for a long time, about a great many things. Lucy is a very private person, and as a teenager, she kept her life to herself. However, she was always very protective of me, and there had been a few upsets over the years when she felt I was too liberated in my lifestyle: sunbathing topless, for example, which was a treat for me, was something she found undignified. She may well have been right, although it was irrelevant now, as it wasn't something I ever saw myself doing again.

Lucy gently suggested a warm bath. 'The nurse has said I must stay with you, and if you need help, to call for her. So if I can cope with seeing you naked, Ma, then I'm sure you can cope with seeing yourself?' she said with a small smile. And she was right, although, bless her, she left the bathroom at that point and gave me a few minutes to myself.

I stood in front of the mirror and took my pyjamas off. Gently pulling the long piece of plaster that held the bandage in place, it came away to reveal the part of my chest where my right breast had been. The skin was smooth and almost flat with a long incision right through the centre. Nothing remained of my nipple although there was a tiny amount of the areole. The once lumpy, cancerous and raised ridge had disappeared, and there was now a deep dent, about six inches down from my collar bone. I placed my hand over the dent, and sensed the somewhat angular shape of the expander through the skin, and then running my fingers down under my arm I felt the hardness of the valve. When I say 'felt,' it was with my fingers only as there was no sensation of touch on my skin at all. I had no feeling over the entire breast area right up to the collarbone. Around my armpit and shoulder was numb too, and to this day I still don't have any feeling there. I lifted my right arm up as far as it would go and put my hand over my mouth so that Lucy wouldn't hear me sob.

It didn't matter to me that the surgery had been carried out to rid me of the tumour and the cancerous lymph nodes, at that moment I would have given anything to turn back time. But I was going to have to get used to this, and work on building my strength up to face the seven months of chemotherapy and radiotherapy.

'Are you all right, Mum?' Lucy called through the door.

I wiped my face roughly with a flannel, telling her I was fine, and was ready to get into the bath. There wasn't really a great deal more to say, but just having her with me helped enormously. She told me sweetly that I honestly didn't look all that different, and she was sure things would improve as I healed. Her calm and comforting presence helped me enormously and, wrapped in a large towel and smelling of bubble bath, I was able to put my darkest thoughts to the back of my mind until bedtime.

# Chapter Fifteen

I don't think either of us slept terribly well that final night in hospital. It was much harder for Lucy, who was sleeping on the floor in my room, but she stayed and had an early breakfast with me before having to head off back to her teaching commitments at school. Roz and Colin were both there to collect me, and Colin, having made space in his car for all the beautiful cards, flowers and gifts that I had been given was first into the room. I had been completely spoiled, not just by friends and family, but by work colleagues and viewers of QVC too! I will never forget Liz Earle's generosity when, having heard my news, she sent me some beautiful flowers, and also provided goodie bags for me to give to all the nurses, which they were thrilled with!

The insecure feelings I'd had the night before ate away at me while I waited for Colin and Roz to make several journeys to the car with all my belongings. My right arm was still very sore, and an appointment had been made for me to see the physio in a couple of days' time. I thought of the beautiful little cottage I was renting, with its views

across the fields, and then I thought of being alone
with Colin. Knowing that I would be sharing a
bed with him that night troubled me. I had missed
him terribly – the physical closeness of him – and
the memory of our lovemaking the night before
my surgery stirred up a whole host of conflicting
emotions. But that was then, and this was now, and
although I finally knew what I looked like under my
bandages, I wasn't ready to show him. I couldn't
see how he would still want me, or fancy me, as I
felt so different physically and mentally.

It was pouring with rain as we left the hospital
with Roz following closely behind, and I watched
the drops of water track down the car windows
creating liquid lines. The closer we got to the
cottage, the more uptight I became. These feelings
were alien to me – I hadn't really entertained them
while I was in hospital, but now they crowded into
my brain like grains of sand in an egg timer. As
the traffic slowed along the high street, our car was
on a level with all the pedestrians, heads down,
umbrellas up, battling the cold wet weather. We
stopped at the lights to allow them to cross, and
watched the wind whipping their wet coats around.
There's always somebody who waits until the lights
are on amber, and then throws themselves on to
the crossing like a lemming, and today it was a
young woman, wearing a very tight pair of jeans,
high heels and a T-shirt. No coat, just a T-shirt,
which was clinging to her large breasts and barely
covering her hard nipples that stuck out like chapel
hat pegs.

I'd been brought up to believe it's rude to stare and to make personal remarks, but I couldn't stop myself from doing both. My insecurity manifested itself in a litany of licentious comments about her. Unkind, angry and uncharacteristic comments that continued long after the lights had changed. 'I bet that made your day eh?' I said to Colin. 'Make the most of it, because I don't have what she has any more.'

He didn't rise to the bait, just looked sideways at me.

'I mean seriously? Why the hell would you be out in weather like this without a coat? Or a bra? They're probably not even her own breasts. Some bloody boob job. She probably didn't have tits at all – flat as a pancake! Hey. Whatever. So much better than what you're going to be looking at now eh? Not exactly a real woman any more am I? Diseased and disfigured. That's what I am. And you're stuck with it. Unless you choose to walk.'

'That's enough!' he said, turning his face to look at me and away from the road. 'Have you any idea how insulting it is for you to suggest that I would want someone else purely because this has happened? So if I lost an arm or a bollock you wouldn't love me or want to be with me anymore? I keep telling you, nothing has changed! I love for you who you are, not how you look.'

I felt crushed and unbelievably weary, and after wiping my tears away, I reached across for his hand and held it tightly. I so wanted to believe him, and having said sorry, I told him I *did* believe him, but in my heart I felt his argument was flawed. He said nothing had changed, but to me *everything* had changed. At the beginning of the year I was looking forward, now all I wanted to do was to go back. I hated myself for hurting him and for doubting him, when all he was trying to do was love and support me. I knew I was risking our recently repaired relationship, but I felt completely out of control – I had no choices. I was on a path that had been mapped out for me by the cancer and those trying to rid me of it, but at that moment in time I wanted to crawl into a corner with my head between my knees and howl.

# CHAPTER SIXTEEN

You know when someone asks you 'What is the worst that could happen?' I don't believe my answer years ago would ever have been to be diagnosed with cancer, in fact, I would have thought it would be far more likely to be either spend time in prison, be buried alive or freeze to death! However, coming a close but far less dramatic fourth, would have been throwing up. I would go to extraordinary lengths to stop myself from being sick. Until January 2011 the first three on the list were highly improbable, and the fourth doubtful, but suddenly the unthinkable had become a reality. I remembered just a week after my initial diagnosis my breast nurse saying in a somewhat gung-ho manner that it was highly unlikely I'd have to have chemotherapy, and that radiotherapy was purely belt and braces. Of course, following the subsequent tests I now knew I was actually going to have to have both, and shed loads of it too! Obviously, recovering from my surgery was the most important thing, but I had been forewarned that they would like me to start chemotherapy just three weeks later.

With such an irregular work pattern, I rarely booked holidays in advance, but something that had been in the diary for months, was a girls' weekend away. For twelve years my friends and I had taken ourselves off to various rural retreats in the UK, and enjoyed extended weekend breaks together twice a year. It was booked way in advance, and involved the same group of friends who had been with me for the infamous hot tub and eyebrow-tinting experience. They'd been as shocked as I was to hear of my diagnosis, but had been totally supportive as always, and I knew that spending time with them just before my treatment would help me enormously. It was an absolute joy being with them, and the bond that held us together had become far stronger over the years. I really wanted to make this happen, especially as now suddenly everything seemed so much less certain.

My breast surgeon sent me a letter explaining that I had been appointed an oncologist and that this doctor would be responsible for putting together a treatment plan for me. Luckily the chemotherapy was to be in the same hospital as I'd had my surgery, and although about forty minutes' drive away, I felt safe there.

Lucy came with me for my first visit to the oncologist, and we arrived with just enough time for me to visit the loo before we were ushered into the consulting room. There, the most charming, personable and kind woman I had so far met, introduced herself to Lucy and me, making sure we knew where to sit in the somewhat cramped space.

Lucy felt for my hand and held it tightly.

On the desk in front of us were my medical reports, and handwritten on these pieces of paper were additional notes my newly appointed oncologist Dr Mei Lin Ah-See, had made. I could see hand drawn diagrams of my breasts, with arrows and a lot of writing. Dr Ah-See began reading from the report in front of her, reminding us of the multifocal tumours, the positioning of them, the fact that in spite of trying to clear the margins as closely as possible, the anterior margin showed the infiltrating tumour was still present even after the mastectomy. Then, of course, there was the fact the cancer had got into my lymph nodes, and more importantly my sentinel node, which was the node next to the larger tumour. She explained kindly yet clearly that the sentinel node is the one that sort of 'stands guard' over the breast, and is the first node that filters the fluid draining away from the area of the breast that contained the cancer. Basically, if cancer cells are breaking away from the tumour and travelling away from the breast via the lymph system, then the sentinel node is more likely than any other lymph node to contain the cancer. Breast cancer can and sometimes does metastasise – this means a rogue cancer cell sets up as a secondary cancer in another part of the body. It has a tendency to affect the brain, the bones, the liver or the lungs, and because of this, chemotherapy would give me my very best chance of it not recurring.

She had worked out a treatment plan, based on my weight, my height, and my diagnosis. I would

start with four treatments of a drug known as FEC.
This is an abbreviation of three separate drugs –
5FU, epirubicin and cyclophosphamide.

I laughed. 'God! Would you believe it?' I said
smiling at Lucy, and then looking at Mei Lin.

'I was married into an Irish family for seventeen
years. "Feck" is the word they used instead of our
four-letter one! It always sounded less rude, but I
think it's more than appropriate for this treatment!'

FEC is pretty potent and reduces the production
of white blood cells by the bone marrow, making
you more prone to infection. This effect can begin
around seven days after the treatment has been
given, with your resistance to infection usually
reaching its lowest point ten to fourteen days
later. Hopefully after that, your white cells should
increase steadily and would usually have returned to
normal levels before the next cycle of chemotherapy
was due. She went on to explain that the drugs
would be administered by infusion and injections
into a cannula or a line once every three weeks
for three months in a special ward at the hospital.
I would also need to have a blood test every three
weeks, on the day before my next treatment was
due. In her gentle yet authoritative voice, she
explained to Lucy and me that there were a number
of common side effects, which I was probably
already aware of. Others, though, were less
common, she said, but all of them were documented
on the pages she presented to us both. My eyes
flickered over the first few words, but before I could
focus on them my attention was drawn back to her,

as she explained that that this was only the first part of the treatment.

She felt it was necessary for me to also have twelve treatments of something called Paclitaxel (Taxol), which would need to be administered once a week. She then handed over a second page of notes that I took with my free hand, the other one still holding Lucy's tightly. Looking kindly on us she asked if we would find it helpful if she read through some of the possible side effects. She did stress though at this point that while some people could have very few, others may have more, but the variety of symptoms would not affect *everyone* having FEC and Taxol.

One of the first things mentioned was the lowered resistance to infection because of the reduction of white blood cells; bruising or bleeding as FEC can reduce the production of platelets (which help blood to clot and stop bleeding); possible anaemia and feeling or being sick. Tiredness, particularly towards the end of treatment; complete hair loss – which included all body hair and may destroy eyebrows and lashes – sore mouth and ulcers, irritation of the bladder, skin rash, upset tummy and occasionally gritty eyes or blurred vision. The less common side effects were blood clots, skin changes – such as a rash or discolouration – changes in the colour and condition of your nails, problems with your liver and maybe even changes in the way your heart works. The second drug Taxol could bring on more of the same – the risk of blood clots, feeling sick, upset tummy, constipation, and a few variants. These included aches and pains in the joints, numbness or tingling in the hands and feet, headaches, breathlessness and feelings of anxiety, low blood pressure, changes in your heart rate and abdominal pain or heartburn.

I do want to stress to you though, as Mei Lin did to me, that all of these things are 'possible' side effects, with the exception of hair loss which is unfortunately a given. Should you have a similar treatment programme you may of course have a completely different reaction. A colleague of mine got through six months of chemo, and all she struggled with was a cough!

My mind was having trouble keeping up with this rather long list but my fear of being sick was paramount, and I wanted to know how likely it was that this would happen. Apparently there has been an enormous amount of research carried out over the years to make certain that with additional medication, the chances of being physically ill have dramatically reduced. An anti-sickness drug would be administered not just with the chemotherapy on the day, but by me injecting something called pegfilgrastim into my stomach for six days following each treatment. These injections I could carry out myself at home. I swallowed, not fancying the thought of that at all, but she assured me that I would have the chance to talk through all of this with the nurses in the chemo unit, who would not only help me with the injections, but could tell me about the cold cap, which was a device that may help to save the hair on my head, should I choose to use it.

I think it's important at this juncture that I reiterate that not all treatment programmes are the same, and pegfilgrastim may not be included in yours. However if it is, I'm certain you'll get the assistance you need, and you will cope as I did!

The doctor paused, and leaned back in her chair. I took a deep breath, and looked sideways at my daughter. There is something terribly sad about putting your child – however old they are – in a situation where they will have to take on the kind of worries that you have always tried to protect them from. At that moment I felt it was a complete role reversal. My girl is made of strong stuff, and has always looked out for me, but her face was pale and her pretty features were taut as we listened to the litany, and she concentrated hard on what we were being told.

I thought I was coping pretty well with it all – hair and fingernail loss just a part of it – but the final comment floored me.

'Because the chemicals within this treatment can cause your skin to become photosensitive, it will be impossible for you to sit out in the sun during your treatment,' the doctor said.

Lucy said. 'Oh, Mum…' and I felt tears prick my eyes.

Anyone who knows me knows of my obsession with the sunshine and getting a tan, and I had joked with Lucy on the way to the hospital, saying that least I would have the whole summer off, I could get a corking tan *and* I wouldn't need a bikini wax!

Childishly, it had made bearable the thought of coping with the treatment and being away from work and my friends for such a long time.

I never seem to have a tissue to hand when I really need it, and was trying to surreptitiously wipe my tearful eyes and running nose with my sleeve. Dr Ah-See pushed the box of tissues towards me. I took one gratefully.

'It's childish really, and probably not very good for me either!'

I missed the irony of my words.

Having clarified that the chemo was given intravenously, and because my veins had let me down so terribly up to this point, she told me she was arranging for me to have something called a 'Portacath' fitted. This is a small device about the size of a pound coin that has a thin soft plastic tube with an opening (port) just under the skin. The tip of this tube sits in a large vein just above your heart, and means that all the chemotherapy can be given via the port, without needing to use a cannula on the arms or wrists or hands.

There are several other methods too which could be offered to you, but it may depend on the length and type of your treatment, and obviously your veins! That was definitely my silver lining, and I thanked her profusely. It might sound crazy, but it made me feel that all I'd been just been told was now do-able. An appointment would be made within the next couple of days to have this fitted, which left just one final thing.

Like millions of women, I had a Mirena coil

fitted. For those who may not be aware, it is a very effective contraceptive device that is inserted into the womb and emits something called levonorgestrel that dramatically decreases the chances of pregnancy. My diagnosis had found the cancer to be strongly positive to both female hormones oestrogen and progesterone – meaning they act almost as a fertiliser for the cancer, and as levonorgestrel is similar to these hormones, the coil would need to be taken out. For many women it's not remotely uncomfortable having one of these things fitted or removed, but despite her valiant efforts, my poor GP had a nightmare trying to fit mine, and I'd had to have it fitted under sedation in the very same hospital I was now sitting in! Bearing that in mind, I was obviously worried about having it removed, but luckily the consultant who had succeeded in professionally planting it in my uterus just a few years earlier, still practised at the hospital. Having told my oncologist this, she said kindly that she would make an appointment for me to see him within the next few days.

There was a moment of silence. I looked at Lucy and she was wiping her eyes, so I hugged her to me. 'I'll be fine, Looma, don't worry.'

The oncologist sensitively gave us a moment before saying, 'I realise this is a great deal for you to take in, and a very distressing situation, and I am very sorry. But I also realise that this hospital is quite a distance from your home, so would it be helpful for you to see the chemotherapy unit now while you are here, and meet the nurses who will be caring for you?'

Really? I felt utterly exhausted.

'I don't want to sound defeatist, but I've got several physio appointments booked over this next week, so could we come back another day? It's just quite a lot to take in…'

'I think that's best, Mum,' Lucy compounded.

'Of course, that's probably a better idea. I'll let you know as soon as I have a date for you to have the port fitted and your coil removed.'

Lucy and I stood up, and having thanked the doctor, we made our way out down the blue carpeted corridor towards the car park.

# CHAPTER SEVENTEEN

True to the doctor's word, within a couple of days the appointments came through for me to have my port fitted, and my coil removed. As QVC had told me to not worry about work and to take care of myself, I was essentially on leave and free to fill my days with whatever was needed. I didn't really want to go to either of these appointments on my own, but realised quite early on, how incredibly fortunate I was to have a large number of people who were happy to accompany me to wherever I had to go. Between Colin, my friends and family there was always someone to support me, but I realise there are a large number of people who face a diagnosis of cancer alone. Although the physical process would be a great deal harder, there are so many organisations like Breast Cancer Care or Macmillan that can help emotionally, so hopefully no one would ever feel unsupported.

Lucy worked as a teacher, and having explained my situation to her Head of Year when I was first diagnosed, she and the school had been particularly helpful and allowed her time off when needed. I was very glad that she would be able to come with me when I had my Portacath fitted.

A different hospital, but similar admissions process, saw us taken to a private room, where having ordered sandwiches for afterwards (it had become a kind of ritual), the doctor who was to carry out the procedure, came and talked me through it. Of course my oncologist had already explained what a port was, and how it would work, but it was very helpful to hear it all again, as my memory – which has never been very good – seemed to be worse than ever! The procedure would need only mild sedation and not a general anaesthetic, so I would be fine to head home soon afterwards, with Lucy driving, of course! Even mild sedation means you're not really road safe for several hours afterwards.

As with most procedures, if you are physically able to walk, then you will end up making your own way to theatre, which I did. As the doctor had promised, only a mild sedative was administered, but mercifully I remembered nothing about the operation, and woke up to find Lucy sitting with me in my room. I had a light dressing over what felt like a raised area just below my collarbone that I tentatively felt with my fingers. It seemed really alien and invasive, but recalling how difficult it had been for the nurse to get a line in when I had the MRI, I was relieved. The fact that my chemotherapy would be administered this way would make my life a great deal easier. Once again I thanked my lucky stars for having such good care. I had six long months of treatment ahead of me, and anything that was going to help get me through it was a blessing. The light sedation had pretty much worn off, so after cup of tea, and our shared round of sandwiches, Lucy drove me home.

As she wasn't able to stay with me that evening, my friend Kathy from work had come over to keep me company. Considering the weird shifts we all worked then, it was incredible that there was always someone available, but Debbie held the diary, and made sure that all those who were able to help out with hospital visits or support generally, knew what was happening and when. She ran it very efficiently. Kathy and I set about making supper. At first, I felt okay, but I'd only been home for about an hour when I started to feel very, very uncomfortable. There was a distinct feeling of pressure across my chest, and although the port was quite prominent, pulling the skin taut under my collarbone, I was worried something else was wrong.

Kathy suggested I called the hospital where the procedure had been carried out, although I didn't think for one moment the consultant would be there as it was after 6 p.m. I couldn't decide whether I would be seen to be making a big fuss or not. Eventually I rang and nervously spoke with the receptionist. I explained that I'd been a patient earlier on in the day, and had had a 'Portakabin' fitted, but was now finding it difficult to breathe. There was just the slightest pause before she responded in a slightly strangled voice 'Ah yes, Alison Keenan, I have you here on our patient sheet. It was a Portacath you had fitted? I will put you through to the doctor now…'

Of course anyone having a Portakabin fitted would no doubt be struggling to breathe, but the receptionist was politeness personified! I then spoke with the doctor who was, as he had been earlier in the day, absolutely charming. He calmed my nerves by explaining that because this part of the body is particularly bony, and the flesh lies quite flat, there's not a huge amount of space to slide the port into. My skin was stretched and probably a little bruised, but it would feel a lot easier over the following twenty-four hours. Knowing this didn't make my chest feel any less uncomfortable, but he had allayed my fears, and so, having taken a few paracetamol as he suggested, Kathy and I cracked on with our evening.

I had my coil removed just a few days later, and although quite sick with apprehension before my appointment, the surgeon, who remembered me from all those years earlier, could not have been kinder. Talking with him about my diagnosis, he told me that his wife had been through a similar illness and treatment, but was now fit and well. Although somewhat incongruous to be chatting away, minus my knickers, with a light shining on my nether regions, this man was such a calming influence that somewhere between confirming the number of children I had, and where I was working, my coil was removed painlessly. Such a relief! I felt quite tearful as I thanked him profusely, and admitted that I'd been more worried about having it removed than I was about my pending chemotherapy!

'Stay strong, and stay positive,' he said as I shook his hand. 'I am sure all will be well.'

His words stayed with me for my entire journey home, and consequently became my mantra.

# CHAPTER EIGHTEEN

The month between me having my mastectomy and the start of my chemo seemed to pass very quickly. Outside of the minor procedures to remove my coil and implant the Portacath, I had to attend endless physio appointments at the hospital. I really had been completely unprepared for the lack of movement and constant discomfort I had in my right arm, or for the numbness, tingling, and sensitivity across my breast, my armpit and the upper and inner arm too. Unfortunately for me the 'cording' which had been mentioned to me during my hospital stay, *had* developed in my right arm, and the unbelievably strong pulling sensation that happened every time I went to reach out or stretch my arm, was excruciating.

My physio was a charming Australian girl, whom I liked on sight, and having ushered Lucy and I into a windowless room the size of a cupboard, she got me to lie down on the treatment table. Lucy had brought me to the hospital as I was unable to drive myself, and she had promised to make notes of the exercises, as my memory still seemed a little unreliable following the anaesthetic. She needn't have worried though as the physio immediately produced a photocopied sheet with all of them printed on it, and gave it to Lucy to look after.

I had to start with my arms by the side of my head and pointing behind me. That was pretty much impossible, and I had to use my left arm to lift my right arm, the effort making me break into a sweat as I strained with the effort. The physio measured each of the stretches so that I could see my progress – you wouldn't believe how far two centimetres can seem! These exercises were a lot harder than the ones I'd had to do in the hospital, but the physio explained the tightening in the arm would get worse before it got better. She told me that one of her patients had spent the entire session effing and blinding because of the pain, and told me not to hold back if I felt the need as she was pretty much unshockable. I don't swear that often, and didn't want to appear a wimp in front of my daughter, but I was being sorely tested! The final part of the session involved me standing, facing the wall, and trying to slide my right hand up it as far as possible. I had to hold the stretch for as long as I could before slowly pulling it back down again. This should have been the simplest thing in the world to do but the burning sensation it produced was vile.

'Shitty death,' I muttered as I tried to slide my hand up the wall at a speed a snail would have been ashamed of.

'That's it, Mum, you're doing brilliantly!' Lucy said and the physio agreed.

Small victories, I felt, but a victory none the less.

I only had to attend two more sessions as the 'cording' did diminish over the following week, and I was finally able to move my arm without any discomfort. It made life at lot easier as even the simplest of tasks like washing my hair or getting dressed had been damned near impossible. I tried to tie those sessions in with my plastic surgeon's appointments just so that we saved on petrol as well as time! You may remember that I had been given an expander implant at the time of the mastectomy, and this fairly rigid but small hollow receptacle needed filling with saline solution to make it larger so that it would stretch the skin across my chest. It felt slightly angular and incredibly alien to me, so I decided to give it a name in the hope I would feel less animosity towards it. I called the expander 'Dolly' and as I watched the right side of my chest inflate at a rather alarming rate on my first visit to the plastic surgeon, I felt a kinship to Ms. Parton! The right side would need to appear larger than the left to allow the skin to stretch sufficiently to accommodate the eventual implant. We hadn't yet fixed a date for this procedure, but I knew the general consensus was that it should happen when I had my second mastectomy, as recommended by my breast surgeon, the following spring. It took just two visits for Dolly to reach her potential, and my plastic surgeon said he was happy to leave things as they were until after my chemo and radiotherapy when he would reassess the situation.

Roz remembers taking me to one of my clinic appointments at this time, where I had my dressings changed by the breast nurse, and she saw me catch sight of myself in the mirror. I had made an effort with my hair and make-up that day, and while the nurse gently applied the new dressing I kept my eyes focused on the mirror.

'You okay, Ali?' Roz asked me.

There was a slight pause before I looked away from the mirror and smiled directly at her. 'I could go back to work now couldn't I? I look normal don't I?'

She of course smiled back, as did the nurse, but as she told me some years later, she knew I had a fair way to go before that was likely.

My six months of chemotherapy was getting ever closer, and to fully accept what was about to happen, I decided to try and buy a few wigs in advance of the inevitable hair loss. My breast nurse had already spoken with me about this, and told me that all breast cancer patients facing chemo were entitled to a free wig on the NHS, but there were several independent suppliers who could also help. Charities like Macmillan, The Haven and Breast Cancer Care are incredibly supportive too, and have specialists who can advise you. Outside of the colour and style of wig there are only two other choices to make – real hair or acrylic – the major difference being the price! Hoping to return to work after my treatment I approached QVC about the possibility of them buying a real hair wig for me to wear, and although it was a vast sum of money, they very kindly agreed. I decided to put that purchase on hold until I'd bought the acrylic wigs, although I didn't tell anyone about either decision, as I thought it may be deemed a little previous! I chose an independent wig consultant who came to the cottage with two of what were possibly the largest suitcases I had ever seen! I wasn't at all sure we'd get them through the door, but after a bit of pushing and shoving she was across the threshold, and having moved the coffee table, we were ready.

I had never worn a wig. Years ago my mum had owned a rather strange ginger coloured one that looked more like red squirrel road kill, but I'd always dreamed of owning a long-haired wig. As a child, my own hair was kept very short, because I apparently made a terrible fuss when it was washed, and so with rather large ears and a very short fringe I was often mistaken for a boy! Long hair would have made all the difference then! Inside the huge suitcases were a wealth of weaves, colours, lengths, and styles all made from acrylic hair, and I inadvertently reached up with my left arm to feel my own shoulder-length locks, before reaching into the suitcase.

'Crikey, that's quite a collection! I'm not sure where to begin!'

'That's what most of my clients say. It's understandable. I say that the best rule of thumb is to choose something that looks like your own hair. A style you like and are comfortable with.'

'That makes sense,' I said, sifting through the vast collection, wondering if I was looking for a needle in a haystack. It took a while but I was rewarded with a soft blonde shoulder-length wig with a fringe.

'Can I try this one?'

Putting a wig on while you still have hair is quite a convoluted process. After tying my hair back I had to pull a tan coloured mesh cap over my head. Think of a pop sock, and now imagine pulling it over your hair so that it completely flattens and contains it. Too far down, and you look like a bank robber, not far enough and you look like Max Wall! There is always a front and back to a wig, but on the ones without a label it isn't immediately obvious. Some of them also had tiny little clips at the forehead, just above the ears, and at the nape of the neck. These were there to help secure the wig by clipping them into your own hair, but as the consultant explained, others had soft tabs that you could attach double-sided tape to for those with no hair.

Which in less than a month would be me.

With a little guidance, I managed to line the tabs up with my ears, so the wig felt balanced, and then I had to go into the dining room to find a mirror. Looking at my reflection, pretty much unrecognisable with this rather large amount of honey-blonde hair I felt suddenly old and scared. It was so obviously a wig, and I stood there wondering why on earth I'd thought this was a good idea. Why was I buying them? To look as though I still had hair? To keep my head warm? To hide from others the fact I had cancer and no hair, or maybe to try and hide it from myself? What made me think I was going to be well enough over the next six months to actually want to be dressed up, wig on, and going out?

'You all right in there my dear?' the consultant hovered in the narrow doorway. 'Yes, fine thanks. What do you think?' I turned to face her.

'Very flattering colour on you, and it's a soft style. How does it feel?'

In truth it felt like a very tight hat, but not wishing to seem ungrateful I said impulsively that it was a good fit and I'd take it. 'Just the one, or would you like to consider an additional wig in a different style?'

'I'm not sure, but then I've not seen them all yet' I said, and having followed her back into the sitting room, I looked through the second suitcase.

It didn't take long for me to find a far shorter layered wig that reminded me of the way my hair had been when I first met Colin. Like many single men and women, we had both started online dating, and he was one of only three men I ever met. It was Sam who had suggested I give it a go, after I'd been on my own for eight months or more. He was also the one who took my photo, in the kitchen of the cottage I was then renting, just two days after I'd had my hair cut. The memory cheered me up, and so having agreed this second purchase, I was then given a whole range of special products that were needed to wash and condition my acrylic tresses. The shorter wig was around £175 but the longer wig was over £200. I stupidly hadn't asked about the price beforehand, but tried to see it as a treat to myself, rather than a necessity.

In spite of my mixed feelings, I wore the longer wig on Mother's Day – the 3rd of April. It was just three days after I'd lost all my hair, and the first time I'd been out in public, having felt too poorly to go anywhere before then. The children took me to a local pub for lunch, and I was thrilled that my wig stayed in place and wasn't too hot, although it itched a little. Scratching your scalp is not recommended when wearing a wig as it moves, but apart from that I think I got away with it! It was just another part of all that comes with cancer and its treatment, and it was my way of accepting the changes in my life.

I know it comes down to personal choice and what makes you feel better, but I found that wearing scarves was a great deal more comfortable than a wig. That was mainly due to Pipa Gordon, a fellow presenter at QVC, who, as a complete surprise, bought a huge bag of beautiful scarves for me from Accessorise! Complete with instructions on how to tie them, she told me that she'd not been sure which ones to choose, but I was to only wear the ones I liked. I loved them all, and used them constantly throughout the following year or so – in fact, I still have two of them! The rest I kept for the first three years after my diagnosis and then gave them to a friend who had lost all her hair through chemo. It was definitely a gift that kept on giving.

# CHAPTER NINETEEN

My sister Jenny is younger than me, but has always seemed far more grown up and in control of her life and emotions than I've ever been. It may be because when we were children I never let her take the lead, and so she's spent the rest of her life trying to reverse the roles. When we were young, we were very close, and would spend the school holidays inventing brilliant games that we never tired of. I remember setting up camp in our back garden, and using the coalbunker as our wagon. We covered the wooden clotheshorse with a tablecloth, and with a skipping rope looped through the lids, the dustbins became our horses. We'd play for hours on end, only stopping to make more banana sandwiches, or go to the loo! I actually worked for a while on an idea that would take away the need for toilet breaks, and it involved an empty plastic bag that was strategically placed between the legs and then sellotaped to the thighs. Clearly I hadn't thought it through as I was wearing trousers the first time I tried it out, and ended up with shoes full of wee!

As we got older, the games became more

elaborate and involved, but I would always take the lead because, as I told her, I was the eldest. So if we were playing Royal Families, I was the Queen, and she was my servant; in the vet's practice we created, I was the vet, and she was my secretary, and I remember once we set up our own hospital, where I lorded it over her as the doctor, while she was the patient! Poor girl, I even made her drink a pint of water with Fairy Liquid in it once, having convinced her it was 'medicine'! Amazingly she forgave me, although she burped bubbles for several days.

Originally trained as a radiographer, she changed the course of her life after having her two daughters, and made the move into education. She has worked as Head of Year at a primary school in Hampshire for the last twenty years and is very highly thought of by her pupils and peers alike, as she's incredibly good at her job. Ever since I left home to get married, we have lived miles away from each other in different counties, and what with work, children, and life generally, we rarely see enough of each other. When I called her on that Tuesday evening to tell her I had cancer, she was as always, kind and sympathetic but above all, practical. She came to see me just a few days later, and realising that I wouldn't be particularly able after my surgery, she helped me to rearrange my cupboards, and sort out the space under the stairs where I'd jammed loads of things when moving into the cottage just four weeks earlier.

It all felt very surreal, but we did talk about the

mastectomy and the possibility of me having chemo and radiotherapy. Mercifully, Mum hadn't had to go through chemotherapy, but the fifteen radiotherapy sessions had worn her out. I was still hanging on to the hope that it might not be necessary for me to have this kind of treatment, and so I didn't really want to talk about it, as I felt it would jinx the eventual decision. Daft, really, but the unimaginable had become a reality, and I felt it was tempting fate. Our mum had moved from Shropshire to Hampshire some years earlier, and after six years of living within spitting distance of me, she found a lovely home just twenty minutes or so from Jenny. They saw each other regularly, and after Mum's surgery Jenny had been key in aiding Mum's recovery. She knew all too well what I would be facing after my operation, and so we decided there and then that it would make more sense for her to take leave from work and visit me *after* my surgery, when she could be of some help to me at home.

I'd only been convalescing for a number of days following my mastectomy, and it was Roz who had been looking after me. Although I was still incredibly tired, and very uncomfortable, she'd had the devil's own job trying to stop me from doing things. I found it really difficult to sit still and do nothing, and remember lugging a large and very heavy metal-framed plant holder down the stairs, to be met by her at the bottom. Understandably she was not best pleased! When Jenny came to stay a few days later, Roz gave her strict instructions to watch me like a hawk. "I've got eyes in the back of

my head. It's a family trait, trust me, she'll be safe."
And safe is something I always felt when I was with
either of them.

Of course by that time, I knew that it wasn't
just chemotherapy I was going to need, but
radiotherapy too. Something else I'd only recently
found out, was that there had been more than one
tumour. Multifocal is how they describe a number
of tumours within the same quadrant of the breast.
Although pretty small, it was the same invasive
lobular carcinoma as the original cancer. When
the initial lumpy ridge was surgically removed
and they found that two of the three lumps were
indeed cancerous tumours, my consultant had
hoped that was the only disease in the breast. These
other tumours had somehow disguised themselves
on the mammogram, ultrasound and MRI, so I
realised how lucky I was to have been seen by the
radiographer who had made the initial discovery.
Invasive lobular cancer is also known as a hormone
receptor cancer, and that basically means the cancer
uses either oestrogen or progesterone – or both – to
grow and spread. My cancer was strongly positive
to both oestrogen and progesterone. Apparently
this type of cancer is more common in women aged
sixty and over, but then, I've always liked to be
different…!

It was only the middle of February, but I knew
from my previous discussion with Mei Lin that
the treatment programme she had arranged for me
would begin in early March. It would continue
through until the end of September, which was

daunting to say the least. Over the years, my way of coping with difficult situations has been to keep my head down, but I don't think it's necessarily the most sensible thing to do. If you are ever in this situation and there are things that trouble or worry you, then my advice would now be to always ask. Something that became very clear to me from my diagnosis onwards, was that the entire medical team believed that the more informed you were, the less concerned or frightened you would be. And of course they were right.

Bearing in mind my diagnosis had been over a month earlier, it was essential we had a start date for the treatment. With my girlie weekend booked for the first weekend in March, my oncologist had kindly said she was prepared to delay it until the following week, but that she did feel I'd benefit from visiting the chemo ward and meeting the nurses before then so that I understood what my treatment schedule entailed. That way they could go through it all with me, and answer any questions I might have. The mastectomy had been very much a hurdle I'd struggled to get over, and I knew I was being an ostrich with regards the chemo – my head planted firmly in the sand. That head of course would soon be devoid of all my hair, and so the cold cap was something else I had to think about too. I knew that it had been created to try and help prevent complete hair loss during chemotherapy by lowering the temperature of your scalp to minus five degrees. I didn't think it was for me at all, but having been brought up to 'never say never' I

hadn't *completely* dismissed the idea. It seemed a
lot to have to think about, and so I was extremely
relieved when Jenny timed her visit to fit in with the
appointment. By way of a thank you, I decided to
get to Harpenden early so we could have coffee and
a bun before the tour!

Having motored my way through a mighty
Eccles cake in Costa Coffee, my mood was lighter
as Jenny and I made our way to the Roundwood
Ward – the Spire's own dedicated chemotherapy
unit – where we were greeted by ward sister Anne-
Marie and her senior nurse Rhoma. They were
both very friendly and welcoming, and there was
a definite sense of calm and normality, which
was not at all what I had been expecting. Call me
dramatic (my mother always has), but I'd visualised
something more akin to a busy A&E department,
with grey-faced, hairless people attached to drips
and wearing dressing gowns, drifting about in
search of somewhere to throw up! My imaginings
couldn't have been further from the truth. The ward
itself included ten individual rooms, each leading
off the wide and brightly lit main corridor. There
was no one else in sight, and only the muted sound
of the busy reception outside was audible. However
I gathered that some of the rooms were occupied,
as after offering us a cup of tea, Sister politely
excused herself to attend to a patient. Her colleague
suggested we made ourselves comfortable in one of
the rooms to our left, and having settled us into our
chairs, she perched on the side of the bed.

The room was identical to the one I'd stayed in

following my mastectomy, which was a relief as I had been thinking it would be something more akin to a chemistry lab! The nurse told us about the unit, which treated men and women with all forms of cancer, not just breast cancer. My treatment would be in two stages with four sessions of FEC being administered once every three weeks for the first three months. I would need to come to the hospital the morning before each session to have my bloods checked, because the cumulative effect of the drugs reduces the number of white cells in the blood and makes it difficult for the body to fight infection. The actual treatment itself would take the best part of four hours, and I could either be in bed or sitting up in the chair to have it, whichever was most comfortable for me. It was going to be important for me to keep an eye on how I was feeling after each session, and to enable me keep in touch with them twenty-four seven, I'd be given a telephone number for the ward and also a mobile number that could be called out of hours if I felt at all unwell. I can't remember if it was Jenny or I who said we thought the treatment was *meant* to make me feel unwell, but Rhoma, with a smile, explained that infection was the main concern, so I should call if I experienced anything like a raised temperature, sore throat, diarrhoea, a cough or shortness of breath, a rash, or bruising and bleeding for no apparent reason. 'I know it all sounds awful, but not everyone reacts badly to the drugs, and we'll help you every step of the way. Is there anything you'd like to ask me?'

I felt my shoulders drop as I breathed out, but I couldn't think of anything to say... Jenny though clarified a few points before Rhoma continued, explaining that if the number of white blood cells destroyed by the chemo was particularly high, it could cause something called neutropenia. This condition might require a short stay in hospital and a delay in the treatment, until I was strong enough to take on the next cycle. My oncologist and the team there at the Roundwood Ward would be responsible for making that decision, but it wasn't something that happened very often.

'Well I'll keep my fingers and toes crossed then.' My words belied the frisson of fear I felt, and the Eccles cake and coffee sat heavily in my tummy as the butterflies joined them.

She went on to tell me that I'd have a three-week break before beginning the twelve week course of Taxol, which was the second phase of my treatment. I would need to come to the hospital twice a week for the following three months, and as before, my bloods would be taken the morning before the treatment was given. I silently thanked the Lord again for my Portacath, which would avoid the need for the veins in my arms to be used.

Jenny had a few more questions for Rhoma, and each question was answered kindly and succinctly. It's not just because Jenny is a teacher, or because she has an ever-enquiring mind, it's because she was looking out for me as she always has, and asking what she believed I didn't feel able to. And she was correct, for I was definitely sticking to my late grandmother's adage 'least said, soonest mended!' Finally I was given a little booklet called 'Your Chemotherapy Record' which not only contained information about my treatment regime and its effect on my blood count and platelets, but also had a section for me to fill in with any side effects I was experiencing, and the severity of them. 'It's really important you carry this booklet with you while you're having treatment, and always bring it with you when you come to see us, as we have to keep up to date with everything too.'

I looked at the cover of the little red notebook, but being in ostrich mode, I decided not to open it at that point. Maybe later when I was home…

'I wasn't sure if you'd been told about the cold cap?' I looked up at Rhoma as she spoke. 'There are a few options, but luckily for us, we've got the most up-to-date version that requires just one cap, and automatically maintains the very low temperatures needed. This is rather than the individual caps you may have heard about, that need replacing several times during treatment because they start to thaw out. It can help to reduce hair loss and works pretty well for some women. If you're interested I can bring one in to show you?'

I was impressed with Rhoma's sales pitch and would have smiled if I hadn't have felt so upset, but having sat almost silently for the previous fifteen minutes or so, I heard myself say very clearly that I definitely wasn't interested.

'I really think you should have a look at it before you make your mind up,' Jenny said.

'I *have* made my mind up. I can't bear the thought of something that cold on my head – you know I hate the cold. And it may not even work, so I don't see the point.'

'Well, let's just look at it at least?' she said.

'Alison, what do you think? You really don't have to, I just wanted you to know it's an option,' Rhoma said gently.

'I think we should have a look and then decide,' my sister said directly to me, and so, looking up at Rhoma, I conceded.

Losing your hair is possibly the most highly publicised side effect of this type of chemotherapy, and is something that, understandably, most women dread. I remember many years earlier, being reduced to tears at a Breast Cancer Care rally when a patient talked very honestly about losing her hair, and her consequent despair. A woman's hair is a sign of her femininity, but breast cancer, its treatment and stark surgery does one hell of a job of robbing us of this. I knew someone who had used a cold cap during her chemo, and although it had saved some of her hair, what remained was wispy and weak. She had needed to keep the cap on for several hours prior to every treatment and several hours afterwards, so she was in hospital for almost an entire day. It wasn't even the same cap, because the warmth from her scalp eventually thawed it out, so it had to be replaced with a new cap from a freezer! Even though she was wrapped in blankets she felt miserable and cold, and as the cap came down so far on to her face, even her eyelashes were frozen. She had to contend with this in addition to the treatment, and although I gathered the Spire's system was less archaic, to me it sounded very much like a bridge too far.

You see, being warm is essential to me. The choice between sunny or snowy holidays never happens in my world, and so when Rhoma brought the large hood with a huge tube trailing off the back of it into the room, I literally froze.

'How does it work?' Jenny asked.

Rhoma explained that the hood was attached to a machine that blew very cold air through the tube to maintain a temperature of minus five. 'It has to be worn for at least an hour before treatment, throughout the entire time the drugs are being given, and then for another hour after that.'

'Are you guaranteeing I'll keep my hair then?' I said.

'No, I can't guarantee that you'll keep your hair, but it may help.'

'You should at least give it a go. Could she do just one session to see how she gets on with it?' my sister enquired.

'How do you feel about it, Alison?' Rhoma asked.

'I don't know,' was all I could muster.

Rhoma looked at us both and then diplomatically excused herself for a moment.

I'd had enough. I didn't want this shit. I started to cry quietly as my sister knelt down in front of me. 'Why won't you do this? What are you frightened of? Surely it has to be better than completely losing your hair?' she said, her eyes searching mine for a clue as to why I wouldn't entertain it.

And this is exactly what this damned disease does. It involves and hurts everyone. Your family, your friends, even people you don't know terribly well. They're not the ones who have the cancer, but they don't want this for you. They imagine you ashen-skinned, hairless and sick. They want to protect not just you but themselves, and that is completely understandable.

'I'm frightened of dying,' I whispered. It was the first time since my diagnosis that I had said what scared me the most out loud.

Jenny's arms were around me as soon as the words were out, and she held on to me very tightly for quite some time.

I didn't try the cold cap, and I lost my hair completely just twenty-two days after my first treatment. For me it was the right decision not to give it a go, but there are a very large number of women who do use it, and haven't had to cope with complete hair loss. You will know, should you ever find yourself in this situation, which way is the right way for you.

# Chapter Twenty

The date that was eventually set for my first chemotherapy treatment was 9th of March, the day before my eldest son Sam's twenty-second birthday. Bearing in mind my mastectomy had been on Jack's eighteenth birthday, I felt it was Sod's law that once again we would have to plan our celebrations around my hospital timetable. We chose a restaurant in Milton Keynes and made an early reservation, knowing that I would need to be at the hospital by 10 a.m. the following morning.

On the morning of the 8th of March, I visited the Spire Hospital to have my bloods taken, the first of what was to become a regular procedure. I decided to go on my own, feeling pretty well in myself, and realising that it was something I was going to have to get used to. As soon as I turned into the hospital entrance I regretted my decision, because I was suddenly consumed with an overwhelming sense of fear. In fact, anyone watching me trying to parallel park my car that morning could have been forgiven for wondering if I'd ever had a driving lesson, never mind passed my driving test! I think it was just the enormity of what I was about to begin.

It hit me that it was barely spring, and I would still be having treatment well into the autumn. How was I going to cope with it all? Would I even survive the next six months? With all this whirling around my mind, and worrying that I would be late, I ran all the way to the Roundwood Ward. I was puffing and blowing like an old boiler when I bowled up to the double doors and was welcomed in by Rhoma. Immediately I felt more relaxed seeing her familiar face. I assured her that my heavy breathing was because I'd been running, not because I was about to collapse on her! I had a distinct feeling of déjà vu when she led me to the same room I had been in with Jenny just a few weeks before. I think with hindsight it may well have been intentional so as to make me feel less rattled. The ten rooms on the ward were all numbered – not between one and ten as you'd imagine, but between 100 and 110. As we had both read the George Orwell novel *1984* it became a long-standing joke with Rhoma that all would be lost the day she booked me into room 101!

Having settled myself into the tall backed chair next to the bed, I watched as Rhoma pulled on a pair of sterile gloves and then busied herself with a collection of things that were laid out on a large stainless steel trolley. I found Rhoma's beautiful Scottish accent very soothing, and we chatted a little as she prepared a number of syringes. She then picked up what looked like a long narrow tube with a round disc attached to the end of it and a short point sticking out – a bit like a very short

sword. 'I remember you telling me that you've got
a Portacath, which is great because it means we
don't have to bother the veins in your arms,' she
said as she moved towards me. I could now clearly
see the line attached to largish needle about half an
inch long. It was this, she explained, that needed
to go into the port to access the vein – the little
circle would stop it from going in any further than
necessary. My port was easy to find, protruding
through my skin, and it still felt a little weird when I
touched it. The sterile swab she used to wipe over it
was cold, and momentarily gave me goose bumps.

'Will it hurt?' I asked.

'I hope not. Most patients say it doesn't, but
I will need to push it in quite firmly, so brace
yourself!' she said with a smile. 'Are you ready?
Take a deep breath in.'

Gripping both arms of the chair I filled my
lungs as she made what could only be described as
a slight stabbing motion. Unfortunately, as I was
feeling anxious, I had sat bolt upright just seconds
before, and as the needle punctured my skin I was
pushed back into the chair with some force. 'Good
God! I am so sorry! I thought you were sitting
back in the chair!' she spluttered, looking totally
mortified.

The only thing that was damaged was my dignity
and I laughed. 'You have nothing to apologise for –
I'll be ready for you next time, like a ninja!'

With the needle in place it was incredibly simple
for the blood samples to be taken, and I genuinely
didn't feel a thing. I hope if you ever find yourself

facing this kind of treatment over a lengthy period of time, and you *don't* have a port, that the PICC line, central line or catheter you need will be painless and unobtrusive.

Rhoma told me that they'd have the blood results that afternoon, and I'd need to bring my chemo booklet in with me the following day so she could write them up for me. She also explained that I had the option to leave the needle in place overnight so I wouldn't have to be 'stabbed' again the following morning, but would be all prepped and ready for my first chemo. 'Put like that I think I will,' I said with a smile, and so she attached two fairly long narrow rubber lines to the needle and, complete with colourful clips to keep them closed, she sticky-taped the lot to my chest.

As this first cycle of treatment was only to be once every three weeks, she said it wasn't usually problematic to have the needle in separately for bloods and then drugs, however, when I moved on to the once-weekly Taxol, the skin over the port could become bruised and sore and so I might want to leave it there permanently. I hadn't realised when I'd agreed to her suggestion that it would be anything other than the needle I'd have to hide inside my bra, and thinking of the dress I had hoped to wear to the restaurant that night, I made a mental note to myself to only leave the needle in when I wasn't going out!

'That's all for now, so you can head off home when you're ready,' Rhoma said.

I thanked her, and having buttoned myself up

and confirmed the time she would need me there the
following morning, I left her, the ward, and a great
deal of trepidation behind me.

Unfortunately I hadn't done a very good job of
disguising the port or its attached paraphernalia,
and once I arrived at the restaurant Lucy spotted
it straight away, and shot me a look of concern.
'Not the most attractive of accessories I know,' I
told her, but having assured her it wasn't the least
bit uncomfortable, I tucked my serviette into the
neckline of the jumper I'd chosen to wear instead
of my dress, and tried to forget about it. In spite of
everything we really enjoyed our time together, and
once again I was reminded of just how much my
children mean to me. It was a bittersweet feeling.
As we were leaving the restaurant, Lucy hugged me
very tightly and said she and Jack would come and
see me the following evening. 'It'll be okay, Mum I
know it will. It's going to make you better, and you
have to get better forever,' she told me.

'That's the plan sweetheart' I whispered.

And yet at that moment, forever seemed a very
long way away.


My son Sam had very kindly offered to take me
in the next day for my first cycle of FEC, which I
really appreciated, particularly because he didn't
and still doesn't like hospitals. He had every reason
to feel that way: following a horrendous motorbike
accident when he was in his late teens, he was
in intensive care for weeks. His injuries were so

severe that his right leg had to be amputated, and he remained in hospital for over four months, having to endure twenty-one very lengthy and serious operations. Twice we nearly lost him. The memory of those months has never left me, nor the sense of overwhelming fear and distress. It will remain one of the best levellers I have ever had when facing things that upset or scare me. Nothing for me so far in my life, has ever been as dreadful as nearly losing Sam.

I'd really wanted to be on my own this first time, just in case I didn't cope very well, or it was uncomfortable. However, although it was unlikely, I had been told I could have a reaction to the drugs, which might then make it difficult for me to drive myself home. So, for this initial appointment, I would have to be chaperoned.

Sam arrived in plenty of time, and seemed keen to get back on the road and to the hospital. I, on the other hand, kept fannying around, checking and double-checking that I had everything I needed – not that I had a huge amount to take! All the rooms at the hospital were kitted out with a TV, and the staff were more than happy for patients to bring in books, computers, music or knitting – whatever would help pass the time more quickly. I know that in some hospitals the chemo sessions can involve quite a number of patients all in the same room, so at least everyone has someone to talk to. Because Sam was going to be with me, I thought it would be rude to take a book, and I don't knit anyway, so having shoved my chemotherapy booklet into

my bag, we headed out of the house. My insides
were churning at the thought of what I was about to
embark on, but I didn't want to worry Sam. I also
felt that considering all he'd gone through over the
past three years or more, this didn't really compare.
Of course as a parent the protective feelings we
have for our children stay with us always – and so
on our journey, we talked about the weather, the
traffic, the past; in fact anything but the present.

We arrived in plenty of time and Sam's car
parking was impeccable. Having been taken to
room 103, I was told that it was entirely up to me to
choose where I would have my treatment, and could
either sit in a chair, or get into bed. I chose to get
into bed, as at least that way Sam was sitting next
to me rather than us looking at each other across
the room. Next to the bed was a large appliance
that reminded me of the monitors used to track a
baby's heartbeat when a mum is in labour. I wasn't
at all sure what this one was for, but decided to wait
and see – sometimes the less you know the better!
Anne-Marie and Rhoma breezed into the room,
and with their easy and friendly conversation they
immediately relaxed us both. Sam was offered a cup
of tea or coffee, and I had a glass of water, before
undressing in the bathroom and putting on my
dressing gown. I snuggled in under the duvet, and
propped my pillows up. I was ready for them.

The girls wheeled in a large trolley on which
were a great many different sachets, syringes and
paper-covered packages. Having confirmed my
name, my medical number and my address, they

read out the name and dose of each of the drugs that I was to be given.

'Crikey is all that for me?'

'Don't worry, you'll be surprised how quickly it's administered with the pump.' Rhoma nodded towards the machine next to the bed.

So that's what it was. Having opened a couple of paper packages they each put on a plastic apron and some blue rubber gloves. That made me smirk. They reminded me of the ones you see farmers and vets wearing when ferreting about inside a cow or sheep!

'We're going to start with a saline solution to make sure the line is clear and then the anti-sickness drugs will be the first ones we give to you. They're all on a timed delivery system which is operated by this pump, so once they're through an alarm will sound and you'll be ready for the next lot.'

Sam was looking a tad fidgety, and so I suggested he maybe go and buy a snack or something from the canteen. He seemed relieved to be able to leave the room, and I told him not to rush back as I wasn't going anywhere.

Rhoma took only a matter of moments to attach the saline solution to the pump, and then attach me to the line, and apart from a cold sensation initially, I felt nothing as it was flushed clean. It was the same with the anti-sickness drugs, which are sometimes given as a tablet, but more usually delivered through the line. The alarm sounded just as Sam returned to the room, and he'd barely got his bum on the seat before Anne-Marie and

Rhoma came back in to set up the first of the chemo drugs. Having both removed their blue gloves they replaced them with a new pair of purple ones. A rather fetching damson shade, they clashed somewhat with the deep pink solution that I could see inside a large plastic syringe they brought over to the pump.

This first drug was called epirubicin (the E within the name FEC) and they read out not just the name, but the measured dose and the expiry date. I wasn't really listening though, as all I could focus on was the extraordinary colour of the chemo drug! Pink has always been associated with breast cancer. Whether it is the branding of the charities that raise money to help those with the disease, or the ribbons that are worn to raise awareness, they're all pink. I mentioned the irony of this to the girls, who admitted it had never struck either of them, and then staying with the subject of colour, I asked them why they'd changed their gloves to the purple ones? I was a little rattled when they told me that as the chemotherapy drugs were harmful to the skin, the gloves were heavy duty and would protect their hands from any spillages.

'What does it do to your insides then?' I asked rather stupidly.

'Well, of course it's designed to destroy all the cancerous cells, so it needs to be pretty powerful, but we will run a saline drip at the same time to hopefully avoid it causing any irritation to your veins.' Rhoma patted my arm kindly. 'I'll stay with you at first, but if I have to leave the room, you can press the buzzer if you feel any reaction at all.'

I looked across at Sam who was staring at the syringe. 'Good job it's going through the line and not with that huge syringe, eh Sam?' I said in a falsely jolly tone.

He looked up at me and said nothing, but just nodded.

The syringe was the first of two, and it took approximately fifteen minutes each time for the solution to run in through the line. Mercifully, there was no sensation or irritation, and having given up on small talk, I switched on the TV and Sam and I watched together in a comfortable silence. The timer sounded, the girls returned, and I was told that the next drug I was to have was the F part of FEC.

Fluorouracil or 5FU is the medical name for this drug and again I had to smile at the initials. This substance was colourless, and came in a large clear plastic sachet not a syringe. No saline was given alongside the 5FU, but within a couple of minutes I started to feel a strange sensation in my nose. The only way I could describe it, would be to liken it to the burning feeling you get in your nostrils and back of your throat if you eat too much mustard or horseradish sauce. Making my eyes water and my nose and throat sting, it was really unpleasant. Not wanting to make a fuss, I thought I'd ask Sam if he could smell anything weird, or if his nose was itching?

'No I feel fine. Why?'

Describing how I felt, and realising it was getting worse, I asked Sam if he thought I should buzz for

Rhoma, but Sam got up and said he'd find her. They both returned within moments, by which time my eyes were running and the pain in my sinuses was horrid. Apparently I was only the second person ever to have a reaction like this to 5FU, and outside of a warm bean bag to lay over my nose and cheeks there was nothing they could give me for the discomfort. Checking the timer, I was told I only had about another ten minutes to go, and so I started counting quietly to myself while Rhoma left to the get the bag. I had to laugh when she came back into the room, because the beanbag was the same size as one you'd put on the back of your neck or shoulders to help alleviate stiff and sore muscles. Trying to balance it on the front of my face made me look like a horse wearing a nosebag! By the time we'd finished faffing around with it, the timer sounded and the infusion stopped, as did the discomfort – almost instantly. 'We'll try giving it to you more slowly next time, my love. It may well help.' she said.

That was a relief to know.

The third and final part of the treatment was to be the drug cyclophosphamide, and the butterflies had started up in my tummy again as I worried about a possible reaction to this drug too. I asked the girls if anyone had ever felt ropey or unwell while having this one, and was mightily relieved to hear that no one in their care had ever had a reaction, and so I laid back against the pillows and told Sam we wouldn't be much longer. This final dose took about half an hour, and was again given alongside a saline solution. I spent most of that time making a conscious effort not to think about just how much of these toxic substances were now travelling around my system. I talked a little with Sam, but again sensing his unease I shut up and checked the timer instead. Mercifully outside of these mental concerns, I felt nothing unusual physically, and when the timer sounded, and Rhoma came in to set up the saline to flush through the line, I let out a huge sigh of relief. As a precaution they wanted me to just relax for ten minutes or so in case there was a reaction, and then they'd give me the additional medication I had to take home with me. So it was done! I'd got through the first one! A little voice inside my head interrupted with 'still fifteen to go' but I ignored that, and holding on to my feelings of relief, I suggested to Sam that we go into Harpenden and get some lunch; an idea he jumped at.

The meds I had to take with me were the anti-sickness tablets and steroids for day one and two, and also the six syringes of pegfilgrastim, to be administered on day three around lunchtime and then again every lunchtime for the following six days. Having never given myself an injection in my life, I was relieved that Rhoma explained how this was done. By pinching a roll of fat on your tummy you then push the needle gently and slowly in, and there shouldn't be any resistance. The clever design of the syringe meant that the needle automatically went back into the casing once the dose was administered.

'Are you going to be all right with that, Mum?' Sam asked in a concerned way.

I told him I was sure I'd be fine, and if not, I'd just come back to the hospital for help.

Because of the syringes, I was given my own bright yellow sharps box, and for some inexplicably childish reason this cheered me! Perhaps it was the colour, but I knew it was something I would be leaving out on show rather than hiding away.

'Takes all sorts to make a world,' my Nanny Timms would have said.

My chemotherapy booklet, which had been duly filled in, was given back to me.

'Don't forget to call if you feel in any way worried, or unwell. Or if you have a temperature, any sickness, pain, or trouble breathing. The numbers you can get us on are written on the back page.' Rhoma said.

I thanked Rhoma and Anne-Marie, and with Sam carrying my bag of meds, we left the hospital.

I don't know what changed my mood, but as soon as I was in the car I felt panicky.

'Sam,' I said, 'would you mind very much if you took me straight home rather than going out for lunch?'

He looked at me solemnly. 'Are you okay, Mum?'

I looked down at my hands in my lap. 'Yes, I am, it's just the thought of suddenly feeling ill in a public place...'

Sam nodded. 'I understand, Mum. Let's go home.'

Grateful, I relaxed back into the seat. As Sam pulled out of the car park, I thought to myself how it was a little like waiting for lightning to strike – I had absolutely no idea when or how the chemo was going to affect me, I just had a gut feeling it wasn't going to be pleasant.

# CHAPTER TWENTY-ONE

It may seem a bizarre comparison, but once I got home following my first chemotherapy treatment, I experienced the same feelings of fear and anxiety I'd had before I gave birth to Lucy. It was all well and good going to the hospital and having the drugs administered, but the all-important 'what happens next' question was one I hadn't allowed myself to think of. The incredibly long list of possible reactions and side effects that I had been given by the oncologist sat inside a drawer in my kitchen. I think I only ever looked through it once – in desperation – throughout my entire treatment. I didn't even know how many days or weeks it would be before my hair fell out, although I knew it was a certainty, but what I wasn't remotely prepared for how my body would react to this incredibly powerful yet toxic drug regime.

I'd been pretty healthy most of my life, and with the exception of a few surgical procedures, had managed to avoid any major medical intervention until my teens, although there'd been the occasional need for first aid.

When I was two, our family moved to Molesey

in Surrey. There was a little cottage hospital half a mile away from our home, and my first visit there wasn't until I was five years old and had a very painful whitlow on my middle finger. I used to bite my nails, and I had a hangnail, which is what caused my finger to expand, throb and become septic. I'm not sure why it was my dad who took me to hospital that day, as he usually worked every weekday, but I was thrilled that it was. I loved my dad, and coveted any extra time with him, so I was even more delighted when he allowed me to push my purple doll's pram all the way to the hospital and then home again. I don't remember much of what happened there except that the treatment itself was the cure. Same situation when I broke, fractured, and splintered the bone in my ankle on three different occasions. After an X-ray, Tubigrip bandage for two weeks and rest, the ankle healed. It was no more complicated than that.

There was however, some mystery surrounding the undiagnosed tummy pains I struggled on and off with for a number of years. I think I am relatively sensitive to stress and difficult situations, and if there's ever been a problem I invariably get a tummy ache. However, I was eventually diagnosed with inflammation of the Mesenteric glands, which are the lymph nodes attached to the abdominal wall. It meant very little to my mum or me, but apparently common infections can cause this to happen, and it is sometimes mistaken for appendicitis. To this day, I'm still not sure whether I actually had appendicitis or not when I was taken into hospital at the age of thirteen with severe tummy pains. It is what I was diagnosed with though, and had my appendix whipped out anyway! Not a particularly pleasant experience, but I have to admit to being more distressed by the fact they shaved off my newly acquired pubic hair! As I explained with some chagrin to the nurse, it had taken me over a year to grow it! Outside of having my wisdom teeth removed when I was twenty-one years old, I had no reason to see the inside of a hospital again until I was due to give birth to my first child Lucy. I lived in Colchester at the time, and the town had a dedicated maternity hospital.

I think I've only ever met two women in my life who've said they had actually enjoyed giving birth, and one of them was my mother! However it was something I refused to think about until I was at least seven months pregnant and started attending antenatal classes. We had a local NCT group that my midwife had advised I go along to, so that I could speak to other women about their experiences of birth, rather than just comparing notes with other first-time mums, as none of us had any idea of what to expect! Until this point in my life I had studiously avoided any films or television programmes that included women giving birth. On the odd occasion when caught unawares, I'd been treated to the vision of a sweat-soaked woman hanging on to the bed head, screaming for what seemed like hours while writhing around in pain, before a squalling baby was hauled out of her bleeding body! It's all changed now we've got

Channel 4's *One Born Every Minute*, which I watch and weep tears of joy over.

As a child of the sixties, human reproduction and sex education at school was brief and to the point. We weren't subjected to Technicolor films of the act itself, or even the process of birth, but instead were told all about the birds and the bees by a very sweet teacher called Mrs Chrisman. She had been married during the summer before term time, and all she said was that when *this* happened between a man and a woman it was just wonderful! At which point, possibly remembering the previous night's lovemaking, she twisted her fashionable and lengthy necklace – 'love beads' they called them back then – and snapped them! We spent the rest of the lesson picking up the beads, but were none the wiser as to the joys of procreation!

My mother, bless her, had often told me that although not exactly a picnic, giving birth was hard work but incredibly rewarding. She always maintained, and I've gone on to do the same, that there is no point in telling somebody expecting their first child what may or may not happen. No two women are the same; some mums' pain threshold is higher than others, and some births more straightforward than others. Very few of us can elect to have the baby surgically removed, and so you just have to get on with it!

I only attended one NCT group, because the second-time mums there frightened the life out of me talking about their experience of birth! My midwife had told me that holding a bag of

frozen peas against my Achilles tendon would
give me some idea of the kind of discomfort I
may experience in the early throes of labour! But
then again I have been told that pigs might fly.
One of the NCT mums talked at length about her
horrendous back pain, the burning sensation, the
stretching and the tearing. She even told us first
timers to try and imagine passing an Ogen melon
out of one of our nostrils, because that is what it
would feel like! 'You'll end up like the Albert Hall
down there if you have a big baby – I don't even
know whether my husband's in or out any more!'
she finished triumphantly. I remember thinking that
hopefully her second baby would just fall out if that
was the case...

My sister Jenny gave birth for the first time
eighteen months after I'd had Lucy, and all I told
her – in keeping with family tradition – was that
it was hard work, stung a little, but would be fine!
She had been in labour for several hours when
she turned to her husband and said that the whole
thing was ridiculous, far too painful, and she'd
had enough. She wanted to go home. He explained
gently to her that this wouldn't be possible, just
as the door to the room opened, and a trolley was
pushed in at great speed. On it was a woman with
legs akimbo, screaming loudly 'Kill me! Just kill
me!' Realising they were in the wrong place, the
staff did a prompt about turn with the trolley, but I
don't know how Jonathan managed to keep Jenny
on the bed or even in the room at that point! In the
final stages of her labour, Jenny's midwife asked

her if she'd like a mirror to see the baby's head crowning. 'Oh, go on then,' Jenny said, expecting to be given a small hand mirror. Instead the midwife wheeled in a full-length mirror, which gave my sister a complete view of not just her sweat-soaked, straining body, but parts of her anatomy she wouldn't normally see, stretched to an unbelievable degree! Her first words to me when I visited her and baby Emily at the hospital were 'You lied!' but I prefer to see it as me being a little economical with the truth. And in all honesty, my experience of giving birth to Lucy had been very different.

It was the morning of 12 October 1985 when my husband drove me to the maternity hospital in his brand-new Astra. He'd made me sit on a Marks & Spencer carrier bag, just in case my waters broke and spoiled the perfect upholstery. My labour was swift, and I was fully dilated after just four hours. I'd been given gas and air which to be honest did very little for me, until I grabbed the handle and whacked myself on the bridge of the nose with the metal part of it, rather than placing the mask over my nose and mouth! Epidurals were only given on a Thursday at the maternity hospital, and as this was a Saturday I had to just crack on with the help of some pethidine, that made me feel as though I'd drunk a bottle of Bells Whisky! Consequently I was then sick as a dog, my contractions stopped, and Lucy decided to stay where she was. It took forceps and unfortunately no additional pain relief to haul her out just two hours later, but as soon as she was in my arms the previous six hours' struggles were forgotten.

And although it may be hard to believe, for those of you who are currently going through chemotherapy, or know someone who is; as with labour and childbirth, the memory of it will dim with time. I can never forget the long road to recovery for Sam following his amputation, but over time it has become less stark. I think the grief I felt when my father died is the only other emotion that brought a similar feeling of pain and distress, and over the years I have found the only way to deal with it is to accept that there will always be a huge hole in my life that can never be filled, but I now walk around the edge of that hole, as opposed to falling in it.

Chemotherapy is temporary, and as we all know life isn't everlasting, but I believe the treatment I've had, has given me my best chance of having a future.

# CHAPTER TWENTY-TWO

I had originally planned to write a diary beginning with the day after my first chemotherapy, but when I mentioned this to my mum she told me she thought it would be better not to document what was happening, as it may be far easier to move on from it if I didn't have a written reminder. She may well have been right – she often is – and feeling vulnerable at the time, I went with her suggestion and didn't record my symptoms. Of course that does make the whole process of writing a book a little difficult, but luckily I kept all my follow-up letters which have jogged my somewhat fuzzy memory and brought back a great deal of how I felt at the time.

The first thing I struggled with, and possibly not something for dinner table discussion, was constipation. It's something I had also had to contend with following my first mastectomy and the general anaesthetic. Once home, I had poor Lucy running around Leighton Buzzard scouring Boots and Tesco for something – anything! – that would get my guts moving! It took glycerine suppositories to shift things, and although the instructions on the packet said you were supposed to hold the

suppository in place for up to twenty minutes, I
only managed ten. It reminded me of the enema
I was given in hospital when I was thirteen years
old and about to have my appendix out! Mind you,
back then, it was a rubber hose and warm soapy
water that irritated my innards and meant a heart-
stopping race to the toilets at the end of the ward!
The suppositories were far less messy but equally
intense! I did call the hospital the following day and
they prescribed something called Movicol, which
you mix with water and take night and day, and that
became a constant for me over the following six
months. I'd have drunk anything providing it did
the trick!

The first couple of days following treatment, the
constipation was a little easier, but accompanied
by terrible heartburn, stomach bloating, and also
a very swollen red face. This was because my
body had to cope not only with the FEC, but also
Dexamethasone, the steroid I had to take for the first
few days. Then, on top of all that, I had the joy of
my pegfilgrastim injections. I clearly remember the
first time I had to try this, and it still weirdly makes
me smile. It's important that at least twenty-four
hours has passed since the last chemo and so I had
to wait until the early part of the afternoon before I
could get my syringe out of the fridge, and leave it
for thirty minutes at room temperature. Apparently
doing this stops the solution from stinging when
you inject it. I sat down, rolled up my jumper, and
grabbed at a roll of tummy fat. I took the cover off
the needle.

'Are you sure you want to do this?' asked Yo who was with me that day.

'Of course not! Would you?' Each time I went to put the needle in, Yo visibly winced and I stopped myself, but after ten minutes of talking myself out of it, I decided to be grown up and get on with it. The best thing of all was that the needle did exactly as Rhoma had said it would, and slid easily into my tummy just as soon as I pressed the syringe. Bingo! The drug was delivered. All done, I rolled my jumper back down, gave Yo a high five, and went to the bathroom to dispose of my first syringe in my bright yellow sharps box. Result!

My treatment had been on a Wednesday, and not only did the symptoms seem to be worsening, but because of them I was getting very little sleep. Something that was making it so much worse was skin sensitivity. My entire body was sore to the touch, so that moving around in bed at night woke me, and if Colin tried to cuddle me that hurt too. Any clothing I wore rubbed my skin and made things worse.

By the Saturday I was feeling very tired and distinctly uncomfortable, as along with the heartburn, indigestion and constipation, I felt as though I'd had a night out on the tiles! Hangover-like symptoms stopped me from doing anything very much, but I had a pre-arranged lunch date with my friend Suzi B, who was over on a flying visit from her home in California to sell her range of jewellery on QVC. I didn't want her to have to get a taxi and was determined to drive her myself,

but on the way to meet her at the Railway Station
I managed to get a flat tyre! I called Sam who
lived just a few miles away and he saved the day
by collecting Suzi from the station, bringing her to
me, and then taking us to the pub and back to my
little cottage. It was so good to see her – albeit a tad
emotional – and although I hadn't lost my appetite,
there just didn't seem to be room in my tummy for
the fish pie I'd ordered. My stomach looked and felt
bloated and so although I picked at it, I was unable
to eat very much of the delicious meal in front of
me. Once back at the cottage, we had a cup of tea
and talked about everything except my on-going
treatment, and then having ordered a taxi, Suzi was
taken back to the station.

That night was difficult. Trying to 'do jolly' for
Suzi had been hard. I hadn't wanted her to have the
long flight home with nothing but negative thoughts
and worries, but some of her questions had been
very direct, and had made me doubt the eventual
outcome of my treatment. I was also genuinely
worried that over time I'd change as a person.
Would I become irritable because of the tiredness?
Angry because of the endlessness of it all? Would
my friends and family want to be with me or would
I be someone they'd try to avoid, as I'd be lousy
company and make them feel awkward? My body
felt sore and heavy and tears stung my eyes as I
ran my fingers through my shoulder-length hair. I
didn't want this... I really didn't, and what if after
the full six months of this shit, and the radiotherapy,
the cancer was still there? What would I do then?

I pulled my knees up to my distended stomach and cried myself to sleep.


The following day I looked worse but felt a little better in myself. I'd spoken to Colin that morning and was very glad to know that he was coming to stay with me that night, which gave me the incentive to get out of bed, put a bit of mascara on and make an effort. Sam had also called, and very kindly took me to get a new tyre for my car. It was while we were driving to the garage I started to feel distinctly uncomfortable. Not emotionally, but physically, as the jeans I was wearing were stretched to the limit across my much larger thighs! I could feel my hands swelling too, and I asked Sam if I looked any different to him?

He shot a look at me as though I was mad. 'In what way?'

'Well, I don't think my legs are normally this fat, and my jeans feel really tight.' I muttered.

Obviously embarrassed that as my son he would have any idea what my thighs looked like normally, he told me I was asking the wrong person, and so I decided it must be something to do with the drugs I was taking, and I should just keep a tin lid on it.

Having sorted my tyre out, and got my car back on the road, I thanked Sam profusely and drove myself home. I'd had to unbutton my jeans and take my jacket off because my arms and hands felt fat and were tingling. I was also having difficulty breathing normally by the time I got home, so I was very relieved that Colin was there to meet me.

'Are you okay?' was his first question as I stepped through the door.

'No not really…Why?' I replied.

'Um, well you just look a bit puffed up that's all.'

'I told Sam something was wrong! Look at my jeans! My legs aren't normally this big are they?'

Colin looked genuinely taken aback at my thunder thighs, and his reaction compounded my uneasy feelings and made my breathing even more laboured.

'My chest feels tight too,' I said, putting my arms around him, and without further ado, he suggested we ring the hospital.

There's something about an A&E Department on a Saturday night that's not pleasant. Whether you've watched *Casualty* or been there yourself. This Saturday was no exception, and I wondered how on earth the staff coped with the large number of drunken patients who, in spite of it being early evening, were loud and abusive, and happy to throw up wherever they're sitting? Some had damaged themselves by falling, or been in a fight, but either way it wasn't pretty.

I was by now in a state of panic. We had rung the emergency number in my chemotherapy booklet, and been put through to sister who was on call that night, and she'd recommended we get to the local hospital to make certain there were no clots or problems with my heart. Bearing in mind this was day four following my first treatment, and knowing that infection could prove fatal with my immune

system already majorly compromised by FEC, I felt
more than a little vulnerable in a place where those
who weren't in pain and bleeding, were hacking
and coughing or vomiting! I had taken my jeans off,
and replaced them with an elasticated waist skirt,
and swapped my sweatshirt for a very loose jumper,
but before I put them on I'd looked at myself in the
full-length mirror. Think Pillsbury Doughboy...
that's what I saw, and feeling utterly dejected
and extremely panicked, I covered myself up and
headed downstairs.

After a two-hour wait, it was our turn, and
we were introduced to a very nice junior doctor.
He took us into a separate room with a row of
cubicles that were separated by dark blue curtains.
Having checked my name and looked through the
chemotherapy booklet that I had brought with me,
he told me to make myself comfortable on the bed,
and then assured us he'd be back as soon as he
could, as he'd need to take bloods before he could
send me for a chest X-ray. I had a moment of panic,
thinking of my veins and his potential problems
taking my blood and then I remembered my port.
Phew! There was a God!

Colin helped me climb up on to the bed, and
as I lay there all I could see was the large mound
that was my distended stomach, my huge legs
and my feet sticking out from under my skirt.
It was uncomfortable for me to be in a reclined
position, as the tightness in my chest was making
it difficult for me to breathe normally, so Colin
adjusted the bed and got me sitting upright, which

helped enormously. The junior doctor returned and informed me that they couldn't use my port at this hospital, so he would have to find a vein. Before I could even start to worry about it, he had a tourniquet around my arm, knelt down, put the needle in, and hey presto! There was blood in the syringe! My face must have been a picture.

I'd barely had chance to apply pressure to the cotton wool pad in the crook of my arm before there was a commotion on the ward, and a young man was wheeled in and placed on the bed next to mine. Colin and I were unable to see anything much because of the blue curtain separating us, but we could hear that he was in a great deal of discomfort having dislocated his shoulder during a game of rugby. It was also obvious that this doctor had treated him just a few days before for the same injury. 'I can't believe you're back here again! You know how uncomfortable this was last time, and I'm now going to have to do the same thing again! What part of 'give yourself a month off' did you not understand?'

Colin and I leaned towards the curtain to hear the patient's response, and gleaned that it had something to do with an all-important play-off.

'Whatever…' was the rather heartless reply.

We were caught with our necks craned forwards, by the junior doctor who told me that they were now ready for my X-ray. He explained it wasn't necessary for Colin to come with me, as it was very straightforward and would take just a few minutes. He was right, I was in and out in a jiffy, and secretly praying that the patient next to me would have been treated and gone home. Not so.

Colin helped me back on to the bed, and I asked him in a whisper if anything had happened with the guy in the next cubicle. Before he could answer, the other doctor and a nurse strode through the double doors and made a beeline for the bed directly beside us. Having told the lad exactly what he was going to do to get the shoulder back into position, the doctor suggested the patient held on to the nurse's hand as it wasn't going to be pleasant...

Something you need to know about me is that I cannot bear the sound of anyone in pain. I made no noise while giving birth to my children, mainly because I didn't want to hear myself crying out, and at one point, while in labour with my third child Jack, I was halfway out of the delivery suite because I'd heard the woman in the room next to me howling like a wolf! The nurse told me it was a dog in the car park and thanks to the pethidine I believed her...

Colin and I looked at each other and both raised our eyes to the ceiling.

'Rather him than me,' he said quietly.

'Take a deep breath...' the doctor commanded and although the command was not directed at me, I automatically did just that, screwing my eyes tight shut and waiting for what I expected to be an ear splitting cry of pain, but the lad didn't make a sound. We did hear his shoulder click back into place, and the doctor say, 'Well done! Good lad!'

I'm sure both doctor and patient must have heard

our sighs of relief, but within moments, my feelings
of respite for the lad were overtaken with my
own feelings of trepidation. I told Colin I wished
we hadn't come, as the risk of infection from the
hospital surely was a great deal more worrying than
the symptoms I was experiencing.

'That's for them to decide, Ali, you're only doing
what the nurses at the chemo unit told you to do.'

I sighed deeply and looked at the clock on
the wall, its hands moving towards midnight. I
was pissed off, and in total frustration I cried out
'For Christ's sake! I feel really ill, I can't breathe
properly, I've got a swollen stomach, fat legs and
one useless tit.'

'I'm doing the best I can' was Colin's response.

I looked at him, leaning backwards in the chair,
his lovely but tired face smiling at me, and the pair
of us started laughing uncontrollably. The junior
doctor returned at that moment, and might have
joined in with our jollity, were it not for the fact
he was facing another eight hours on shift before
he finished. Having told us that there was nothing
to worry about on the X-ray – no evidence of a
blood clot – he said it was probably the steroids
that were causing the swelling, and I should contact
my oncologist for advice. I also had a low calcium
count so he was going to send me home with
calcium supplements. We thanked him, wished him
luck with the rest of his shift, and made our way out
of A & E into the car park, my fat thighs chafing
and my elasticated waist stretched to a frightening
degree. Home had never seemed more welcoming.

# CHAPTER TWENTY-THREE

B y day eight following my first chemo, I was feeling a great deal better. My thighs and tummy were less swollen, and my frighteningly red face had returned to a more normal hue. Because I'd ended up in A&E my oncologist was notified and an appointment made to see her on the Wednesday, which was my birthday! She could not have been kinder or more sympathetic, and was genuinely sorry that I'd had to come in at all… Having talked through everything, she prescribed Lansoprazole for the heartburn, and also made an appointment for me to see a consultant cardiologist for an echocardiogram. This was because she was concerned about the shortness of breath and tightness I'd had in my chest, and wanted to rule out any issues with my heart. I had wondered if some of the discomfort across my chest was due to the expander, but she thought that was unlikely. As I was due to the see the plastic surgeon on the Friday, she suggested I speak with him then. We arranged to meet again the following week, when I would be five days away from my second treatment, and as I was leaving, I asked her when she thought my hair would start to fall out.

'It may well have started by this day next week, but it can take up to a week for you to lose it all.'

I gave her a half smile and a little nod.

'I'm sorry. It's not easy I know' she said.

'It's okay. I've got the children and my mum coming for dinner tonight, and Sam's cooking, so that'll be nice. Anyway, it's one down, only fifteen to go!' I added, hoping I sounded positive.

'I'm sure you'll have a lovely evening. Take care, and I'll see you next week or earlier if you need me,' she said, holding the door of her room open as I thanked her, and headed to the hospital pharmacy to get my prescription.

The Lansoprazole worked well, and virtually rid me of the heartburn I'd been experiencing, although I was constantly struggling with the weird cramping pains in my chest, behind and around Dolly my expander. There was no apparent reason for them, and indeed the echocardiogram had showed my heart was normal, but I felt my body was trying to reject the hard, rugby-ball-shaped implant.

Apart from this, each day I felt a little better, and as I got stronger, I filled every waking hour. Not working was really strange as I've been employed pretty much all my adult life, and although I didn't miss the journey to Battersea, I very much missed my friends. I used this time to see as many of them as possible, and felt far more like a lady who lunched, than someone with a life-threatening illness! That said, niggling away at the back of my mind was the thought of the cumulative effect of the chemo, the hair loss, fatigue, general discomfort and

build-up of toxins. Each treatment would be harder
to recover from, and so I treasured the time I had.

Something else I made time to do was to answer
every one of the incredibly kind and supportive
comments that the QVC viewers had written on my
fortnightly blog. Social media has changed the way
many of us work, and since 2008, it had become
part of my job to keep in touch with our viewers by
writing not just about my time at work, but home
life as well. Over the previous couple of years I had
built up a pretty healthy following, and genuinely
enjoyed writing and responding to the ever-
increasing number of comments. The blog worked
well as a support network too, and when someone
wrote with a problem, we all chipped in with our
advice or support.

When I was diagnosed with breast cancer I spoke
to my manager, as I felt I should tell my friends on
the blog about my impending surgery and treatment.
She agreed and said it would also make life easier
for my colleagues at QVC, who had initially been
asked by the management to say nothing other
than I was unwell. Sitting down to write that blog
before I even had my surgery was harder than I
imagined, but I was very honest. However, when it
was submitted, our marketing team felt it necessary
to keep to a minimum the details of my surgery and
treatment. They believed it could upset and worry
some folk, and with hindsight I know they were
right. It was difficult though, having laid my soul
bare, to be told to skirt around the truth. I trimmed
out most of the details, and was overwhelmed and

humbled by the hundreds of people who wrote to me with messages of love and support. It was just the beginning of what would become a huge part of my recovery and a link to so many viewers I would never meet, but without whom those long days and nights when I felt so ill would have been interminable. They named themselves 'Ali's Army' and truly made all the difference, not just while I was away from work and on chemo, but for all the weeks months and years since then.

I wanted to keep the QVC blog upbeat and positive, and more like a journal, but among the supportive and concerned comments, there were questions about my surgery and treatment. A great many women wanted to know what a mastectomy involved, how much chemo I was to have, and how I was feeling. As I'd been working with the charity Breast Cancer Care just four months earlier, they contacted me as soon as they were told. Having spoken with QVC's marketing team they wondered if I'd be prepared to write a blog once a month for their forum? I could link from my own QVC blog to it, and it would be a more appropriate site for me to include details about my treatment. I agreed immediately, and it was a very useful tool not just for those who found the answers they were looking for there, but for me to read back, and realise how far I had come.

# CHAPTER TWENTY-FOUR

As the side effects of the chemo lessened, my apprehension about losing my hair grew. For the first two weeks I'd been so preoccupied with my heartburn and general malaise I hadn't really given it much thought, although I remember I was fiddling with my hair more than I would normally. By the beginning of the third week following chemo I noticed that when I ran my fingers through my hair, small amounts of it came away. It was very fine, but I had a lot of it, and although it was just a few strands to begin with it was nonetheless upsetting.

I'd tried on my acrylic wigs a couple of times when I was alone in the cottage, and each time I felt I looked ridiculous. I still hadn't shown them to Colin or even Yo, but had stuffed them as far under the bed as possible. I think in the back of my mind I was half hoping that I'd be well enough between treatments to go back to work for a couple of days a month, but I didn't think I'd have the confidence to sit in front of a camera with either one of those options on. I'd also been told that in studio lighting they tended to shine in a rather unnatural way! I

spoke with the girls at Breast Cancer Care, and
they said it was possible to buy a real hair wig,
but they were pretty pricey. Bearing in mind my
intention to get back to QVC I wrote to the Director
of Broadcasting and he very kindly said that the
company would cover the cost of a real hair wig for
me, and so I set about sourcing a supplier.

Something that dawned on me while I was doing
my research was that as hard as it may be for those
of us who lose our hair through chemotherapy,
hopefully it would only be a temporary situation.
Many of the reviews I read online when seeking
out a supplier were from women with alopecia –
permanent hair loss – and once again, I thanked
my lucky stars that although this was going to be
difficult, it hopefully wasn't going to be forever.

Each day a little more of my hair fell out, and
just before I was due to see my oncologist for
my follow-up appointment, I managed to get into
London to see the lovely Richard Ward, who had
been cutting and styling my hair for a number
of years. He had called me as soon as he heard I
was off work, and said that if there was anything
he could do then I was to let him know. You may
remember me telling you that once I knew I was
definitely to have chemotherapy, I had gone to a
local salon and had the length cut away. Now I was
facing the total loss of my hair, once again, I felt it
might be easier to deal with if there was less of it to
lose. I know some women prefer to have their heads
shaved in advance – maybe it's their way of taking
control of the situation. That wasn't an option I'd

ever considered, and when I got to the salon I asked Richard to cut what was remaining as short as possible. His patience was immense, his kindness heart-warming, and his sympathy for my situation clear. Each time he ran the comb through my hair to cut it, more came out. However, the eventual result was a fabulous pixie cut that I was thrilled with!

'You're going to be okay, Ali,' he told me as I stood up to leave, 'and best of all is that you're one of those women who can carry a really short style and look great. As soon as it grows back I'll style it for you again.'

He refused to take any money, and I left feeling lighter physically and mentally.

The following day I was due to see my oncologist, and then journey into town for my appointment with the real hair wig maker. Although I'd showered the night before, I hadn't washed my hair as I was trying to hang on to it as long as I could! I found a fair few hairs from my pretty pixie cut on the pillow that morning but checking my reflection in my dressing table mirror, I was relieved to see the majority of it was still in place.

I was one week away from my second FEC treatment, and as my echocardiogram had come back normal, and there was no inflammation or infection behind Dolly my expander, Dr Ah-See suggested that this time, we switch to a week's course of Filgrastim (the tummy injections) in place of the one pegfilgrastim injection I had given myself with the first cycle. Colin had driven me to the hospital and I was feeling quite positive and well that day, so I told her I'd prefer to stick to the original plan, as I felt my body would be better prepared for the second round. She conceded, but did suggest that if I was struggling with the same kind of symptoms, we could consider a dose reduction for cycle three.

Amazingly, I continued to feel stronger each day and enjoyed a wonderful joint birthday celebration at Kathy's family home. She'd invited Clare, Deb, Simon, Barbara and a few more of my closest friends from work, and as we blew out the candles on our shared birthday cake, I made a wish, and hoped against hope that all would be well.

It was the morning after my second cycle of FEC and Colin had to leave early for work. I'd had a disturbed night with heartburn and tummy pains and as I couldn't get back to sleep after he left, I decided to shower and get on with my day. I was enjoying the feeling of the warm water hammering down on to me, when I realised it was pooling around my feet and not draining away. Wiping the soap out of my eyes I looked down at the plughole, and saw it was crammed full of my hair. I took a deep breath in, and just stood there, not daring to touch my head. Reaching behind me I turned the shower off, and stepped out on to the mat. In front of me on the windowsill was the only mirror in the bathroom. A free-standing vanity mirror that was angled away from my reflection. I grabbed my towel, wrapped myself in it and then turned the mirror to face me. The face that looked back at me was initially unrecognisable. Most of my hair had gone, although there were a few very long fine strands left, and strangely, a rather random little fringe. My ears looked huge, my face resembled a plate, and my scalp was grey and smooth.

'Oh my God…oh my God…' I leaned against the sink and started to cry. Reaching up with both hands to touch my head, my towel fell down revealing the livid scars across my chest and my lopsided body. My arms were smooth, as were my legs, and the pubic hair I'd valued so highly when it had first made an appearance all those years ago was completely gone, leaving a slightly obscene and literally stripped bare version of myself. I felt broken and helpless. I understood why I had to have the surgery and treatment, but at that precise moment I felt it had robbed me of my femininity, taken away so much of what I felt made me a woman, and left me feeling vulnerable and insecure.

A loud choking noise interrupted my self-pity, and I realised that the water was still trying unsuccessfully to drain away. I grabbed some loo roll and wiped my eyes – I still had my eyelashes at least – and then I leaned into the shower and scooped out handfuls of my hair. There seemed to be so much of it, and as most of the highlights had been cut off the week before, it was my natural shade of brunette! I dug into the plughole with my fingers, worried that the hair might block the pipe, and having put the last of it into the sink, I turned the mirror away from me and left the bathroom.

I called Lucy once I was dressed, and my lovely
girl was with me within the half hour. As always,
she kept a brave face when I opened the door to
her, and in spite of how she was feeling inside she
greeted me with a smile and a big hug. She'd barely
got through the door though before I told her that I
wanted her to cut the remainder of my hair, and as
I wouldn't entertain a razor, I suggested scissors.
I don't know why I couldn't have done this for
myself, and not involved her, but I was struggling,
and once again the roles had been reversed. She was
looking out for me.

It used to be a standing joke in our house when
I was a child, that there was never a sharp knife or
pair of scissors when you needed one. Dad would
manfully hack away at whatever needed paring
down, complaining bitterly that the tools were 'as
blunt as Ben Busby's boots!' I never did find out
who Ben Busby was, but like so many memories
attributed to my father, I kept them alive and quoted
him regularly to my children and my friends. Lucy
and I rummaged through the Man Drawer, full of
all those bits and bobs that men are meant to make
good use of, but rarely do; then my sewing box
and even the garden shed before finally coming up
with an old pair of kitchen scissors that I used to
cut flowers with. I will never forget sitting on the
floor between Lucy's knees while the blunt blades
chewed away at what was left of my hair. She told
me years later that it was something she'd sadly
never forgotten either. It made it real. I decided I'd
like to leave the little fringe, and was really chuffed

when, having tied one of my pretty scarves around my head, the wisps of hair across my forehead belied the baldness beneath. Simple pleasures and all that…

Mothering Sunday was just three days later, and the children took me to a local pub for lunch, where I proudly wore the longer of my two wigs and full make-up. Granted my body had already started to swell again because of the second treatment, and my face was a rather unflattering shade of red, but I was happy.

Small victories, is how I saw it, and silver linings.

# CHAPTER TWENTY-FIVE

L ooking back, I so wish I hadn't planned to visit the wig maker the day after my appointment at Richard Ward's salon as I'd felt quite buoyant. Unlike my experience at the Metrospa my experience at the wig maker's was unpleasant and I was handled insensitively. I have written this account without naming the supplier, and have given the stylist a false name, because I'm well aware that there are hundreds of places who treat their clients with the kindness and support they need, but not this one.

Bearing in mind any company who make and sell real hair wigs rely quite heavily on a client base that may have cancer or alopecia, there wasn't a hint of sympathy or understanding from Derek. In fact, he wasn't remotely interested in knowing why I was there or indeed why I needed a wig! A one-time hairdresser to the stars, he was now using his somewhat limited talent and bijoux accommodation to try to convince those of us suffering with hair loss – temporary or permanent – to buy one of the company's wigs.

Derek smelled: he clearly didn't wash regularly, had bad teeth and grubby clothes. But he had me in his mirror, virtually bald and definitely vulnerable, willing him to make me 'as I once was'. He leaned all over me, breathed all over me, told me of a party he was going to be attending in Croydon with an old school friend who'd known him way back when he styled the likes of David Essex and Adam Ant. There was no evidence of those folk on the walls of the incredibly hot basement studio, just pictures of round-breasted beautiful women, pert and pouting. Hair styled by the likes of Nicky Clarke, staring with their sightless eyes at my bald pate and lopsided shape and willing me to stand up and say 'I was beautiful once…'

Derek took out a pair of clippers that reminded me of the ones they have in the type of men's barbershops that has a red and white pole sticking out over the street at a somewhat inappropriate angle. He fired them up and approached my newly styled cut, the fine and fragile hairs only just covering my head. 'Some women don't like this,' he said as he pulled the skin tightly just above my ears.

Funny that, I thought, but said 'No it's fine… really I'm fine.'

It wasn't to be an all-over shave thank God, as I wanted to hold on to my pretty pixie cut for as long as I could. But Derek was on a mission, aiming for the middle of my forehead, above the ears and on the nape of the neck where I would have to stick the double-sided tape. Of course I'd been told about the tape when I bought my acrylic wigs, and it would be the same with this one, as I'd have no hair to clip the wig on to. Therefore it was necessary to hold it in place with tape to stop the unmentionable from happening. Derek pushed my head down as he cut a neat square above my ear, and as I stared up and out at my reflection in the mirror, I had a memory of my son Jack's first haircut: his head bowed forwards; beautiful almond-shaped eyes with his camel-like long dark lashes settling gently on his cheeks; his brown baby hair falling on to the black nylon gown he was wearing. Where have the years gone I found myself thinking, and then that thought was replaced almost in a heartbeat with, how many of them do I have left?

A strong waft of sweat broke through my self-pity and I found myself looking up at Derek's sphincter-shaped mouth, while his wet underarm moved above me. 'I'm not going to take that much off as once it's gone, it's gone. It won't grow back.'

Does he really think I don't know that? Has he any understanding of the circumstances that have brought me here? Does he actually give a shit? The clippers were really noisy, and left my skin white and smooth where there had once been a fine covering of hair.

'You told our receptionist that you wanted blonde and long, is that right?' he said, banging the clippers down so hard that I jumped.

'Umm yes. I think so,' I murmured nervously, but he'd already turned away from me and was rustling his way through layers of tissue paper that lined the inside of a large grey box.

And then suddenly there it was, the wig I had dreamed of owning since I was a little girl. I wondered who she was – the woman whose head this beautiful blonde hair had been cut from, and whether it had started to grow back. Was she cold without it?

'It's not been styled yet, so once you decide how you'd like it to be cut, I can do that for you. There will of course be an additional cost.'

As there would be for the incredibly large and heavy wig stand I would need, plus the pins that were necessary to secure it for washing and brushing through... With a certain amount of flair, Derek flipped the wig inside out so we could see the four tabs on the mesh cap. 'We need to stick the tape to these so the wig will stick to your head,' he told me, and cut inch-long sections from a little roll of double-sided tape. Taking the backing off the tape he secured the sections one by one to the tabs, and then with very little ceremony or thought, he pulled the wig down over my head. I was suddenly blinded by a mass of incredibly soft tresses, that dropped down almost to waist level. With a little bit of pulling and pushing, the wig was secured to my head, and then Derek's hot hands parted the front of it for me.

'Would you prefer a fringe or layered parting?'

I decided to opt for a bit of both - a fringe and then layered around the face, and having agreed that I'd need at least eight inches off the length, Derek started to peel the tape off my head. I couldn't help but notice the fine wispy hairs sticking to the tape, and wished for the umpteenth time, that I'd waited until I was hairless before coming to see him.

I was told that it would take a couple of weeks
to style and finish the wig properly, and when I
came to collect it, I could also pick up the stand,
the pins, and any other extras Derek felt would be
necessary. He turned away from me and wrapped
the wig in tissue paper while I looked at myself in
the vast mirror. The bald squares above each ear and
right in the middle of my fringe looked ridiculous –
thank God I was driving myself home and not going
by train! This thought was almost immediately
replaced with another far starker one. The next time
I looked at myself in this mirror I wouldn't have
*any* hair… how ridiculous would that look? Dolly
twinged painfully, and after giving Derek my phone
number so he could contact me with a return date,
I thanked him and climbed up the narrow staircase,
out of the basement and into the spring sunshine.

# CHAPTER TWENTY-SIX

One of the most difficult things to adjust to once I'd lost my hair was how incredibly cold I felt most of the time. It was particularly draughty around the back of my neck and behind the ears. Daft, really, considering the number of times I had worn my hair up, but there's a vast difference between an 'up-do' and a 'no hair do!' The scarves I wore helped a little, but they were too uncomfortable and weighty to sleep in, and I felt there was a strong chance I may get strangled by the very length of them if they unwound! I had considered keeping my wig on in bed, but there was a limit to the strength of the double-sided tape! They also made my head itch, and I felt it would be a little like sleeping with false teeth in – you just shouldn't! So I was determined to find something soft and warm to cover my bald pate in the wee small hours. I don't know if it's any different for those who lose their hair over time, or if the gradual thinning allows one time to get used to the change in temperature, but for me, it was like sleeping in a constant draught.

By the sixth day following my second cycle of FEC, I was struggling yet again with the same symptoms as before: major swelling in my arms and thighs and also around my neck, with increased sensitivity of my skin. There was no evidence of a rash, but it felt so sore to the touch. The tightness in my chest made it difficult and uncomfortable for me to breathe easily, and the spasms I had across the right side of my chest and behind Dolly were particularly strong. In addition to all this, I felt distinctly hungover, though no alcohol had passed my lips, and indeed the desire to drink had disappeared completely! The steroid Dexamthasone I had taken for the first three days, had wired me to the ceiling, and along with my puce face, increased heart rate and frozen scalp, I was struggling to get a good night's sleep.

It was on one of these nights, when Colin was with his family in Watford, that I felt particularly poorly. I didn't want to bother Lucy again, and knew that Jack would be out, and so I called Sam. I guess I was worried things might get worse and I'd have to head to A & E again, but I was also lonely and scared. I think Sam realised I wouldn't have called him unless I was desperate, and so he came over and lit the log burner for me and then we settled down to watch the amazing Attenborough series *Frozen Planet*. As Sam invariably wore a woolly hat during the day, I had asked him to bring a spare one for me to borrow, without stipulating a colour or style. Ultimately this was a decision I would live to regret, as the tartan deerstalker, complete with sheepskin earflaps, made me look like a dead ringer for Elmer Fudd.

Luckily, and in much the same time-scale as before, the more extreme of my side effects wore off within twenty-four hours and I had rallied a little by the time I met with Dr Ah-See the following day. It was the first time she'd seen me since I'd lost my hair, and as we talked about that and my other symptoms, I was able to tell her how I'd been feeling, relieved in the knowledge that she would make sense of it all. Of course we'd been here before (apart from the hair loss) just three weeks ago, and I had chosen to postpone the adjustments she had suggested then. She ran through it all again, reminding me that with the third cycle, I should omit the steroid on day three, and give myself Filgrastim injections from day five for six days, rather than having it all in one dose. As this part of my treatment helped to combat the decrease in neutrophils in the body – the blood cells needed to fight infection – it was important I continued with it.

'You're halfway through the course of FEC and in spite of all these side effects, I think you're coping incredibly well. You have been unlucky as very few patients have to contend with this kind of reaction,' she said kindly.

I thanked her for her constant advice and care, and for keeping an eye on me, and as I stood up to leave, I flicked the tail of my scarf behind me in a hopefully carefree way, and said I'd see her after my third treatment.

Each day I felt a little better and each day I walked

the three-quarters of a mile to the top of the lane
and back again. It wasn't a straight road – there
was a particularly steep incline at one point – and
there was also a riding school and stables halfway
up that hill. The tarmac was littered with large
piles of horse poo, which called for some pretty
fancy footwork to avoid the fetid waste! Some
days that walk was harder than others, but I always
felt better for having done it. Exercise has always
been important to me, and following Jack's birth,
I had been an avid gym user. I'd even employed
a personal trainer just before my fiftieth birthday
so that on reaching half a century, I'd be in my
best shape ever. After my diagnosis in January, I
never went back to the local gym, but had made the
decision to walk at least once a day in order to keep
up my energy. That wasn't the only reason though:
I felt very strongly that it was important for me to
'have' to do something each day, and it gave me a
sense of purpose to walk up the road and back. I felt
I'd achieved something even when I was at my most
poorly. If I remember correctly there were only two
days in the entire seven months of treatment when,
if I was home, I didn't make this walk.

I continued to have a large number of visitors to
my little cottage, not just my family but also friends
from work too. Simon who had joined QVC a few
years after me, arrived one morning with a whole
heap of freshly chopped logs for my wood burner. I
was weeding my borders – as you do – and I popped
up from behind the wall as soon as I heard his car.
Poor man, he hadn't seen me since I'd lost my hair,

and as the sun was shining I hadn't bothered to put a scarf on. I must have looked like Yoda peeping over the parapet, the sun's rays warming my scalp! All credit to him though, as there was no sense of alarm on his face, just a genuinely warm smile.

Claire Sutton was another one of my QVC compatriots who came over to see me on a number of occasions at the cottage. I also spent some time at her home, and we met in Harpenden after my blood tests on a couple of occasions to have brunch in a charming little tea room there. For those of you who may never have seen Claire, she's stunning: long blonde hair, a beautiful face, and incredibly elegant and feminine. The first time she visited me at home was a couple of days after I had lost my hair. I remember her arriving in a pair of jeans and a loose jumper, no make-up and her hair pulled back tightly in bun. To me she still looked beautiful, but it meant a great deal that she had kept her appearance as low key as possible when she knew I felt like shite. Ali Young, QVC's resident beauty expert, had called me not long after my mastectomy and had gone through my skin care routine, highlighting what I would and wouldn't be able to use while on chemotherapy. She then sent a collection of natural oils that she had mixed specifically for me. Lovely Lisa, who worked at QVC as a director, also came to see me several times with batches of pies she had baked, to make sure I ate properly. Her husband was at that time fighting his own battle with cancer, and I know how difficult life was for both of them, so the fact she had taken the time to do all this meant a great deal. I filled my good days with good times, and stayed over with Deb, went out and about with Kathy, and popped into QVC and saw as many of my friends as possible. I must mention dear Charlie, whom I once rang just after midnight, when I was alone and feeling particularly low, and who talked to me for nearly two hours until I felt able to sleep. Their love and support, plus my family and friends, helped me to believe there was a light at the end of the tunnel. I never underestimated how healing that support was.

It was just before my third cycle of FEC that I received a completely unexpected invitation. Singer and songwriter Lulu had brought her own range of Time Bomb Skincare to QVC just a couple of years earlier, and I had been lucky enough to work with her on a number of occasions. The range was an instant success, and Lulu a joy to spend time with. Lulu is incredibly modest and self-effacing, and it was a great thrill for all of us whenever she was in the building. That April, out of the blue, I had a call from her PR manager Gill, inviting me to accompany Lulu to the O2 to see Kylie Minogue in concert! Lulu and Kylie had known each other for some years, and of course Kylie had been diagnosed with breast cancer herself. Initially I was panicked about the way I looked, and not sure I had the confidence to get dressed up and get out there. However, I accepted the incredibly kind invitation and as I'd taken delivery of my real hair wig just a few days earlier, I decided I'd be okay – besides, my children would never have spoken to me again if I'd have turned it down!

Not only did Lulu send a car for me, which took me to her home, we then travelled together – after a glass of wine and some nibbles – to the O2, where we were ushered into the VIP lounge. There I met Danni Minogue, David Walliams and the *X Factor* winner Matt Cardle, to name but a few, and after another glass of wine we took our stage-side seats to watch the incredible spectacle that was Kylie Live at the Aphrodite Les Folies Tour. I didn't know where to look until the show started and then all eyes were on the stage, which was filled with Roman Chariots, winged gods, water fountains, fireworks, scantily clad men and women, and of course, Ms Minogue... all set against a backdrop of The Acropolis! Amazing! It was a great night, with a wonderful ending when Lulu and I shared our taxi back and she sang to me... Just the best time.

As with any cancer treatment, there are good days and bad days, and following my third cycle of FEC, in complete contrast to the constipation that had caused havoc initially, this time I had a really upset tummy and felt awful within just twenty-four hours. I dropped the steroid on day three, and a couple of days later I began with the first of six daily injections of Filgrastim. We had hoped that this change would lessen the side effects of the drug, but unfortunately all it did was spread them out! I had the same skin sensitivity, accompanied this time by a sore throat and a cough, and very little energy. My tiredness was exacerbated by my lack of sleep, constant indigestion and general feeling of being hungover and jetlagged. I also noticed that this time it took longer for me to feel better and guessed that this was due to the 'cumulative effect' of the chemo that I'd been told about. I felt quite tearful too, and worried that I wouldn't be able to cope, bearing in mind I still had such a long way to go.

But I did cope, because I had no choice, and because I also knew – and reminded myself regularly – that this treatment was giving me my best chance of beating the cancer. I do admit though, to crying copious tears while snuggled up with Colin on the sofa a few days later, as we watched Prince William marry Kate Middleton. It was such a beautiful ceremony, so full of hope and promise that it made me wallow in self-pity. In the past Colin and I had talked of marriage, and although I knew I loved him and he loved me, I'd been so badly damaged by my divorce, I didn't feel completely able to commit. I wanted to feel safe and secure; to be myself and not to be controlled as I had been before. That said, my own future currently looked far from rosy, so what was I able to bring to a relationship? Of course, not working meant that I had far too much time to think – and overthink – things, and although when talking to people I always remained positive, sometimes when I was alone, my thoughts would turn to my diagnosis, the treatment regime and the endlessness of it all, making me feel completely overwhelmed.

# CHAPTER TWENTY-SEVEN

They do say you can get used to anything, and I've always felt it to be true, especially when the things we are referring to are things you can't change. My treatment rolled on, and I knew I was almost at the halfway mark, having become very familiar not only with the hospital routine, but also the somewhat unpleasant side effects of the chemo. I was never sure how I would react after each cycle of FEC, but it kept life interesting, and with my fourth and final cycle, the cumulative effect became more evident, and I was able to add blurred vision, mouth ulcers and a somewhat worrying list to the right when walking, to my already numerous side effects! My tongue also swelled up for a couple of days and weirdly my teeth felt sensitive, but most of these symptoms – with the exception of the ulcers – lessened in the second week. I had also felt very sick for the first few days, which was different, but with the help of Lansoprazole and Gaviscon, it had worn off, along with the heartburn. I had absolutely no hair left on my head by this point, and my eyebrows and eyelashes had started to thin, which upset me.

Something though that had cheered me, was the purchase of a small lavender-coloured fleece hat that I wore at night, and which kept my head lovely and warm. I had tried several alternatives, one of them being a black fleece balaclava that my son Sam used to wear under his motorbike helmet. It was actually quite comfortable but was discarded after I'd woken suddenly in the middle of the night, seen my reflection in the large mirror on the wall, and scared myself half to death believing there was a burglar in the bedroom! I was at a loss.

Edna came to stay, and timed it so she could come accompany me to the Spire for my treatment. She'd been in constant touch ever since my diagnosis and had taken me to the hospital when I'd had my echocardiogram, understanding my inherent fear of heart failure, bearing in mind my father's untimely death. One of the many things I loved about spending time with her was that she always made me feel better. She never thought I was making a fuss, and listened to me without interrupting while I whinged on about life generally. She comforted me when I cried; she told me it was completely understandable that I'd feel as wretched as I did, and that she thought I was being incredibly brave. Basically I was able to tell her how it was, and although for the most part I was able to just get on with it, there were days when I found it really hard.

That morning when we arrived at the chemo unit, we discovered that both Rhoma and Anne-Marie were away. The junior doctor who looked after me that morning had struggled to connect the line through my port, and although it hadn't troubled me unduly it had upset Edna. We'd rallied though, and after an evening meal in a lovely Italian restaurant and a few episodes of Victoria Wood's *Dinner Ladies*, life felt good. The following morning she'd peered round my bedroom door but could barely see me as I was completely covered by my duvet. I heard the door creaking and sat up.

'Did you sleep well?' I asked.

'Yes, thank you. Lovely and cosy. How about you?' I saw her eyes focusing on my hairless scalp.

'Just so flippin' cold with no hair!'

'You must be! Don't you have a hat or something? Ian and I bought fleece hats from Millets when we went trekking in Iceland. They worked a treat.'

'We've got a Millets in Leighton.'

'Well, why don't we go there then? They're bound to have something.'

She was right of course, although the girl on the till was more interested in scanning Facebook on her phone than serving us that was until Edna spoke up.

'We need a fleece beany hat for Alison. She's going through chemotherapy and is far from well. What would you suggest?'

The sales assistant looked up lazily. 'We might have some upstairs, but I can't leave the till to look unless Letitia is down here.'

'Well can you please call her? As I've said, Alison's not well, and we don't have all day!'

When Edna locked eyes with the girl's, her slightly

insolent demeanour changed, and within seconds she was reaching for the intercom and speaking to Letitia. Having left the shop to buy stamps and some cotton wool, we returned to find a little family of fleece beanies for me to choose from. God bless you, Edna.

My hat was one of the first things in my suitcase when I packed in readiness for a surprise break to Benidorm. Colin had timed it for the third week following my final FEC, so that I would be feeling as well as I could, and although Dr Ah-See was a little concerned about me leaving the country while on chemo, she accepted that Spain wasn't the backend of nowhere, and that the change may well do me good. It would also be the last time I would have any significant breaks in treatment, as my three months of once-weekly Taxol would begin on my return.

Sadly my children weren't able to come with us because of their work commitments, but four of Colin's five children joined us, and we had a great time considering. The weather wasn't particularly good, but just being together somewhere different was fun. I was quite used to wearing my scarf and my wig, and so that side of things didn't really trouble me, but I was apprehensive about wearing a bathing costume and being on the beach for the first time since my mastectomy. Colin's girls were so sweet with me, and pretty much held my hand throughout our entire stay there, so I didn't feel self-

conscious or insecure, in spite of the fact they were
all in their mid-twenties and looked fabulous! We'd
had plenty of holidays together before then, and I'd
always felt incredibly blessed to have been accepted
by such a lovely family. While we were in Spain, I
played crazy golf, rode the mechanical bull in a bar,
and even danced the night away, complete with my
wig, false lashes and a Kiss Me Quick hat!

The four days flew by, and on our final night we
found ourselves in a club listening to a particularly
good Michael Bublé soundalike! This guy's
rendition of the song 'Hold On' had me crying
into my Prosecco. I blamed it on the booze, but
the children were upset too, and unwittingly the
adage 'all good things must come to an end' sprang
to mind. I didn't want to go home. This break
had been sheer escapism, and a chance to put the
previous three months behind me. But with another
three months still to go and radiotherapy after that,
I was feeling apprehensive. I didn't know how I'd
react to the new drug Taxol, or indeed the once-
weekly regime of treatment. Something I did accept
of course was that it was an essential part of my
'getting better', and as Lucy had said to me all that
time ago, I had to get better forever…

Because I'd had a break, returning just a little later
than I should have done, it meant that my days
of the week at the hospital changed. Rather than
having my blood test on a Tuesday and treatment
on a Wednesday, I now had bloods on a Wednesday

and treatment on a Thursday. My ever-responsible oncologist had taken time out to run through the side effects of Taxol, but felt confident that I wouldn't react as badly to it as I had done to FEC. She told me that this type of chemotherapy interfered with the division of the cancer cells, and that part of the treatment used solvents to dissolve the drug so they could get into my bloodstream. Of course the very nature of solvents might mean it would be difficult to tolerate, and so the side effects she reminded me of were very similar to those she'd told me about previously for FEC. They included low white blood cell count, susceptibility to infection, neuropathy – numbness in the fingers and toes – nausea, vomiting, constipation, taste changes, ulcers, fatigue, muscle joint or bone pain, and changes in the finger and toenails! Being reminded of all these made me momentarily feel as though I had taken a mighty step backwards, but on the plus side it was only one drug that needed to be administered, and so I guessed the whole process should take less time.

'In comparison to so many of my patients, I think you've been very unlucky with your reaction to FEC, but I am really hoping and trusting that you will tolerate Taxol far better,' she told me. I so wanted to believe her, but in truth I was worried about the next twelve weeks. I knew my body was finding it harder to cope with the drugs and the whole 'settling' process was taking a great deal longer – my good days were few and far between. Something else that troubled me was my lack of energy. On holiday I had done a great deal of sitting around and relaxing in the daytime, but once I was home, I found that it was taking far more effort to galvanise myself into doing anything, including walking the mile and half up and down the lane. In fact, there'd been a few days when I hadn't felt like getting out of bed at all. I thought it was just post-holiday blues and talked to Roz about it, who said it was completely normal considering all that my body had to contend with. She suggested I find somebody to accompany me on my walk, and that way I may feel more inclined to do it. I chose Nina, my next-door neighbour's beautiful black Labrador who was super-excited to be getting extra exercise while Mummy was at work. I can't truthfully remember who was drooling and panting the most after our first foray as a couple, but it was definitely a win–win situation, and one I was very grateful to Roz for suggesting.

While the walks got easier, the memory loss definitely worsened! It is one of the lesser-known side effects of chemotherapy and the medical profession has a name for it: 'chemo brain'! Along with 'baby brain', something many pregnant women have to deal with due to erratic hormone changes, let me tell you this is 100 per cent real and incredibly debilitating! Never mind trying to remember who I'd spoken to on the phone that day, or what I had arranged to do the following week, I genuinely couldn't remember what I'd walked into a room for, or where I'd left my car in Tesco's car park!

My first round of Taxol brought with it sensitive skin and aching muscles and the onset of hot flushes, particularly at night. I had my treatment on Thursday but by lunchtime on Saturday I really didn't want to be anywhere other than at home. Colin kept me company, and although I felt pretty grotty until Monday, I then rallied and had a lovely couple of days in the garden. I was really hoping that this was to be the way of things in the months to come, as I had decided to take part in Cancer Research's Race for Life on the 11th of June and had received monumental support and donations from the readers on my QVC blog. Not that I was planning to actually run it, you understand. Although my hairless form made me far more aerodynamic, I intended to walk the course with family and friends, and didn't want to let them or myself down. Colin and I had decided we'd have a bit of a do after the event, and so planning for this, as well as catching up on all my blog responses, kept me preoccupied until my next treatment.

After the second treatment I lost all my eyelashes and eyebrows, which was a blasted nuisance when out walking as tiny thunderbugs and small insects that seem to fill the summer sky, now had unimpeded entry into my eyeballs! It was not a good look… Joking aside, I found losing my eyelashes and brows far worse than losing my hair, as I felt I was now devoid of all facial expression. My face looked as flat as a plate, and who ever said it was easy to stick false eyelashes on to lash-less rims had clearly never tried! Losing my hair had been difficult, but least I could disguise my baldness with a wig or a scarf. This was tough, and made me feel surprisingly vulnerable, but if you find yourself in this position, remember that there's help out there from the likes of Breast Cancer Care, Macmillan and The Haven. They all hold classes to teach women how to apply make-up following hair loss, and the results can be astonishing. I didn't personally get involved, choosing to leave things as they were, apart from perhaps a little lip-gloss on special occasions. With the exception of digging out my discarded balaclava, I had no choice but to make the best of what I had, trying to remind myself that this, like so many of the other side effects, was only temporary. When I was in my more positive frame of mind, it was something I found hugely comforting to hang on to.

'Do you think people know that I'm bald under this scarf?' I asked Colin one evening.

'No, I don't think so,' he replied.

'But do you think I look weird?'

'No, sweetheart, you just look poorly. You look like you've got cancer, and you're doing your best to deal with it.'

He was watching TV at the time, and I looked sideways at him, in the gentle light of the log burner. He wasn't being unkind; it was an honest response. Stark but honest, and sometimes the starkness of this disease, and all that it takes from you, needs confronting rather than avoiding. It takes a great deal of support, love and self-belief to get you through it, and I will always count myself

incredibly lucky to have had bucket loads of the
first two, and constant promotion of the third.

I did manage the Race for Life, and although my
legs were like a couple of Rowntrees Jellies at the
end, it was worth it. The warm up beforehand nearly
killed me, and caused Lucy – who through her own
admission is somewhat adverse to any form of
exercise – to hiss at me through gritted teeth, 'Isn't
it enough that we've just turned up?'

I raised a stonking sum of money thanks to the
donations from my lovely QVC bloggers, and was
very grateful to them for their incredibly supportive
messages. The constant correspondence from them
was very much a lifeline to me, and I would spend
hours replying to every comment that was posted,
especially at night when I was unable to sleep.
Although I was communicating with people I didn't
really know and would probably never meet, it was
a comfort to me. But what was most humbling, was
that they felt able to write to me about their lives,
and all they were having to deal with. Women who
were going through the same treatment, husbands
who were grieving having lost their wives,
daughters caring for parents with dementia, and
mothers trying to come to terms with losing a son.
Words of support would fill the pages of the blog
for each of these individuals from all the others
who posted there, and these comments were a stark
reminder to me that however difficult I felt my life
was, there was always someone somewhere who

had far more to contend with.

The blog and my continued contact with my friends at work meant I still felt connected to QVC even though I wasn't physically there, and having celebrated my ten-year anniversary with them just two months before my diagnosis, it was the longest period of time I had ever had spent employed by the same company.

# Chapter Twenty-Eight

L ife was very different when I left school in 1976. University was for those who'd been to Grammar School and had plans for a professional and profitable career, unlike me with my secondary modern education. I had seven O levels, three CSEs, and very little idea of where my future lay! I applied for several jobs that summer, and was interviewed by a variety of employers such as the NatWest bank and the Milk Marketing Board. In spite of being offered the job after each interview, I think it would have helped me enormously if I'd have had some idea – any idea! - of what I wanted to do, but apart from the pipedream of becoming a TV newsreader, nothing particularly enthused me at the time. Our careers lessons at school hadn't inspired me either, consisting mainly of reading through a selection of cards on which job titles and the relevant skills required were given. One of my favourites was for the position of 'egg packer', the specific skill set being 'nimble fingers'.

As Mum was bringing us up on her own, money was tight, and I knew that unless I had something definite in mind requiring A' levels, she would need me to work.

There were far more job opportunities available to young people then, so we were spoiled for choice. I decided to take a job at Shell International Petroleum on the South Bank at Waterloo, because my initial training would involve me learning how to type, for which I'd be paid. I thought this would be a useful skill to have, and although there had been over five hundred applicants for just twelve positions, I was lucky enough to be chosen. The thought of commuting into London every day excited me. So different to when my own children were that same age and I wasn't even happy for them to travel by train in rural Bedfordshire from Leighton Buzzard to Milton Keynes!

I stayed with Shell for two years, learned how to type proficiently, and was promoted to the position of administrator for their in-house magazine. From a daily routine filled with typing internal correspondence and memos (as they were known in those days), my role included writing and typing copy for the magazine. Most of it revolved around Shell's global affairs, with a great deal of emphasis on raw materials and the oilrigs. I once made a glaring error on a piece of copy that read 'All hands on dick, the cry went up, as the large piece of machinery slid into place...'

With the promotion came a slight salary increase, but more importantly an invitation to lunch with the CEO or Chairman as he was then addressed. Shell Centre is built on twenty-four floors and I worked on the 13th. I had only ever once been to the top of the building and that had been when I accepted the job. We were given a guided tour and while enjoying the unspoiled views of our fair city, the guide gave us a rough estimate of the number of folk who had thrown themselves from the top of the building! 'If you can visualise the huge hole a one-pence piece would make in a concrete paving slab when dropped from this height, just imagine what damage a human body would do!' I didn't think the paving slabs should have been his primary concern, but having caught sight of the rather complicated series of net and wire around the edge of the roof, I instinctively moved away from the edge as our guide clarified that this had been put in place to deter 'would-be' jumpers!

The invitation to lunch was very welcome, even more so because it was to take place in an executive dining area on the twenty-third floor. Having been ushered out of the lift, we were taken to the most incredible room with windows on all sides. I was just eighteen years old at the time, and somewhat shy, but I do remember listening to a gentleman talking about various career opportunities within the company. 'You could always make a sideways move into tankers' he said enthusiastically, and because I was well brought up I nodded in agreement, and then concentrated on my dessert. I didn't want him to think me ungrateful, but I knew there and then that my future was not going to be with this company. The sun shone through the clear glass windowpanes and afforded me the most amazing view of the city of London. I had my whole life ahead of me, and choices to make, and

I didn't want to make a sideways move anywhere. I wanted to try and carve a career for myself that would involve something far more exciting.

I spent weeks searching for jobs and surreptitiously sneaking off for interviews in my lunch break, but it wasn't until I found a position with Michael Joseph, a hardback book publisher in Bedford Square, that I felt happy. The job was to work alongside the publicity manager as her secretary although the position had come with a warning; "It's not all razzmatazz and parties you know.". At 18 years old, I so hoped it was! This prominent business commissioned biographies, fiction and non-fiction, and counted among their authors James Herriot, Spike Milligan, Dick Francis and Stan Barstow. I have always enjoyed reading, so to be surrounded by shelves full of literature, and also be involved in organising launch parties, TV/radio interviews and general publicity for the authors was beyond exciting! I'd only been working there for a couple of weeks when Sophie Loren's autobiography was published. Not only was there a signing session at Selfridges on Oxford Street that required police assistance and road closures because of the crowds, but I was entrusted with a pair of Ms Loren's stockings (the ones she'd been wearing the day before) and told to guard them with my life as they were to be put up for auction to raise money for Help a London Child! I met some lovely people during my time there, made many friends, and did a lot of growing up. I thoroughly enjoyed the job and there was never a dull moment, with plenty of opportunity to experience all the best our great city can offer.

I remained there for two years and was promoted to assistant publicity manager of their sister company Pelham Books, before I married and moved to Colchester. Commuting from Essex to the city and then across London was a nightmare, and so with some regret I left my literary friends, and found employment closer to home.

My move into the world of advertising seemed a natural one, and after a brief spell as PA to the Managing Director of a small agency, I took on the role of account executive with a larger company, and handled many of the regional clients, overseeing above and below the line campaigns. I wasn't sure initially what that meant, but basically it involved all mediums of advertising – from local press, poster sites and local radio, to national TV. I found the job great fun and really challenging, and my commute – on a moped - took only fifteen minutes!

I left their employ not long before Lucy was born, and set up my own little company 'Relsec Services' – an abbreviation of Reliable Secretarial Services! Using the government's Enterprise Scheme, which paid out seventy pounds a week, it helped those of us determined individuals to set themselves up in business. I did my due diligence and within a fortnight had my first client. Having found a reliable child-minder for Lucy, I increased my workload to three mornings a week with this small and local advertising agency, and after six successful months, I decided to go back to school and study English at A level. It was a pretty intensive thirty-six-week course, but at the end of it I got both A level English language and literature. My dad died very suddenly just before I was to take my exams, and although it seemed incongruous even to attempt to sit them, I was so glad that I did. Mum said that he would have been proud of my determination and eventual achievement – Grade B in both exams.

I kept my workload to a minimum so that I could spend as much time with Lucy as possible, and did a fair amount of typing from home, managing to make a few pounds in profit! It was around the same time that I stumbled into voiceover work for a local radio station. I say stumbled, there was actually a great deal of hard work involved to make it happen, and I really have to thank my lecturer from the Wolverhampton College where I'd studied, as without him, I doubt I would have ever given it a thought. Jim Bell helped me make a demo tape and put me in touch with a host of local radio stations. Having always wanted to work in radio or on TV, I was thrilled when That'll Do Productions on the Tettenhall Road in Wolverhampton, asked me to come in for an audition.

They were affiliated to Beacon Radio, and having given them a number of different voices, and choices of delivery, I was taken on. It was a great place to start, and I happily accepted ten pounds a script to record radio advertisements for them. The first voice over I took on was for Berlei Bras, and for some inexplicable reason they wanted me to sound like a robot! Everything after that seemed easy, and I was thrilled when six months later, I was given the opportunity to take over from Beacon Radio's regular travel reporter as she was off to have a baby. I took on the job as their travel girl five mornings a week, and within a fortnight I was double-heading the mid-morning show for Beacon Radio in the West Midlands.

A year later I was given my own show on their Gold station, and from there I had a fabulous three years with BBC Radio Shropshire with my own afternoon show. In those days as a presenter you were expected to research, produce and present the show, so trying to find sufficient content to fill two hours was sometimes challenging! We had our own Outside Broadcast van, and I notched up quite a few unusual features on subjects as diverse as sausage-making at a butcher's in Much Wenlock, an interview with an individual who kept huge live snakes in purpose-built drawers in his home in Bridgenorth, and a very enjoyable, if slightly smelly afternoon at the local sewage works!

The success and increased audience I gained for the show gave me sufficient confidence to audition with my second husband for ITV's flagship daytime TV show *This Morning*. Over the following four years we presented more than a hundred shows as the regular anchors whenever Richard Madeley and Judy Finnegan were absent. It was my first foray into TV, and I have to thank Dianne Nelmes – who launched *This Morning* and was the director of daytime and lifestyle programming for Granada TV – for giving us this monumental chance. I will never forget my first live show, waiting for the title music to end and thinking the beating of my heart was so loud it would be picked up on my microphone! It was an incredible place to begin my TV career, and I learned a great deal from the crew and production teams. Celebrity interviews, fashion features, and topical phone-ins were all part of the brief, but my most vivid memory is having to present the show the day after the Dunblane tragedy. By that time, the full horror of what had happened was only just emerging, and I will never forget the enormity of having to hold the show together while struggling with my overwhelming feeling of sadness.

I stayed with Granada TV for a number of years, and worked for their independent channels too, presenting six of my own shows on a range of different subjects, such as historic homes, fashion, cooking and health. This led to several years working as a reporter on the BBC's *Watchdog Value for Money* series, and also their highly successful *Holiday* programme. None of this work though was full-time, so alongside raising my three children I formulated programme ideas for TV, working for several years as a contributor for Channel 4's *Dispatches*. I also wrote storylines and scripted several episodes for BBC 1's daytime drama *Doctors*, and successfully placed a TV drama with Sally Head Productions Ltd. My voiceover commitments continued to grow, and I was lucky enough to be credited with working for clients like

Sainsbury's, Halifax Building Society, Thomson Holidays and for also being the voice of the Alpine satellite navigation system, which can be found in most Jaguar and Honda cars. The *Sunday Times* wrote a double page spread on satellite navigations systems, having spent a morning with the sound engineer and myself as we pieced together the somewhat monotonous but meticulous audio. I had to pose for a number of photographs too, some inside a car, and some in the studio, complete with headphones ruining my carefully coiffured barnet! They chose one of these to accompany the article, and it was set alongside a headline that read 'The Dominatrix of the Sat-Nav Systems'! Another string to my bow?

I began working for QVC The Shopping Channel in the year 2000. I was with an agency who searched out TV work for their many clients, and although I knew very little about QVC, I thought I'd give it a go. When I arrived for the audition, I was taken to a room filled with a large number of men and women, and all kinds of products – including cosmetics, electrical items and household appliances. We were all asked to choose something we felt we could comfortably talk about for at least eight minutes, and then given time to prepare. To say I was nervous was an understatement. I was completely out of my comfort zone, but grabbed hold of a hair straightener and took it out of the box. Twenty minutes later I was in a small studio, standing in front of three people I'd never met before, extolling the virtues of this high-tech piece of hair wizardry. Amazingly, they liked me, and were impressed with my knowledge and retention of information, and so I was given the job.

That was seventeen years ago, and I'm still enjoying it.

# Chapter Twenty-Nine

I think it was two days after my fifth cycle of Taxol that had me retching into the sink ... God I felt so sick. My skin hurt, even my bones felt sore, and I was struggling to sleep. I felt defeated, and didn't think my body could cope with much more although I knew I had another seven weeks to go. The problem with a long-term treatment plan is that it pretty much takes over your life; you eat, sleep and breathe it. Your world is built around hospital visits, contending with the side effects of the chemo, and trying to keep a hold of some sort of normality.

Unfortunately for me, the side effects hung on for days, and apart from a couple of visits from my sister, a few friends, my children and of course Colin, I stayed in and did very little. If I was having a good day, I'd try and do something positive, even if it was just going out for a coffee, but I became wary of driving and being too far from home, as I had very little warning of when I'd start to feel lousy.

I was approaching my sixth treatment, and due to have my blood tested, but one particular morning I woke up feeling pretty groggy. I put it down to being tired as I'd not slept at all well. Colin hadn't been able to stay with me, and I'd had a disturbed night without him. However, my bladder was urging me to get up, and I knew I couldn't remain in my warm flannel sheets forever. The bathroom in the little cottage was downstairs, so while mentally reminding myself to google commodes, I had no choice but to head there! Of course, once you're up and out of bed, you may as well stay up – well, that was my theory – and it gave me the incentive to crack on with my day. My mouth ulcers were giving me grief that morning, and so I had a bowl of porridge for breakfast. Having put on my loosest clothing in an attempt to lessen the irritation to my skin from the fabric, I tied my favourite scarf around my head and set off for the hospital.

The ward when I arrived was as always, quiet and calm, although I guessed I must have looked pretty peaky as I pushed through the double doors, because Rhoma who was at the reception desk seemed a little taken aback when she saw me.

'How are you?' she enquired as I walked over to her and leaned on the desk.

'Not so good today' I replied.

'I'm sorry to hear that, love,' she said 'Do you fancy a chat?'

I nodded, and followed her in search of a comfy chair, a cup of tea, and a place to talk. She led me into one of the treatment rooms and I flopped down on to the blue chair in the corner while she went off to get the tea. Having given me my brew, she perched on the corner of the bed and told me to tell her all about it, which I did – at length. It was only after she'd given me several tissues for my tears and told me how brilliantly I was coping, that she gently informed me she wasn't actually expecting me in until the following day as it was only Tuesday and bloods were on a Wednesday! Twenty minutes earlier and I would have no doubt burst into tears, but instead I shook with laughter 'You're kidding! What am I like?'

'You're just like every other patient who has to contend with this rotten routine, but remember you're over halfway through it now!' she replied, just as Sister came into the room.

'Chemo brain!' I said cheerfully to her, wiping my lashless eyes.

'We're always happy to see you, Alison,' she said with a smile, and I got up from my chair and hugged them both.

Professionals like Rhoma and Anne-Marie carry their patients, like myself, through what can seem to be a never-ending tunnel. I would have struggled so much more without their constant care, and I will never forget their kindness and understanding, because it made all the difference to me.

The seventh and eighth cycle of Taxol saw my fingernails begin to discolour, and the skin behind them start to rot. Dramatic shades of purple, green and black coloured the nails, while behind them the nail bed was soft and putrid. I was losing the sensitivity in my fingertips too, and in frustration when the rather nasty oozing had stained my clean sheets, I dug the nail bed out with the end of a screwdriver because a) I had nothing else to dig it out with, and b) I hated the smell of it. It didn't hurt, but left me with deep hollow channels behind the disturbingly discoloured keratin. My big toenails were also affected, although my smaller toes just felt numb. Of course this was one of the side effects that I had been warned about, but had hoped wouldn't happen, and I can honestly say that I have yet to meet anyone else who was on the same treatment, and reacted in this way! Indeed, while writing this book, I've spoken to many women who were on a similar treatment regime to mine, and all they had to contend with was just mild discolouration and weakening of the nails. The great thing for all of us, was like the hair loss, it was only a temporary problem, so if it happens to you, try not to fret because I promise you, your nails will grow back.

Once the nail beds had dried out, the whole business was far less troubling, although the lack of feeling in my fingertips was definitely worsening. I decided to ask Colette my manicurist if there was any way she could disguise the rather lurid hue of my existing fingernails, and her suggestion was to paint them in a very dark nail polish! I have always been totally inept at painting my own nails, probably because I've never had to, but when I began working at QVC in 2000 I started to have my nails professionally painted. When your hands are on screen, they are mightily magnified and need to be perfect! I hadn't known quite where to start in my search to find this service locally, but our then neighbours Keith and Jeannette Batten, came to the rescue and introduced me to their future daughter-in-law Colette. She worked at Champneys Health Resort and Spa and had been awarded the prestigious title of Manicurist of the Year for Natural nails, and also had been personally requested by Demi Moore to look after her hands and feet while filming in the UK! During the fourteen years she looked after me, we became great friends and my nails had never looked better! She married Dave, had two daughters, and when she and her family moved miles away to Bournemouth, I knew I was going to miss her. She was very much a part of my metamorphosis in the years following chemotherapy, for which I will be eternally grateful.

The deep plum shade of nail polish did a corking job of hiding what lay beneath, but the loss of feeling in my fingers and toes had become something of a problem. In addition to this I had developed nosebleeds that I found to be a flaming nuisance! My skin had become far more photo sensitive, so that even the slightest amount of time in the sun – which let's be frank is pretty much all one can hope for in England – brought me out in a horrid strawberry red rash on my forehead and arms!

When I met midweek with lovely Mei Lin, I told her about my problems and along with arranging for me to see the hospital dermatologist about my rash, she prescribed a different type of mouthwash for my ulcers. She also touched on the possibility of giving me a week's break from treatment to try and let things settle down, should my reactions to the drugs get any worse. I was fiercely against this as mentally I'd accepted the number of weeks and months it was all going to take, and I could almost see the finishing line in the distance. I so wanted to be through all the treatment by the end of the year. Having listened to my argument, she accepted that it would be difficult for me change anything, but told me that she would monitor the situation closely.

It was always gratifying to hear that what I was experiencing although unusual, was not unheard of. Picture, if you will, a bald woman, dabbing at her nose to stop the blood flow, while scratching her itching forehead with numb fingers and purple nails, and that's completely discounting the ulcers or the lack of feeling in my toes! I had developed an upper respiratory tract infection, which presented itself as a rotten cough, but there was no chest infection, thank God, just a little more effort required to get to the end of the lane and back on my daily walk.

Weeks six and seven saw me continuing to battle with the annoying cough that I didn't seem able to shift, and so I was prescribed antibiotics for the following week, in the hope it would clear the infection. I was using Corsodyl and Difflam on a daily basis to help with the mouth ulcers and along with saltwater mouthwashes these did help. I'd also been told to try fresh pineapple, because there was something in its fruit acid that was thought to be beneficial, whereas I knew to avoid fresh tomatoes as eating them was torture! Dining out on my good days had been a pleasure, but now I was wary of finding myself faced with food I couldn't eat. It felt very much as though the cancer was fighting against the chemotherapy and appeared on occasion to be winning. It wasn't all doom and gloom though, and I remember a lovely evening with Chris and Roz at their street party, where I drank Pimms and danced in the street until my feet hurt. However, the gaps between the rough and the smooth were getting smaller. The endlessness of it all was beginning to get me down. I felt very vulnerable and self-conscious, and because of this there were more occasions when I only wanted to spend time with those who understood how I was feeling, and didn't put me under pressure to 'do jolly'.

One day in particular, having planned to spend it with my friends at QVC, I'd woken up feeling too poorly to drive, and had abandoned the trip. Because they were all on shift that day, they couldn't come to me, but I assured them I'd be fine, and had spent the day on my own in the cottage, watching TV for a bit and then sitting in silence feeling sorry for myself. The sun set, and the daylight turned to dusk. The phone rang but I didn't answer it. The frozen ready meal I had defrosted sat on the beech wood worktop in my kitchen, leaking icy water into the sink. My all-familiar view was less visible in the shadows, but still I remained quiet and unmoving. It must have been around nine o'clock that I had to head to the bathroom in what was left of the light, and probably around that same time I decided to get the bottle of whisky from the cupboard by the fireplace and pour myself a large glass. It went down very easily. As did the second glass, and as the sky darkened and the shadows deepened, I became completely self-absorbed... I think whisky has a tendency to do that, but I'm not a heavy drinker, and wasn't prepared for the fall out...

Judging by the light of the moon it must have been around midnight when I shut the front door of the cottage and headed up the lane in my jeans, trainers and a fleece sweatshirt. It was very quiet and very dark – no street lamps on our lane – and no police cars either, which was extremely fortuitous. I'm certain that if they had stopped to question me, I would have been immediately booked for being too drunk to even walk in a straight line! But I wasn't walking. I was running. The cold wind blew unimpeded over my bald head, my lash less lids failing dismally to stop the tears that were falling from them. The night sky was clear, and the stars were bright, and I ran the entire way up the hill, turning without stopping to run all the way back again. My chest was pounding with the effort, and I felt physically sick when I slowed down on my approach to the cottage, narrowly missing my car that was parked up on the verge. The little wooden gate slammed shut behind me as I flopped down on the old bench that was set next to the brick wall. 'I can't do this anymore!' I cried out loud to no one in particular. 'I don't want to be like this! I hate it. I fucking hate it. ' I cried whisky-soaked tears into my fleece top, until the cold and damp air forced me to go back into the cottage and finish what I'd started five months before.

# CHAPTER THIRTY

Following my premature visit to the ward having got my days muddled up, I'd written all my remaining treatment dates down on my calendar in the hope no more mistakes would be made. I'd arranged to meet Claire the next day in Harpenden after my blood test, so we could celebrate the fact I was on the eve of my penultimate treatment. I felt good, and we had a lovely morning together. I was loath to leave her, but as it was the school holidays she had to get home for her children. We were still wittering on to each other as we headed back to our cars, and without even looking, I stepped straight out into the road and almost under the wheels of a white Fiesta! 'For fuck's sake, Ali!' she shouted as she grabbed my arm and pulled me back on to the pavement. 'Jesus! Can you imagine me having to tell your kids that you'd survived the chemo, but had been killed by a car while out with me?'

I laughed out loud, not because what I'd done had been particularly funny, or even because I'd scared Claire half to death, but because I'd never heard her swear like that before! I apologised profusely and hugged her tightly, promising to Google the Green Cross Code as soon as I was home.

It's strange but that little episode reminded me of a phrase I'd heard so many times since my diagnosis: 'It must be really scary living with cancer, but any one of us could step off a pavement and under a bus tomorrow!' It's true, of course, but not particularly helpful, and I have ranked it right up there with the question asked by someone who will remain nameless, when enquiring about the intimate side of my life while I was on treatment: 'It must be difficult for Colin not to be repulsed by the way you look?' Luckily for me, Colin never made me feel less of woman, or any less attractive to him following my surgery or throughout my treatment, which meant everything to me.

I overslept the following morning and then wasted a good ten minutes or so trying to find my chemotherapy notebook, which was right where I'd left it, in the bathroom! I left the house in a panic, hitting the A5 like a madwoman. While waiting at the traffic lights I took my notebook out of my bag to check my platelet count – as you do – and I noticed that it wasn't my eleventh treatment after all. It was my tenth – I still had two more to go! I couldn't believe it... I was so shocked that I sat there immobile, while the lights turned green, causing the man in the maroon Mazda behind me to hoot at me and gesticulate inappropriately.

I drove the rest of the way to the hospital in silence, and having parked the car, I cried. I didn't want to go in and go through it all again, but I knew I had to. Did I have a choice? What if I stopped now, and then the cancer came back and was incurable? How could I live with that? Well, I wouldn't live with it would I, because it would be incurable! I wiped my eyes and shook my head, pulling down my sun visor to look at my face, expressionless without my eyelashes and eyebrows. 'You're an idiot,' I told my reflection, and got out the car and headed into the hospital.

I reached an all-time low the following Monday when I found it impossible to untie my trainers after my walk. My fingers had been so numb and yet so painful that morning that I'd had to accept I was unable to hold Nina the black labrador's lead, and so I had walked alone. I had continued wearing some of my favourite jewellery throughout my treatment, but was now finding it almost impossible to fasten a necklace or put my earrings in. It was even difficult to use my touch screen phone or to get a grip on anything, as my nails had begun to peel away from the nail bed. I'd also noticed a profound heaviness in my right arm, which on closer inspection appeared almost Popeye-like in proportion! My hand and fingers seemed swollen too, and so somewhat alarmed, I rang the chemo ward for their advice, and they organised for me to see Mei Lin and a breast consultant as soon as possible.

It transpired the swelling in my arm was caused by something called lymphedema. The consultant was perplexed as it taken hold 'somewhat earlier than normal', although that said, it can apparently happen any time after the chemo is finished, but it's unusual for it to start while you're still on the drugs. Unfortunately if you have a complete clearance of the lymph nodes as I did, there is a 10 to 20 per cent chance you could fall foul of this condition, which basically arises because of the lymphatic system's inability to drain fluids away. Well, this was the first I'd heard of it, and I wasn't best pleased to be given the news! The consultant went on to say that he would arrange for me to have a CT scan, to exclude the risk of a thrombus or blood clot. If that was clear and it *was* lymphedema, then I would have to begin a course of lymphatic drainage. What on earth was that? I had no idea, but it sounded as though I'd need to employ the services of a plumber rather than someone in the medical profession! The consultant clarified that it was a specific form of massage, and would require regular visits to a specialist. I was told I'd also need to protect my arm in the future, never to have blood taken from it, or even a blood pressure cuff put on it, and I should also avoid shaving under my arm! Any form of injury could prove problematic, as it would take so much longer to heal.

'Will it wear off?' I asked hopefully, while trying to pull my fat arm through the narrow sleeve of my cardigan.

'No,' he said gravely, 'unfortunately, not. This condition is for life, and your arm will be for ever compromised.'

'Seriously? On top of everything else I'm

going to be stuck with a right arm that puts Serena William's to shame?' I spluttered.

He looked over his glasses at me. 'The lymph nurse will measure you for a compression sleeve which will help over time, I'm sure.'

'Great!' I responded rather rudely, and then apologised immediately before reaching for my bag with my heavy hand. We both stood up, I took the note on which he'd written the name and address of the lymphedema nurse with my numb fingers, thanked him for his time, and left the room.

Dr Ah-See had arranged to see me following this appointment, which was a real bonus, as I wanted to talk through with her what I'd just been told. I also needed to let her know that the neuropathy had definitely worsened, as had my mouth ulcers. In light of all that we discussed, she decided that I should have a small dose reduction of Taxol for my final two treatments, which would hopefully help. She also talked to me about the adjuvant endocrine therapy that would start a month after my chemo finished. It would involve a drug called Tamoxifen that I would need to take daily for a total of five years. As with most drugs there were side effects – in particular hot flushes, arthralgia (joint pain), a slightly increased risk of blood clots, and a very rare risk of endometrial cancer.

'It may be that we extend this therapy after the five years with Letrozole, but if you are still pre-menopausal, then it may be better to have your ovaries removed,' she said, her eyes locking with mine across the desk. I sighed, prompting her to say gently that none of this needed to be discussed again until that time arose.

'It's okay,' I lied. 'I'm just feeling a bit rough today. I'll be fine.'

Once again I reached down for my handbag, and then stood up to leave. Mei Lin stood up also.

'You really are doing very well, Alison. Almost there now,' she said kindly. I smiled and thanked her before heading out of the hospital.

It wasn't like me to be defeatist, but my head was a total jumble with so much information to contend with. Never mind the Tamoxifen and its side effects; to be told that I had lymphedema and would have to wear an ugly compression sleeve for the rest of my life really upset me. It would be a constant reminder of this bloody cancer long after my hair and nails grew back, and it felt really unfair. Since the 9th of March, when my chemotherapy had begun, I'd counted the months, watched the seasons change, and accepted all the grotty side effects, because quite frankly I didn't have a choice. I had endured it all because the treatment was deemed to be curative, devised to make me better. During this time, in conversation with various people, I'd heard about other patients who hadn't been able to cope with the way the chemo made them feel, and had given up on it. God knows there had been many times, especially since I'd started on Taxol that I too had felt beaten because it was tough, and continued to be, but to give up on it? Lucy had said to me that it was just nine months out of my life, and I was stronger than I knew. I found that the fear made me stronger, and although I hadn't told her, I knew of several cancer patients who'd not been able to contend with their treatment and were then diagnosed with secondary breast cancer some years later. Who's to say that it was as a direct result of their decision, or whether it would have happened anyway? When I was told 'this is what you have to have', I didn't question it. I knew there would be no guarantees or promises that the big C wouldn't appear somewhere else in my body at a later stage in my life, but I knew that everyone involved in my care had done their level best to bring that risk to a minimum. The rest I felt was in the lap of the gods.

When I got home Colin was there. I hadn't been expecting him, and wasn't sure I'd be the best company, bearing in mind how negative I was feeling. Sitting with him on the sofa I ran through all that I'd been told, trying to put a positive spin on it.

"I know it's not fair, none of this is, but whatever happens you'll get through it Ali, and if it means you'll be here with me for longer, then it's got to be a good thing."

"Even if I've got a right arm that's bigger than yours?"

"It'll be an advantage if we ever arm wrestle," he said smiling at me. I snuggled into him, and for a short while at least, closed my mind to what was ahead, preferring the here and now and just being with him.

A few days later, and as a complete surprise, I was contacted by the charity Breast Cancer Care, who asked me if I would be prepared to make a speech at their annual fashion show to be held in October. As I mentioned in my introduction, BCC have been QVC's charity of choice for many years, and as the official broadcaster we tended to position the event at the beginning of the evening. Before accepting what I saw as a monumental challenge, I got my calendar out, and checked that this would fit in with my three weeks of radiotherapy that was to begin in September. Amazingly I would have my last appointment the Friday before the fashion show, which was to be on the following Wednesday. Determined to look on the bright side, I got in touch with the charity and said that although I might be a tad tired and possibly 'sunburned' I would love to represent them alongside my employers. Deep down I knew that if I wasn't well enough to step up on stage, one of my colleagues would be more than capable of taking my place on the podium!

Trying to decide what to write for my speech was in itself pretty daunting, but I also faced a whole new challenge… what to wear? Looking at myself in the full-length mirror, I felt more than a little discouraged. I couldn't remember what I looked like before my surgery and the chemo. The face staring back at me was as alien as the lopsided, hairless, and somewhat scarred body – never mind my huge right arm! Not a pretty sight. Sod it! I'd think about it nearer the time – a wig and professional make-up would make all the difference, and perhaps I could get a snazzy compression sleeve to dress up my outfit! Okay, maybe not quite as exciting as choosing a pair of killer heels or luxurious lingerie to go underneath a strappy number, but hey! If I survived this ruddy treatment, and made it to October, then that was surely worth celebrating. Marginally mollified I grabbed my dressing gown and headed downstairs.

Suffice to say, the next couple of weeks were tough, and I didn't venture out much at all. Apart from Colin and my close circle of family and friends, the only person I spent any time with was Liam in his Ocado van. He had delivered my Ocado shop, and then collapsed in his van just a little way up the road. Ocado had called me, and after hacking up the lane to find him, I'd called for help, and waited with him. He'd had some kind of a seizure, and I don't think the ambulance men knew which one of us to take to hospital as I looked equally poorly! Mercifully Liam made a full recovery and I got £25 off my next Ocado shop. A win win situation.

I will always remember the Thursday I had my final treatment. Although it was the middle of August, it was drizzling and pretty chilly. I had woken up early and watched the raindrops running down the window. From where I was lying in bed I could see across the lane to the hedgerows and the fields beyond. It was a beautiful view even when the weather was rotten, and it was one of the many reasons I loved living in the cottage. I still found it hard to believe I'd only lived there a month before being told I had cancer, and although the past six months following my diagnosis had changed the direction of my life entirely, essentially the worst was over.

The thought of finishing my chemotherapy brought about a funny mix of feelings: relief obviously, but also a strange sense of uncertainty. Since the 18th of January, my life had been mapped out for me. I'd spent a great deal of time in hospital with the same lovely staff caring for me, and although I hadn't always felt my best, I'd felt safe. The slightest twinge or unexplained pain was investigated, and I was never made to feel as though I was making a fuss. When I was struggling they had told me I was brave, and their positive comments and endless kindness had bolstered me through the worst of it. To know that after today I would have no reason to visit Roundwood Ward again made me not only sad, but scared.

I'd had umpteen offers from family and friends to accompany me for my last treatment, and although I knew Colin particularly wanted to be with me, I felt it was something I had to do alone. I needed to say my goodbyes, to thank the nurses, and also to try and get my head around the fact that the times were changing. I had cancer, but now my treatment was done, did that mean I was free of it? Could I just go back to how I'd been before, and not worry about this wretched disease returning? I had further surgery planned in less than a year, when I

would lose my left breast too. I tried to think back
to what my life was like before this had taken over,
but on that day I found it impossible...

When I arrived at Roundwood Ward, Rhoma
and Anne-Marie were in great form, and I had my
photograph taken with each of them before getting
into the hospital bed for the last time. With the
intravenous line attaching me to the unit, I found
the familiar whirring and pumping noise along
with the powerful antihistamine, had, as always, a
soporific effect, but this time, as the toxic treatment
dripped slowly into my body, my tears stopped me
from sleeping. I lay there watching the rivulets of
rainwater run down the double-glazed windows
and thought back over the last six months. Had all
of this changed me as a person? Would I have the
confidence to return to work? Would I be able to
put it all behind me, or would I allow this cancer to
define me, to turn positives into negatives, and to
take away simple pleasures by overlying them with
fear? I had no answers.

Leaving the hospital and my weekly routine
was hard for me. I had spent six emotional months
living a totally different kind of life that had been
mapped out for me by my cancer. The treatment
and subsequent side effects had been hard to bear
at times, and yet those who had administered this
highly toxic treatment, were the people I trusted and
had become reliant upon.

Rhoma and Anne-Marie had been incredible:
never stinting, never complaining, constantly caring
and always understanding. It takes a very special

kind of person to take on this kind of role, and I will never forget how between them they carried me through this sometimes seemingly endless tunnel of despair. Their kindness, their conversation and sense of calm had got me through my chemotherapy, and made me realise that whatever the future held, I was lucky enough to still have a life worth living and fighting for. Having said my somewhat emotional goodbyes, I wanted so much to be able to be able to put it all behind me, to wave a magic wand and have hair again, pretty nails, both breasts and to go back to work.

In time I would, but before all that, there was the radiotherapy.

# CHAPTER THIRTY-ONE

Those first few weeks without chemo found me floundering. It was a bit like flying without a safety net. Although I was relieved to find that my mouth ulcers, and nose bleeds improved dramatically within days, the dark ringed eyes topped by a bald head stared back at me every time I looked in a mirror. I'd managed to squeeze in a family holiday to Brighton with Colin and my children to celebrate the end of my treatment, and although the weather was blustery, it had gone pretty well. We all stayed together for the bank holiday weekend, and then Colin and I continued alone along the Dorset coast to Swanage, Corfe Castle, Lulworth Cove and Durdle Door.

I inadvertently left my fleece beany hat at the B & B in Lulworth Cove, and although they made a 'thorough search' it was never found. I had to make do with a thin jersey replacement that was next to useless, although after a couple of weeks I noticed a fine grey fuzz on my once bald pate which cheered me immensely. Emotionally I felt like a piece of cotton in the wind – nothing anchoring me and with very little direction – but I only had a couple more weeks, before I began my radiotherapy.

It was around that time I found out that my mum had also been diagnosed with lymphedema – rotten luck considering the incredibly low number of women who do have it. It was her right arm too, and she had been to her GP for advice. My own right arm continued to be problem, and so I duly made an appointment to see the lymphatic drainage expert, who luckily for me, lived just fifteen minutes away. I spent a very entertaining hour in her treatment room, as she regaled me with tales of her training and nefarious time as a nurse! She was quite insistent that MLD - (Manual Lymphatic Drainage) - should only be carried out by a trained therapist, but that she could show me a few 'movements' that I could do for myself at home. It's nothing like a sports massage or an aromatherapy massage as it's carried out with quite a light touch and no fragrant oils sadly. The aim is to encourage the extra lymph fluid to move away from the swollen area that is devoid of lymph nodes, and into other parts of the body, so it can drain normally. MLD improves lymph drainage in the healthy nodes, which in turn helps keep fluid away from the swollen areas.

My therapist's touch was gentle as she made a series of number seven shapes, starting at the wrist, and then continuing up my arm and across my dented chest. It wasn't uncomfortable, although I felt a little self-conscious lying there with just a sheet over my lopsided top half. It took about half an hour, and once she'd finished, she spent ages with a tape measure wrapped around and across my mighty right arm and hand, calculating in what seemed like code, before giving me a card full of measurements that looked more like a lesson in map skills! 'I have to be completely accurate with this, because although it'll feel tight, we don't want it to stop your circulation. You'll need the sleeve and glove as your hand's affected too, but this style is all in one, so if you take the prescription to your GP, he'll know what to do with it,' she told me. 'Oh, and don't let them fob you off with a wait time. They can turn it around in less than a week if they use the contact I've written on there,' she added.

Before I left, I set up my next appointment, as although she felt the compression sleeve should help pretty much immediately, she believed it would be wise to continue with the MLD for a couple of months. If I left it, and the fluid was allowed to build up, it could cause the arm to become solid, and that would bring with it another set of problems. 'Ain't life grand,' I said sarcastically as I shook her hand and left the house. It may sound dramatic, but to me this really felt like a slap in the face. I'd struggled with the surgery, and then had to cope with the chemo, but this was such a bloody nuisance, and I was genuinely concerned that it could delay my return to work. How was I supposed to sell beautiful jewellery with a stonking great right arm and hand? Of course, my fingernails were pretty dreadful too, I had no hair, eyelashes or brows, and Dolly was a completely different shape to my natural left breast. What if I lost my job? Hadn't this cancer taken enough from me already? Feeling more than a tad sorry for myself,

I headed home via the surgery, where I dropped my meticulously written prescription for the compression sleeve and glove.

The day I took delivery of it was also the day I received the planning date for my radiotherapy at the Mount Vernon Cancer Centre in Watford. When Mei Lin had originally talked through this part of my treatment with me, she'd explained that it was an incredibly effective and targeted therapy for breast cancer. She was recommending five days a week for three weeks, and although it sounded like a monumental amount of time, each treatment would only take about ten minutes. I wasn't particularly receptive that day, as I was almost at the end of my chemotherapy and feeling pretty ropey, but I'd held on to a couple of things. I recalled that the treatment can sometimes cause a rash almost like sunburn on the skin, and that some patients find it makes them very tired. My mum hadn't been given chemotherapy, but had finished her course of radiotherapy on Christmas Eve. She had been very tired afterwards, and understandably quite emotional. I had shut all this away in a box in my brain, and kept the lid on it. It was very much a case of needs must, and I didn't want to think about it until I had to.

Colin was born and brought up in Watford, and as he was still living there when we met, I knew the area pretty well. The Mount Vernon Cancer Centre is part of a much larger general hospital,

and is extraordinarily well equipped with fabulous
scanners and up-to-date technology. I was to
have external beam radiotherapy, and to enable
the radiographers and my oncologist to work out
exactly what the treatment should be, I would
need to have something called 'mapping' carried
out beforehand. When I'd called to confirm
my appointment, I was told that I should wear
separates, and bring my own dressing gown in, as
it would speed up my wait time. I was happy to
oblige, having found that most hospital dressing
gowns felt more like a loofa against the skin, and
played havoc with the red and rather sore rash I still
had on my left arm and hand.

I hadn't the foggiest idea what to expect when I
got to the hospital, but having spent nearly half an
hour looking for a parking space and then realising
I didn't have the right change, I was pretty stressed
when finally I arrived at reception. Why do so many
hospitals have so few parking spaces, and then
charge you to park there? I felt anxious enough, but
couldn't help imagining how much worse it would
be to have to circumnavigate the car park so many
times with a passenger who might be seriously ill,
or maybe a mum in labour! I had wanted to rant on
to someone – anyone – about this lunacy, but having
arrived at reception and been ushered into a room
with several similarly hairless and pretty poorly
looking people, I thought better of it.

I sat in silence, clutching my dressing gown to
me, and because I was late, it was only a matter
of minutes before I had to get changed. 'You can

keep your trousers on, but take off your bra and top please.' The incredibly tall Antipodean nurse showed me into a tiny cubicle, where I did as I'd been asked and then tied my dressing gown tightly around me. She was waiting for me as I came out, and trying to make small talk I asked her which part of Australia she was from. 'Melbourne,' she told me, as she hurriedly ushered me into a large and mainly empty room. The door we had to go through was incredibly thick, and reminded me of the ones that usually secure a bank vault. However, rather than a huge wheel on the front of it, there were several sinister yellow and black signs with warnings about radioactivity on them.

'If you could take your gown off, we're going to need you up here now, so you might want to stand on this?' She pointed to a small stool that stood at the side of a narrow metal-framed bed. It was almost chest height.

'I could always take a run at it?'

'Not such a good idea.' she said frostily as I clambered inelegantly on to the flat surface.

I felt distinctly chilly having removed my dressing gown, and even though I'd had Dolly my expander for six months or so, I still felt awkward and embarrassed without a top on. I was relieved to see Mei Lin's familiar and friendly face, who having introduced me to the radiographers asked for the lights to be dimmed so that the mapping could begin. What a bizarre business! I had to lie incredibly still with my arms above my head while Mei Lin and two other clinicians worked over me.

It wasn't the most comfortable position to hold because of the scarring from my breast surgery, but it was very important that I maintained it for almost thirty minutes. God! It was so cold in the room I was more concerned that extreme shivering rather than cramp would cause me to move! Using bright red and green beams of light, they shifted me, and the bed I was lying on, so that they could create a map of lines over my chest. Each movement was almost imperceptible, made with extreme care and often repeated. Each position was said out loud with a series of numbers, before my skin was marked with a felt-tipped pen. Hearing them converse with each other was like listening to an audio version of the enigma code, but as I discovered afterwards, this numerical language meant they could work out my exact position in degrees. It seemed to take ages, but finally they were done, and having put down the felt-tipped pens, they told me they were ready to tattoo me!

I had been rather excited about the prospect of getting a tattoo in my fifties! I had lain awake at night thinking about the kind of thing I would ask for, but when it came down to it there wasn't a choice, just a plain black dot no bigger than a pin head right in the centre of my chest, and one each side under my arms. If I'd have joined them up, I could have created a kind of wide pyramid shape.

Finally it was done, and with huge relief, I was able to move my arms from above my head. Having sat up and put on my dressing gown, I was told that they'd need me to be at the hospital, at the same time every week for the next three weeks. Each treatment would take around ten minutes, but I would have to be there on time as there were a large number of patients treated each day. While I'd been lying there in the semi darkness, trying not to think about radiation and the dangers associated with it, I'd decided to ask my son Jack to taxi me to and from the hospital, as he had offered to help on many occasions. If he could drop me at the hospital, within half an hour I should be in and out. I'd pay him of course, as he didn't have a job, and I felt it was only fair if he was making this kind of commitment. I decided to mention to the staff the problem I'd had with the parking that day.

'Oh, you won't have to worry about that. Any cancer patient who is here for treatment can collect a token and use that to park with each time. If you go to the main reception, they'll be able to help.' Apparently there was a sign to explain this on the ticket machine but I'd been too agitated to see it! I was very relieved that I hadn't vent my spleen earlier, and having clambered off the bed on to the stool, I was given an information booklet with my start date on it. Once they'd heaved open the enormous door for me, I thanked them all and left the hospital.

I do want to say at this point, that for those patients who don't have chemotherapy but are given radiotherapy instead, the whole process is understandably more daunting. The fact that the treatment is radioactive is alarming, and as with all things in life, those who've had a bad experience are always more than happy to share it! I hope this isn't the case for you. Luckily for me I'd only spoken with my mum, and apart from the fatigue, she had found the whole experience strangely comforting, as she knew it was a targeted treatment, and deemed to be very successful. I think that attitude is absolutely the best way to deal with it.

I actually enjoyed my journey in that first Monday morning with Jack, and was delighted to be able to leap out of the car this time, although it left him with the frustration of finding a parking space! The room was exactly as I'd remembered it, and although initially I was a little apprehensive, I think that was more to do with the fact I had to get myself back into *exactly* the same position I'd been in when they'd done the mapping! This was essential as the radioactive beams needed to be directed only at the affected areas. The room felt incredibly cold – a little like the freezer aisle in a supermarket – and the nurses' digits dug into me. 'Why is it so blooming cold in here?' I asked, having kept my cardigan over my jeans when I lay down. I had a different nurse this time, with a Home Counties accent and sensible shoes. 'When we turn the machine on, the radiation causes it to heat up, so we keep it cool in here.'

'Oh. I see,' I said, while wondering what it would do to my insides. But then I remembered… Mei Lin had told me exactly what it did. I shut my eyes tightly. The nurse had to take direction from whoever was in the control room and so a disembodied voice gave her the all-important instructions, and having gently pushed and prodded me into position, she left, closing the incredibly thick metal door that separated me from them.

Some days there was a radio playing, but other times it was very quiet. I would lie there waiting for the high-pitched siren noise that indicated the radiation was being beamed into me and I'd count... slowly... It only took thirty seconds or more and then the machine silently swung up and over me so that the tiny lines of light were focused directly on to the tumour site. Another thirty seconds and it was done, but I didn't move until the nurse came back into the room just in case. There were more than a few days when I felt like leaping down and getting out of there, but as the bed was too high, I had to wait for it to be lowered.

Looking back over those initial appointments, I had a distinct sense of unreality. It was difficult to believe that a treatment that took so little time, and had seemingly no side effects – unlike chemo – would actually make a difference to me in the years to come?

However, during the second week I had quite a lot of tightening around Dolly my expander – not painful, more uncomfortable – and that by my third and final week, there was a livid red rash across the right side of my chest. I duly applied the aqueous cream I'd been given and although it didn't get rid of it, it certainly helped the itching. I noticed also the first autumn leaves in the hospital car park when Jack dropped me off that Friday... I had almost come full circle.

# CHAPTER THIRTY-TWO

From the moment I was told I had cancer, I knew that I'd be facing time away from work, and strangely what helped me through the hardest times was the thought of returning. Sometimes with longing, other times with apprehension, but always believing that as soon as I was back in the building, I could put the previous nine months behind me.

I loved the challenge of the job, but it was the sense of belonging to a community that was most important to me.

There's a modern-day expression FOMO – fear of missing out – and although the phrase maybe new, I think it's something I've always had. Looking back over the years, I remember how important it was to me to be one of the crowd. In addition to ganging up with as many members of my class in infant school, including Debbie Guardhouse and Arthur Fishpool, I found my *raison d'être* when at seven years old, I was allowed to join the Brownies. It wasn't just the uniform and bright yellow badges that appealed to me, but the fact that I could spend

every Tuesday night with my best friend Jeanette
Pemberton and be officially known as an Imp!
The groups were called sixes because there were
six of us in each, and Jeanette and I, having sworn
our allegiance to this small blue being, became the
proud owners of a badge bearing an embroidered
likeness to this unnaturally flexible and double
jointed creature. My mum's rule of thumb was that
if we joined anything we had to stick at it for six
months minimum. She was firm, had limited funds,
and I think looking back, it was fair. Life was tough,
money was tight, and the cost of a Brownie uniform
meant no brightly coloured Corona fizzy drinks for
almost the entire summer.

I loved being taught how to tie knots, embroider
my name on a hanky, and boil an egg. For every
activity I performed, I got a badge, which, thanks to
my needlework training, meant I was able to stitch
it on to my uniform myself. 'Dog's tooth stitches,'
my mum said, which I felt was a little unjust,
but looking back and remembering the large and
uneven threads that held the badges in place, it was
probably true. I used to polish my brown leather
belt, and dream of being a Brown Owl and owning
a silver whistle. Although that was only when I was
there in the school hall, as once I got home, I was
more than a little daunted by the responsibility of
being even remotely committed to Baden Powell's
minions. However, my Aunty Eileen, mum's sister,
had been involved in the Girl Guide movement for
years, and she actively encouraged me.

Those of us who attended regularly and

continually contributed sixpence a week, climbed
the ranks and were taught the Brownie Guide Law.
If we showed real promise, we were taught how
to furl and unfurl the Union Jack at the beginning
and end of our meetings, and while the other girls
formed a circle, and stood in groups of six, the
'chosen one' was allowed to stand right next to
the plastic mushroom that graced the centre of our
circle. Not quite one of the Seven Wonders, but to
a small person, being that close to the large red and
white spotted plastic mushroom, complete with a
slot in the top for the sixpences, took on an almost
religious quality.

We were quite a diverse bunch. I met a girl who
put Vaseline on her eyelashes as someone had told
her they would grow longer if she did. I learned
about tampons – well, I say 'learned', I was told
what they were – and spent three sleepless nights
worrying about internal bleeding and losing the
end of the piece of string up your front bottom! I
was only eight years old after all! Brown Owl was
supported by Tawny Owl, and she worked as a
nurse in our local cottage hospital. I remember her
telling us all in stark detail about the first baby she'd
had to lay out, its tiny orifices filled with cotton
wool and its eyes open. It was definitely a learning
curve, and although on occasions a tad disturbing, I
felt I belonged.

Life at home was more than a little fractured.
My father was far from faithful, and my mum
understandably struggled. I remember one night
sitting on the stairs and overhearing a conversation

between her and our neighbour June. Mum was crying and June was trying to comfort her.

'Has he been leading you up the garden path again?' June asked, her voice a little distorted and distant because they were both in the kitchen. The stair carpet was itching my bottom as my nightie was quite short, but even that distraction couldn't stop my mind from wandering. Why would Dad have led Mum up the garden path? The only thing up there was the shed? And why would it have upset her if he had? The last time I'd seen him, he'd been packing a pair of paisley pyjamas into his black overnight bag, and having kissed us goodbye, had turned on his heel and left the house; a small piece of toilet paper still stuck to his chin where he'd cut himself shaving. We just accepted that it was part of his job to be away, and made the best of it when he was home.

I think it was the promise of 'summer camp' that made my Brownie nights at Sunnymede Infants School even more exciting. I knew that once I was in my final year I would be allowed to go. Money was even tighter that year as Dad had left home, but it strengthened my resolve to become a Girl Guide. This and the lure of the periwinkle blue shirt and bright red tie made it impossible for me to resist! I enrolled the following spring, and Mum scraped together sufficient funds for me to go to the summer camp, which that year was in Dorset. My sister Jenny had only just joined the Brownies, but after Mum had a quiet word with Captain, she was allowed to come too. I wasn't best pleased about that, because I was on a mission to find out more about the Boy Scouts who met on the same night as the Girl Guides, and just a few hundred yards up the road. I knew they may well be coming to the same camp, and with the thought of romance never far from my mind, I would loiter with intent once our evening finished, in the fervent hope I might get to meet one of them. I pestered the Scout Leader known as Akela, for a place in the Scout band, and was delighted to I was accepted. Apart from a tambourine or triangle, the only other instrument on offer was the flageolet. I didn't even know how to pronounce it, let alone play it, but even now it sounds more like a marital aid than a musical instrument! It's actually something made from tin, that resembles a recorder, but as I was keen to impress, I decided to choose the only other – and far larger -instrument available. The bagpipes. My attempts to master this unbelievably unwieldy instrument were quite painful to listen to, but they did catch the attention of a particularly smiley, sandy haired and freckled Scout called Paul. He was eleven years old too, but his instrument of choice was indeed the flageolet.

Although the Scouts didn't travel with us, they were set up in the field next to ours, and arrived at camp about an hour before us. Remembering our mode of transport it's a miracle we arrived at all. Picture 40 Girl Guides and several Brownies crammed into the back of a removal lorry, jammed to the gunnels with tents and our personal paraphernalia! No seats or safety straps, with the roll down door left up so we all faced out, allowing us to spend the entire journey trying to catch the attention of the drivers following us!

Our Guide Captain had chosen a site that afforded us an uninterrupted and stunning view of Corfe Castle, but the field on which we were to make camp, was undulating, and set on quite a steep gradient – about a one in six! Having brailed our bell tent – not a euphemism, merely a technical term for rolling up the edge of the canvas as it was hot – we zipped ourselves into our sleeping bags, and spent hours peering through the gap, trying to spot a Scout in the adjoining field. The corner of the field we'd had to pitch our tent on had a particularly savage incline, and meant that one of our number, a small Chinese girl called Mai Mai Lilywhite, rolled out of the tent in the night, under the canvas, and was found wrapped around the flag pole in the morning. That was just one of the more memorable mornings we had, waking up to porridge made with condensed milk, and chocolate spread sandwiches. Apart from washing in cold water and having to empty the Elsan latrines – it was the stuff dreams were made of.

I think all those years of enjoying that sense of belonging had led me to truly value the colleagues at QVC I'd worked with for ten years. They had become my friends, and without their gentle support I know I would have floundered. I often wondered if I'd have had a different kind of job – like I'd had all those years ago - in a bank maybe, or an office – would I have wanted to carry on working during the early part of my treatment? However, that was never really an option as QVC were understandably concerned about my health and how my diagnosis might impact on some of the more vulnerable viewers, or those facing a similar diagnosis. Indeed, as I've mentioned, the first blog I had initially written, with details of my surgery and how I was truly feeling had been severely edited so as not to concern our customers. Obviously if this was something I was going to share publicly I understood it needed to be tempered, although there was a part of me that still felt the need to 'tell it how it is'. However, once I started reading through all the kind, funny, supportive and compassionate comments that appeared on a daily basis, I knew my employer had been right. As I think I've said previously, the blog became very much a lifeline to me, and reading and responding to the hundreds of messages and comments meant that I never felt alone. Even in the wee small hours of the morning when sleep eluded me and I felt beaten by it all, these wonderful missives brought me comfort.

Having finished my radiotherapy on the Friday, I went shopping that weekend for an evening dress to wear for the Breast Cancer Care Fashion Show. I wasn't going to be on the catwalk, thank heavens, but I would be taking to the stage to talk about my experience of breast cancer. The speech itself was difficult to write. I had just six minutes in which to cram a corporate introduction and eleven months of my life, and it stretched me, mentally *and* emotionally. I had represented QVC at this event on many occasions before, and had always enjoyed searching for a dress, deciding on how to wear my hair, and being given a fabulous professional makeover. This year was different. The excitement and exhilaration were replaced with something closer to apprehension, and instead of the stunning Amanda Wakeley number I'd worn the year before, I chose a rather uninteresting flouncy frock in TK Maxx. I had thought initially of searching out something that would work well with my skin-coloured compression sleeve, but instead I opted for a rather shiny grey fabric. I'd had my real hair wig 'dressed' – I think that's the technical term for an up-do – and decided to wear it en route to the venue, rather than risk it being spoiled in transit.

'I know women who would kill for hair like that!' my make-up artist remarked, as she added colour to my sallow complexion.

'I'd be happy to lend it to them,' I said.

I suppose it was because she had a blank canvas to work with that she took her time being creative, but it wasn't until she'd applied my lipstick, that I was allowed to take a look in the mirror. I didn't want to spoil my long false lashes, but it was hard not to cry when I saw the transformation. Looking at my reflection, I forgot all about my dented, radiation-scorched chest, and my incredibly tight compression sleeve. I felt happy for the first time in forever.

I gave my speech at The Grosvenor House Hotel on the 11th of October, and was so buoyed up by the entire experience that I knew my decision to return to work was the right one. It was agreed that I'd start with two days a weeks, but with the proviso that if I felt ready, I could increase that in the New Year. Television is a funny business, there is no escape from the all-seeing eye of the camera, and the introduction of HD certainly hadn't helped those of us entering the autumn of our years! Unlike other TV companies, at that time, as QVC presenters, we applied our own make-up, and quite frankly there's a limit to how much a full face of foundation can hide, even if you slap it on with a trowel! Age isn't kind, and neither is a mastectomy, chemotherapy or lymphedema. I knew it would have been evident to anyone watching, that I was no spring chicken, and that all those wonderful attributes that make a woman feminine, had long since changed for me. Although hair was beginning to grow back on my head, and I had eyelashes and brows once more, I'd also developed a fuzzy covering over my face and neck! Blonde fuzz, yes, but much more like kitten fur than the desirable peach skin I would have preferred! I was concerned about it, as my first hour back on air was to be presenting jewellery. If the director decided to take close up shots of me wearing earrings, I was worried I might look like a bearded lady! My fingertips were still numb, and my nails paper thin and deep purple. Luckily they were masked by the beautiful nail polish Colette had applied, but my right arm and hand were still Navratilova-esque! I felt acutely aware of the dent in my chest and the fact I was noticeably lopsided, but I refused to resort to a polo neck sweater. Apart from anything else, I'd be far too hot under the lights, and that was bound to bring on a hot flush. Would my make-up melt? Would the sweat patches under my arms be noticeable? These thoughts and many others were running through my mind as I drove the forty-four miles from Bedfordshire to Battersea. The roads were familiar, as was the endless stream of traffic that crept its way down the Finchley Road. I had made this journey hundreds of times over the previous ten years and could have driven it blindfold – all very much the same, although somehow different. But then everything was now.

When I was at secondary school I read an incredible short story called 'A Sound of Thunder' by Ray Bradbury. It involved time travel to a Wild Game Safari, where the would-be hunters were allowed to shoot any animal they wanted to. Having chosen to go back 60 million years there were strict instructions for the men directing them to the carefully targeted dinosaurs they were allowed to kill. Those dinosaurs that would have died anyway and at exactly the time calculated. Each hunter had to stay on a cleverly constructed floating path, from which they were forbidden to step. The path would take them to their target, and all hunters were warned not to inadvertently kill any other creature en route, as this could irrevocably change the future.

Faced with a furious Tyrannosaurus Rex, one of the hunters took fright and stepped off the path. Returning to the present with their trophies, they find everything is the same but somehow different – just a whisper of something imperceptible. The tiny green and gold butterfly embedded in one of the time traveller's boots had changed the course of the future and nothing would ever be the same.

As I drove towards work that day, I felt the same sense of unreality that the hunters must have experienced. Everything seemed the same, and yet so much had changed, and although I was returning to the job I loved, I realised I would be facing different challenges.

There were two entrances to Marco Polo House, and I parked my car in a spot furthest from reception, having decided to sneak in with my bags and my wig before meeting everyone. It wasn't that I didn't want to see my colleagues, I just needed to take a deep breath and centre myself. My dressing room hadn't changed – crammed full of clothes, shoes and products – the photos of the children, Colin and I still glued to the mirror. So many memories of our holidays in the sun with all of us bronzed and happy. Me bikini-clad and whole. I looked at my reflection and pulled my scarf a little further down onto my forehead.

'You can do this. You wanted to do this.' I said placing my stonking great wig stand on the dressing table, and dumping my bags on the floor. 'It's going to be fine…'

And of course it was. My friend Charlie chose

the dress I wore, and he was with me for my first hour back on air, metaphorically holding my hand all the way. Wendy our floor manager was there too, with a fan for when I had a hot flush, and the producer and director couldn't have been kinder, avoiding any close ups of my fuzzy face, and my concave cleavage. All in all, I really enjoyed being back on air.

I was just about to leave the building when a guest who no longer works for QVC, crashed through reception armed with his plethora of cleaning products.

'Hey Ali, you're back then?'

'Yup. Just had my first show.'

'How are you feeling, 'cos you look good to me.'

'Why thank you kind sir! I doubt you'd have said that if you'd have seen me a couple of months ago, and without this wig!' I reached up to my blonde tresses.

'Well I think you're incredibly brave to come back after all you've been through. Knocks the confidence I would imagine?'

'It does, but it's all smoke and mirrors in this business eh?'

'Yeah! And God knows, you don't need tits to sell a steam mop!' he concluded.

I took a deep breath in, taken aback by his bluntness, before responding

'Well that's lucky for me then' I said through gritted teeth, and struggling to maintain my composure I walked out into the cold night air.

# CHAPTER THIRTY-THREE

It was as though life itself was turbo-charged, rushing through Christmas and into the spring with barely a nod to the New Year. I had taken things slowly at work for the first month or so, but felt strong enough to extend my days in January 2012, and although I found the driving very tiring, my shifts were short and my hours uncomplicated. In February Colin and I took a three-week break to Australia to see my brother Peter. He had moved out there some thirty-odd years before, and I hadn't seen him since 2003, when my sons and I went to spend Christmas with him and his family. We had an amazing time, and I could see immediately why he had chosen to make a life in Australia and to bring his two children up in Sydney. He'd been back to England a fair bit in the interim, but once he started his own business, he had very little spare time, so this trip was particularly special.

When Mum was diagnosed in 2010, Peter was understandably shocked and concerned, but was unable to return to the UK, managing instead with regular phone calls and emails to Jenny and I to keep up with her progress. His son James was living

in Sweden at that time, but his daughter Clare was
still living at home with him and his wife Sarah.
Because Mum had a two-month wait between her
breast cancer diagnosis and her mastectomy, she
decided not to contact Peter initially, preferring
him to have his summer holiday without worrying.
Having been told he then decided not to tell his
children until after our mum's surgery. They were
both understandably concerned, but Clare had taken
the news particularly badly. She was upset because
she had been the last to know, and desperately
sorry that she lived halfway around the world, and
couldn't be with us all.

I was acutely aware of this the morning I
phoned to tell my brother of my own diagnosis, yet
ironically it was Clare who answered.

'Hi there, Aunty Alison great to hear you! Dad's
out at the moment I'm afraid, but how's everything?
How's Colin?'

'He's fine, thanks love, but I'm afraid I'm not so
good pet.'

'What's up?'

I made the decision to tell her there and then.

'I'm afraid I've just been told I have breast
cancer, the same type as Nanny. I'll have to have a
mastectomy and possibly—'

'No!' Her voice cracked. 'How can that be?'

'It's okay, sweetheart. Now they know what it
is they can treat it, and so I'll be fine like Nanny.'
I could hear her sobbing down the phone. 'Please
don't cry sweetheart. I'm really sorry I didn't mean
to upset you, I just know how important it is to you

to be told about these things…'

'But how can this happen to you as well? It's awful!'

'Darling, I'll call back a little later, but please try not to…' She interrupted my falsely felt, yet hopefully comforting response.

'It's Dad! Dad's back! I'll get him for you.'

The phone hit something hard, and I heard her running down the hallway to the front door, crying.

'Clare? What's wrong? What's happened?' I heard Peter's voice in the distance cut through her sobs and her muffled response.

'It's Aunty Alison…she's on the phone.'

I felt my shoulders drop as I heard his feet hitting the solid wooden floor – the sound getting louder with each step.

'Alison? What is it? Is it Mum?'

'No, it's not mum, she's fine. I'm sorry. It's me. I've just been diagnosed with the same breast cancer and I've got to have a mastectomy and probably chemotherapy too.'

There was a small silence.

'Oh Ale… I'm so sorry' he said quietly, his use of the nickname my dad had chosen for me, making me cry. We didn't talk for very long, just touching on the proposed dates for surgery and clarifying a few details about the diagnosis. He promised to be in touch and sent me his love, but I don't think I've ever felt the distance between us as great as it was that day.

Just over a year later, Colin and I arrived in Sydney and were met at the airport by Peter and his wife Sarah. I was wearing my favourite auburn wig, which hid my very short jet-black curly hair, and as it was the first time they'd met Colin, they didn't instantly recognise us walking towards them through the busy arrivals hall. Nine years is a long time, but some things never change. I dodged past the trolleys being pushed interminably slowly towards the exit, and threw myself at my brother. I felt his arms go round me, and then he gently pulled away, smiling.

'Ale, you look great.' He said, and that was all I needed to hear.

I don't remember exactly *when* I was told that there was a chance the cancer could spread to my left breast, but because of this potential risk, my consultant felt it was necessary for me to have that breast removed also. The fact that following my lumpectomy when two tumours had been found, then the subsequent tumours hadn't shown on my mammogram, ultrasound or MRI made us all a little twitchy, and there was almost an element of having 'been there, done that' which played on my mind. I always knew that I would have to have Dolly replaced with an implant, but because I had gone pretty much straight into chemo after my first mastectomy, this and further surgery had to wait. Radiotherapy, which finished in October 2011, had delayed things further, but working alongside my oncologist, a spring date was set for the second 'risk–reducing' mastectomy. Because I wouldn't need any further chemotherapy, I would have reconstruction of the left breast at the same time, making it easier for the surgeon to match the implants and make me as symmetrical as possible.

Reconstruction is something that is offered to most women who have had a mastectomy, sometimes at the same time as the mastectomy, sometimes after treatment. You may choose to delay it a number of years until you feel stronger, and more able to deal with all that you've been through, and of course it may be that you would rather remain flat-chested, as my mum did.

Because the cancer had been missed during my examination and ultrasound in the summer of 2010; following my diagnosis and subsequent treatment I should have been checking myself constantly to monitor any changes, but I hadn't. Why go searching for something that could cause problems? A rhetorical question of course, but I really didn't want to touch or be touched there. Following my surgery, I had no feeling on my right side, other than a constant tightness and discomfort due to the expander, and as far as my natural breast was concerned I avoided any contact there too. Perhaps it was the knowledge that I would soon have the same stark surgery carried out, and would then lose all feeling on that side of my chest also? Maybe I was just trying to bolster myself, as this all felt like a continued assault on my femininity. It was something I found difficult to talk to Colin about; not because he wouldn't be supportive, but because so much had changed for me, and it felt like a mental hurdle I needed to clamber over every time we made love. Avoiding that part of my body that had previously been so responsive and was now numb… I was unwilling to look too far ahead, as I felt we'd already managed to put a great deal of what had been wrong right, and I was worried that yet more change could jeopardise that.

Being constantly monitored by my oncologist, I was happy to leave any breast examinations for her to carry out. However, I was shell-shocked when at my regular check- up in March 2012 she found a lump in my left breast and felt the second mastectomy should be brought forward. She also thought it would be sensible to have a sentinel node biopsy carried out at the same time to make sure there was no cancer in the lymph.

I had a horrid feeling that the previous year's events were about to be repeated, and I couldn't help but be worried. Sensibly, I knew that with all the treatment I'd had, the chances of the lump being cancerous were slim, but then again, as some of you sadly know, it can happen. I tried to stay positive, but had a number of sleepless nights before I was booked in for my operation.

'You'll be fine!' everyone said.

'Worst case scenario, you'll have to do it all again, but you know you can get through it!'

'If it keeps you with us, it's got to be worth it!'

These were just some of the comments made by those around me and although I would agree with them at the time, in truth, the thought of potentially having to cope with another six months of chemo terrified me. Worse still, was the thought of secondary cancer lurking somewhere else in my body, which would be terminal.

Lucy, who had been so brave for so long, and always so positive for me was with me at the cottage when I told her that there was a possibility that I may have to have more treatment. Looking back, I should never have shared my worry in this way.

'You can't go through that again. What if it doesn't work and it's too late. I can't lose you.' She crumpled on to the steps that led into the kitchen.

I knelt down and gathered her to me 'You're not going to lose me Looma, it's going to be okay. I promise you.'

I felt as though I was on one of those horrible solid-wood roundabouts they used to have in children's playgrounds. Someone would set it off and then you had to jump on and sit there while they spun it round really fast. Even if you wanted to, you couldn't get off as it was turning so quickly that it forced you down on to the wooden surface. I always felt sick as a parrot, and terrified of catching my legs underneath it when it eventually slowed down and I made a desperate attempt to dismount! It was that sense of being out of control and possibly in danger that I hated. I felt I was making promises I couldn't keep, and that made me feel even worse.

My breast consultant saw me a few days before my admission date, and took a fine-needle biopsy of the lump, telling me that he would carry out the sentinel node examination while he was performing the rest of the surgery. The waiting game had begun again.

My lymphedema had been pretty bad over the previous months, and necessitated my arm being bound in an almost comical way with masses of padding and crepe bandage. Once removed, I needed to wear my compression sleeve every day – even at work – which I loathed, and so I made a conscious decision not to wear it to hospital. Apart from anything else, it was incredibly difficult to get on and off as it was so tight, and as I wouldn't be able to exert any pressure with either of my arms after surgery, it wasn't going to be possible to pull it on. I'd had to invest in a very weird frame thing called an arm butler, which was shaped like a bridge, and was something you had to pull the compression sleeve over, before putting your arm inside it and then pulling the frame off! Complicated, time-consuming, and quite frankly, a bloody nuisance! I resented it and was glad that I now had a genuine reason not to have to use it.

Colin took me into hospital and was with me when my breast consultant arrived, wearing a charcoal grey suit that blended perfectly with his silver tie. He had with him a large black marker, and once I'd removed my gown, he drew thick lines and arrows across and around my chest before asking me to sign the consent form.

'You remember that there will be two of us performing the surgery today, just like last time?

You'll be in theatre a little longer as we're working on both sides. The plastic surgeon is operating at the moment, but you'll see him before we call you.'

'Okay, that's fine. Any idea how long it might take though, as Colin could maybe go home for a while, rather than sitting here all day?'

'I'd say between six and seven hours.'

'You may as well go home then, pet,' I told Colin, who was helping me back into my robe.

'I guess so.' He turned to face the surgeon. 'I know this is meant to be pretty straightforward, and more of a risk-reducing procedure, but Alison and I are very worried that the cancer may have already set up on the left side. Do you have the results of the biopsy yet?'

The consultant's warm brown eyes focused on me. 'The results came in this morning and are clear which is good news. So as far as the cancer having set up on the left side, as I said to Alison last Friday, it's pretty unlikely.'

'Let's hope you're right, because I don't have the best track record, do I?' I said forcing a smile in the hope that my words sounded less aggressive.

He returned my smile. 'Not the best, no, but while you're in theatre, I'll take five lymph nodes including the sentinel node, and the breast tissue, and it will all be sent for analysis. They'll know from this whether there's any evidence of cancer in the lymph or the breast, and *I'll* know just as soon as I have the pathology report.'

'How long is that likely to take?' Colin asked, his arm heavy around my shoulder.

'I'm not sure, but I promise you I will make it a priority to inform you both.' His well-manicured hand reached out to shake Colin's, as if sealing a deal, before patting me on the arm.

'See you in theatre Alison' he said as he turned and left the room. His words had been of small comfort, but a comfort nonetheless.

I was relieved to find that many of the nurses who'd cared for me last time were still on duty at the hospital, so I felt safe. The operation to remove Dolly and replace her with an implant on my right side went smoothly, and luckily for me, very little encapsulation had occurred over the previous fourteen months. Encapsulation is when the body creates a shell-like coating around the expander or implant, and it can become quite tough and difficult to remove. I wouldn't recommend you search the Internet, as I did to find out more, because there were some ghastly images of this tough layer being hacked off that I rather wish I hadn't seen! A corresponding size and weight of implant was put into the remaining cavity after my other breast was removed, and some strattice was added to pad out and protect the skin. Strattice is made from pigskin, and acts as a kind of buffer between the implant and your own skin. Not that unusual a concept apparently, but one which made me a tad wary of using oil when sunbathing, in case I created my own crackling! My right breast looked much larger than the left, and felt firmer through my pyjamas, but it was early days, and I felt happy to remain bandaged and wait for the unveiling, which I knew wouldn't be far off.

Debbie came to see me the following day but I slept through most of her visit. I kept waking up, throwing a few random words at her, and drifting off again. Bless her, she said she didn't mind – it's probably the first time she's ever got a word in! I don't think Kathy fared much better the following day, but it was good to see her too.

When the bandages were removed to check the area, I felt able to look at my new shape. The implant in place of my breast on the left didn't look all that different to the original, although of course the nipple had been removed, and in truth it was probably a little firmer than my own. It was the total lack of feeling that was evident within a few hours of surgery that saddened me more than the physical appearance. I knew some of it was due to the anaesthetic, but that the majority of it was permanent nerve damage. I was becoming completely detached from what had always been an important part of me, as without any sensation it was difficult to make the connection. I tried not to think about it, focusing on getting better instead, and making sure I had plenty of laxatives to stop my bowels from seizing up because of all the pain relief!

Unfortunately, two days after surgery, my left breast began to swell, and on examination, was found to be bleeding internally, which also caused major bruising down my left side. Not the most comfortable situation, but I did laugh through the pain when the ward sister was instructed to text photographs of my ever expanding breast to the plastic surgeon, to see whether it was necessary for him to come back that night and operate! Not so, apparently, but with some pretty hefty painkillers and great nursing, I got through the night and was back in theatre at some ungodly hour where they drained it all so I felt more comfortable. I remember I slept for most of the day following the procedure, but unfortunately in the evening my left breast started to swell again, which placed enormous pressure and discomfort across my entire chest. The only thing I can equate it to is the feeling you get a couple of days after you've given birth and your milk comes in for the first time. Your breasts feel like boulders and the pain under your collarbones is horrid.

The general consensus was that this wasn't going to get better by itself, and so a unanimous decision was made to take me back to theatre to investigate the cause of this pressure. Colin was with me, but as we'd had supper together at 5:30 p.m., I was told I'd need to wait until the morning to have the procedure carried out.

'I don't believe it!' I said a la Victor Meldrew. 'It's bloody ridiculous! This was meant to be straightforward! I was supposed to be going home tomorrow!' I kicked my covers off as an all too frequent hot flush made me sweat.

'It's probably just bruising, Ali. I'm sure they can drain it like they did last time.'

'Yes but this didn't happen last year. What's gone wrong? Why does it keep going wrong?'

'I don't know, sweetheart. I really don't.' Colin had been sitting in the high-backed blue leather chair next to the window, but came over to the bed and held my hand. He couldn't do a lot else as I had numerous drains and drips in, and was completely bandaged across the chest.

'I wish you could stay the night with me... Why don't you hide in the wardrobe?'

Colin's laugh reverberated around the small room. 'I wouldn't even get my leg in there Babygirl,' he said his tired eyes twinkling, but as a compromise he pulled the chair next to the bed, and laid his head on my tummy with his arms around my hips.

'I miss you,' I said, stroking his thick wavy hair.

'I miss you too, but it's not forever, sweetheart.'

Long after he'd gone I lay there in my room, the lights low, and very little sound on the ward, wondering how this had all happened. A year or so back I had been blissfully unaware of the effect cancer can have on a life, and now it was all I thought of. The crisp sheets caught around my legs as I tried to get comfortable, and I bitterly resented my diagnosis and the consequent surgery. I had to lay on my back as the drains and bruising made it impossible for me to adopt my usual foetal position, and swearing under my breath through my tears, I pulled at what I thought was one of the drains, but was instead the nurse's call button. With a performance that would have challenged Dame Maggie Smith, I apologised profusely to the night nurse who crashed through the door and rushed to my bedside, blaming my tears on my physical discomfort.

'You mustn't put up with any pain, we're here to control it and to make sure you are comfortable. Please tell me if you're hurting, because I can help,' she said, resetting the alarm.

I was hurting, but not just physically. I was trying to claw back some of what cancer had taken from me, but once again I felt as though the disease had the better of me. I took the sleeping tablet and the painkillers she offered me, and truly enjoyed the cup of Horlicks before finally I slept.

Yo – who'd come up the day before – was back in the hospital the following morning in time to take me to theatre for 7:30am. Having compared the bags under our eyes following her early start and my lack of sleep, I reached for her hand.

'Do you think the cancer's spread across my chest? Do you think that might be why it's not healing properly this side?'

'I'm sure it's not that, pet. It may be just to do with the pressure building up, or perhaps a small bleed?'

I looked directly into her brown eyes. 'That'd be it then.'

'Yup I reckon.' She squeezed my hand, and smiled at me before standing up to remove her coat.

When I got to theatre, the anaesthetist played the all too familiar game of 'hunt the vein' for my cannula – oh how I missed my port! – but this time, before I could even start counting, I was asleep.

Apparently a small piece of tissue or debris had blocked my drain and so the fluid had built up. The surgeon removed the offending article, replaced the implant, and gave me new drains! Such a treat! When I awoke Yo was there waiting.

'They could have got Dyno Rod in for that surely?' she suggested, presenting me with a rather large toasted sandwich. We passed the time watching television. Well she watched and I dozed until Colin arrived.

'I'll head off now, love. I have to get Pheebs to school early tomorrow.' She came over to kiss me goodbye. 'You're doing brilliantly, Ali. Brave as a hedgehog.'

I hugged her to me, remembering how we used to say the same thing to her daughter Phoebe when she was tiny. Having thanked her profusely for being with me, I let her go, and watched as Colin walked her to the door where they chatted for a short while. After she'd gone, Colin attempted to play a game of Scrabble with me on the iPad, but at 10:20 p.m., he kissed me goodbye and told me I'd won the game! I'd slept through the entire thing but he'd used my letters and played for both of us, telling me I had a winning streak! His words stayed with me that night, and I found myself wondering if I'd win this battle outright, or if I still had a host of different offensives to fight off.

Luckily the right side of my body was never a problem, healing well, and causing me next to no discomfort now that Dolly was no longer with me!

I prayed very hard over the following forty-eight hours that everything would settle down, and was delighted to have my prayers answered when I was told that if things remained stable, I could go home the following day. I was beyond excited! Although my care had been exemplary, I'd had enough. I picked up my mobile to share the good news. Roz had already arranged to visit me the following day, and as she wasn't working, had said she would sort things out, and bring me home, which was a great help as Colin was out on a job. I know he would have cancelled if I'd have asked, but to be fair, he'd been juggling his life and responsibilities for an interminably long time already.

Friday morning dawned and the doctor on shift called in to see me. Her cropped hairstyle suited her elfin features, and even her navy blue scrubs seemed stylish. She'd be the kind of woman who'd look great in a paper bag, I thought enviously.

'How did you sleep last night? Any pain or discomfort?' she asked, perching on the edge of the bed. I didn't really want to answer as to be honest would mean admitting that I'd felt my left breast tightening up again in the wee small hours, and had been awake since about 4 a.m. with the discomfort.

'I pretty much slept through the night, luckily,' I lied.

'May I?' she said, rubbing her hands together to warm them before lifting my pyjama jacket. I took a deep breath in, feeling suddenly weary.

'This looks swollen to me. How does it feel to you? Is it tighter do you think?'

'Well, maybe a little, but I have been lying down, that's probably what's caused it.'

'It doesn't feel particularly hot, but I'm not certain. It definitely looks bigger than it did yesterday.'

'I'm meant to be going home today…' I said lamely. What should have been a three-day stay had turned into a ten-day nightmare, and so I sat in silence while she checked my blood pressure and temperature. Having made her notes, she stood up, running her long fingers through her short hair.

'I really think we need the consultant to examine you before we can let you leave. You've been very unlucky this last week, and I don't want you to find yourself in a lot of pain, and miles from the hospital. If you're here and need to go back to theatre, it can be arranged very quickly.'

'Do you really think that's likely?'

'I very much hope not, but your consultant's in shortly, and I'll make sure he knows to see you first before he goes to theatre.'

'I just want to go home…' I said, tears pricking my eyes.

'I know, I understand. I'll go and tell Sister now. I'm sure everything will be fine, Alison.'

I thanked her, and waited until she'd left the room before bursting into tears – again.

Although I'd warned Roz that I may not be able to leave after all, she came to see me anyway, and arrived before the surgeon did.

'It is what it is, Ali,' she said in her calm quiet voice, having listened to me bleating on. 'You know how awful you felt the last time this happened, and I wouldn't want you to be at home, in pain, and unable to get to the hospital if Colin wasn't there. Even if it means one more day, I'll make sure I'm here to get you home.'

It transpired that she'd already spoken to Sister on her way in, and my consultant who'd been called to theatre for an emergency, would be with us before midday. And he was, this time in his theatre scrubs rather than the usual beautifully tailored suit.

'I'm sorry I couldn't see you earlier, but we had something of an emergency to deal with. Can I have a look?' He leaned forwards and I that noticed he smelled of aftershave rather than disinfectant.

'It does feel a little swollen, but you've had a lot of interference there over the last ten days. If you keep the drains in and monitor the amount of fluid over the next five days, then I'm happy for you to go home.'

I was like a dog with two tails!

'Do you have the pathology results?' Roz asked

Having been so preoccupied with the horrid side effects of the surgery, and pretty much sedated for the most part, I hadn't allowed myself to think about the analysis that had been carried out on the breast tissue and lymph nodes.

'Yes I do. The sentinel node and the other four nodes were clear of cancerous cells, as was your left breast. There was however evidence of lobular neoplasia.'

'What's that?' I asked, suddenly alert.

'It can be a pre-cursor to invasive cancer. We

see it quite often as the body can mirror what is happening one side and replicate it on the other. The breast is gone now, so it's not a concern.'

'God, Ali, that's such a relief.' Roz hugged me gently.

I felt a little dazed. Almost as though the news was for someone else and I had inadvertently overheard it.

'I'll arrange for my secretary to make a date to see you in a week's time, but you'll need to monitor the amount of fluid from the drains and come back here in the next couple of days to have them removed.'

'I'm staying with Ali, so I can keep an eye on that for her,' said Roz.

It should have been champagne all round, but with the enormous collection of pills they gave me to take home I was advised to stick to fizzy water. As promised, Roz got me back to my cosy cottage where she set me up with a concise list of my medications and the correct times to take them. She even found a couple of bottle bags – the pretty ones you buy if you're gifting a bottle of wine – and put my drains in them. It certainly was easier for me to lug them around, but also made it look as though I was heading for a roaring night out, rather than yet another night in! We spent a great deal of time talking about life generally, our children, and yes, the cancer. Having spent more than three years as a palliative nurse in a local hospice, she understood more than most the effect this disease can have on patients and their families. Of course, the very fact that those she nursed were at the end of their lives brought home to me once again, that I had a great deal to be grateful for.

I've always had huge admiration for all those in the nursing profession, but if I hadn't have talked with Roz about her work, I doubt I would have known much about the incredible role she had taken on and that she managed so well. In some respects it is the complete antithesis of our understanding of nursing, as these patients will never recover, and the weight of responsibility to make the end of their lives as easy as possible lies heavily with their carers. I believe it takes a very special kind of person to take this responsibility on, and in my darker moments when I was first diagnosed, I had asked if she would consider looking after me should the situation worsen. Knowing me as she does, she had already spoken with her senior at the hospice, and told me that I was never to be afraid or worried, as she would be there for me whatever the future held. The relief I felt from knowing this was immense.

Roz stayed with me for several days and was not just an enormous help, but an incredible comfort too. When Colin arrived to take over the reins, she fully briefed him on my meds, before gathering up her bags. I knew I would miss her, and felt a little apprehensive about coping without her.

'You must promise me you'll take it easy and let Colin do any lifting or carrying?'

'Well, hopefully I'm not going to need to be carried anywhere!'

'Not you! You know what I mean' she laughed. 'And if there's anything you're worried about, don't sit there stewing about it, just call me.'

'I will, and thank you. For everything. Love you.' I said, following her to the front door. She turned back to face me.

'Love you too. I'll see you soon, but keep in touch.' She hugged me to her, and once again I thanked my lucky stars for having friends like Roz in my life.

Some days were better than others, but I continued to heal, and had both of my drains taken out within the first five days. My chest was still very bruised and swollen, although there was no feeling or sensation on the skin, which was probably a blessing! The wide and tight strapping I had to wear to keep the implants from moving, left welts above and below my ribs, but to have breasts under my chin at fifty-two years old would have been incongruous!

I was away from work for over two months, and as I healed, I was disappointed to see that the left side of my chest was much larger than the right, and a fair bit lower! It may well have been because of the weight of the implant as my plastic surgeon had placed a larger implant on the left side in the belief that both breasts would match once the swelling went down. Unfortunately they didn't, but my memories of the recently extended stay in hospital and the discomfort following each surgery, meant

I had to accept things as they were. Three general anaesthetics over a six-day period isn't ideal, and with the chemo and radiotherapy, my body had been through more than enough. I was going to have to leave things as they were – for the meantime, anyway. On the plus side, I was finally able to wear a normal bra, and although a little loose on one side, the mismatching was less obvious when I was clothed, so that was definitely a bonus. In fact I wore a bikini for the first time when Colin and I had a week in Turkey that summer. He told me I looked gorgeous, and that no one would know, as the rest of my body looked the same. I was happy to remind myself of that wonderful phrase 'beauty is in the eye of the beholder' and was once more grateful for his generous and loving spirit.

Whether it was the sunshine, the beautiful scenery or just how much we'd enjoyed each other's company, once we were back, we both decided that it was time to find a home of our own. Although we were spending most nights together, it was between my cottage and Colin's flat, which wasn't ideal for either of us. This was a firm commitment, and I felt it was a huge positive. Although QVC had by then moved their studios to Chiswick Park, I was still finding the sometimes two-hour commute each way, completely exhausting, and so Colin found us somewhere to live that would cut my journey time down dramatically.

'You've spent far too much of your life hacking up and down the M1. It's time to change all that.'

"Do you know I worked it out the other day, and

it's over 500 hours each year I spend in the car!'

'Christ what a waste of time! Far better things you could be doing instead.'

'Such as?'

'You need to ask?'

# CHAPTER THIRTY-FOUR

In spite of my initial acceptance of the breast reconstruction and its vagaries, within a relatively short space of time, it became obvious to me that what I now had was nothing close to what I had been promised. I struggled with the concave appearance on the right side of my chest, and the far larger implant on the left. Initially I had believed that once the obvious swelling following surgery had dissipated, my breasts would be more symmetrical, but sadly that wasn't the case. I gave up wearing normal bras, and resorted to softer shape-wear. I felt my breasts were the 'Little and Large' of the mammary world, and they knocked my confidence. I was trying so hard to move forwards, to put the negative side of the surgery to the back of my mind, but I was reminded of it every minute of every day. I tried to explain how I was feeling at a follow-up appointment with my plastic surgeon, but I didn't think he was particularly receptive. His suggestion to change the size of the implant and possibly pad out the dent in my chest didn't fill me with confidence.

'Isn't there another way? Maybe a different-shaped implant that would look more natural, or maybe use a bit of me from somewhere else?' I asked.

'I think these are the best shaped implants for you, and as it would take a great deal of tissue and major surgery to create new breasts for you, I don't think it's an option.'

'Why would we need to change both? The right side looks okay.'

'One implant and one tissue reconstruction would never match. You wouldn't attain symmetry and they would always look different.'

Well, they certainly looked different, and not in a good way. I was racked with doubts. Was I self-obsessed? Was I being vain? Was I hoping to turn back the clock, or was I just trying to make the best of a bad job? It was probably a mixture of all these things, but not content to leave things be, I decided to pursue some of the alternatives.

Lucy had found a very comprehensive booklet about reconstruction written by Breast Cancer Care, and had given it to me before I even began my chemo. To be honest, I'd only looked at it once, accepting my suggested surgery without question. However, when I went online to look for myself, I was staggered at just how much information there was out there! It was overwhelming. My advice would be for you to take your time, and perhaps talk it through with your oncologist, breast nurse, or someone close to you, before you make any decision.

Depending on your surgeon and your diagnosis,

there are currently a number of different ways to surgically reconstruct a breast, and most of them are available to the majority of women. The first option would be what I had – using only a silicone prosthesis inserted under the skin and muscle of the chest to replace the volume of breast tissue that had been removed at the time of the mastectomy. It's quite a simple operation, on a par with a cosmetic 'boob job', and it doesn't involve scarring anywhere else on the body. The three main reasons for choosing this option would be if you don't have sufficient spare tissue to use; you are not well enough for a larger operation, or you simply don't want a procedure that will leave more scars. You can choose pert breasts to replace what may have headed south with middle age, but there are a number of different options if you want something a little less bouncy! Nipples can be tattooed on to the skin at a later date, and there are some truly talented artists who can create a realistic 3-D effect for you. Or, by using a skin graft from another part of your body and some fairly intricate surgery, nipples can be made for you. Once healed, you could choose to have them coloured using a similar tattoo procedure.

There are a couple of other possibilities, but they involve major surgery and a longer recovery period. You may be offered a latissimus dorsi breast reconstruction, using the latissimus dorsi muscle in your back, which is then rotated around to the front of your body in order to recreate the breast. It's a fairly long-winded process but you will have a natural-looking breast at the end of it, as well as a fairly large scar on your back.

The second option would be skin and fat taken from the lower tummy – i.e. a tummy tuck! It's quite a convoluted process requiring either a small piece of muscle, blood vessels, skin and fat (free TRAM flap), or no muscle involved and the blood vessels carefully dissected when the flap is raised (Free DIEP flap). There is a third procedure known as a free SIEA flap, and this is when some of the more superficial blood vessels on the tummy are used and no muscle is dissected or transferred. Although you'd be pretty sore for a week or so, the results are usually stable and permanent, and particularly effective because they avoid irradiated tissue and skin.

There is a third but rarely chosen option, and that is to use fat or muscle from the buttocks or thighs. This involves an even longer recovery time, and leaves pretty prominent scarring, but does avoid irradiated tissue.

With these options in mind, I scanned the BMA list of recommended reconstructive surgeons and arrange to meet with a few of them to find out more. The first plastic surgeon I saw told me that he didn't feel an implant was suitable on the right side, as the radiotherapy I'd had would cause capsulation, which is the hardening and scarring around the implant. He suggested that by using tissue from my thighs he could create a new breast for me, but it would be no bigger than a B-cup. That would mean any implant on the left would need to be smaller than my existing breast, and I would need a matopexy (a lift) to bring it up to the same level as the right side. Before surgery, my bra size had been a 32F, and I really wanted something a little closer to this. Although the photographs of the consultant's handiwork were impressive, the pictures showing the donor sites were pretty gruesome. Huge scars around the tops of the legs that he explained would take a long time to heal. I thanked him, and said I would give it some thought, but by the time I'd walked back to my car I'd decided it wasn't for me.

I went back to my list, and then chanced upon a chap who worked out of the Royal Marsden. A colleague of mine had told me that he'd done a marvellous job for her sister who'd also had a bi-lateral mastectomy.

This time Colin was able to come with me, and we decided to make a day of it. As I was a private patient my initial consultation was at the surgeon's private clinic on the King's Road and not at the Marsden, so we spent several hours in and out of all the fabulous shops there before my appointment. It was definitely retail therapy, as I felt apprehensive and a little awkward, knowing that once again I'd have to undress and be examined.

'Do you think I should have worn my big knickers?' I asked Colin as we sat in the waiting room.

'He's only meant to be looking at your breasts!'

'I know, but the other man suggested using fat from my thighs, so he may want to see them too.'

'But I thought you'd already decided you didn't

want that done?'

'I don't really, but they sometimes suggest using fat from your buttocks.'

'There's no way I'm going to let him touch your bum!' Colin retorted so loudly that the receptionist looked up and over her computer at him.

I burst into laughter. 'You better tell him that then!' I said.

The consultant's rooms were impeccably furnished and finished with the same expensive designer look as the smart suit he was wearing. Having welcomed us warmly, he could not have been kinder, sensitively asking the more awkward questions, and making copious notes from my responses. Colin mentioned his reservations about having other parts of my body 'spoilt' by surgery, accepting of course that the mastectomy had been essential.

'It's not easy for a man to see things from a woman's perspective,' the consultant explained, 'but my rule of thumb is to imagine what I would want for my sister or my mother, and of course I'd want the best and safest option. I've used many implants over the last twenty-five years, but latterly I've tended to use tissue transplants from various donor sites, including the back, abdomen, buttock or thigh. If the patient has substantial amounts of tissue available it can be a very positive experience, particularly if the tummy tissue is used. However,' he continued, turning to me, 'with you, all of the potential donor sites have very limited soft tissue availability because of your slim frame. I definitely wouldn't use your tummy tissue, and I'd have significant reservations about your thigh or buttocks.'

'Glad to hear it!' Colin interjected.

Smiling, the surgeon continued, 'The back can be used with repeated fat transfers, but again I'd have reservations about the volume that we might eventually achieve.'

'What if I were to put some weight on? Would it be possible to use my tummy then?'

'Unfortunately not, because as soon as you lost the weight again, which I have no doubt you would, your breast would decrease in size too.'

'You're welcome to some of my tummy, I've got plenty to spare.' Colin said kindly.

'If it was possible then that would be perfect! It's not, unfortunately, which leaves us with little option but to pursue an implant-based reconstruction, and there would be limitations because of the irradiation on the right.'

'So, there's not really much you can do then?' I asked tentatively.

'My dear, there is always something we can do, but the last thing I'd want is for us to make the wrong decision, and to harvest tissue that may not achieve the desired effect, and could potentially damage your muscles and expose you to risk at the donor sites. What I'd like to propose is for you to come to one of our multidisciplinary meetings at the Royal Marsden Hospital where I can discuss future management with one or two of my colleagues whose opinions I greatly respect.'

'You'd better wear your big knickers for that then!' quipped Colin, who sneakily grabbed my bum as we left the room.

I'd never been to the Royal Marsden Hospital before, but I had heard of the marvellous care, treatment and support given by the staff and specialists who worked there. The multidisciplinary meeting, though, was about as far removed from my initial consultation with the surgeon, as Stoke-on-Trent is from Sydney! Six surgeons were all seated in a row, and I had to stand in from of them wearing nothing but my knickers. Colin was the other side of the room behind a green paper curtain.

'Apologies gentlemen. It's not a pretty sight,' I said, more to myself than to them, but it didn't matter because there was no response. In fact, none of them spoke to me at all for the entire ten minutes or so that I had to stand there. They talked about me though, to each other, using technical terms that meant nothing to me. The longer I stood there, the more emotional I felt, but it wasn't until my consultant asked them if they were satisfied with what they'd seen, that they thanked me and left.

He handed me my gown. 'I am sorry you had such a vast crowd of surgeons, but once we get our heads together I'm sure we can come up with a workable solution for you.'

I felt myself shiver. 'That's okay, and thank you for arranging it,' I said politely, pulling the gown tightly around myself.

'Before you get dressed I'd like to have a few photographs taken of you for reference. Do you have time?'

'Well I—'

'You go ahead, Ali, and I'll move the car,' said Colin, emerging from behind the curtain, unaware of how upset I was feeling.

I was directed to a different part of the hospital and in a small room a young man took photographs of my tummy, my legs, my bottom, and my chest. Once again, I questioned myself: who I was doing this for? Why was it so important to me? Surely the fact that the cancer had hopefully been destroyed was all that mattered? Colin was the only person who ever saw my breasts, and he constantly assured me he was happy with the way I looked.

Travelling home, he reassured me again. 'Honestly, Ali, if you decide to leave things as they are, it's fine with me. I know it's not the same, but it's okay. You're still here, that's what's important.'

'I know you're right. I should be grateful, but I'd love it if they could make me look a bit more normal.'

'I'm sure once they take Dolly out and put a silicone implant in it'll look fine, and hopefully it'll be a bit more comfortable for you too.'

'Let's hope so, and then I could have the other side to match!'

That night, I listened to Colin breathing, as we lay together like spoons, his arm protectively tucked around me. I tried to remember how things had been for us before the cancer, but in the same way that

I could no longer feel his arm curled around my expander-filled chest, I was unable to breathe life into my memories.

It was just after my fifty-second birthday that I received the consultant's summary of the multidisciplinary and his suggested solutions for further reconstruction. Presented on beautiful cream manila paper, it outlined in great detail all the options available to me, and the proposed surgery. The biggest problem was the limited soft tissue available on the right side, and the fact the entire breast and implant were irradiated. Fresh tissue from my tummy could be used in conjunction with an implant to create volume, although he didn't feel it would be enough for total reconstruction. The surgery would be complex, requiring six to eight hours in theatre, and would leave me with a large transverse scar across my abdomen. I would then need to take a break of several months to heal, and if I was to proceed with a mastectomy on the left, then he felt the only way possible to create anything approaching a decent reconstruction would be to import muscle and tissue from my back on *both* sides. This would not only require extensive surgery, but would leave large scars too, and the harvesting of the tissue would cause damage to the muscles in my back and shoulder. I could have cried.

Colin was in the kitchen making toast.

'Do you want a cup of tea, Babygirl?' he asked.

'No thanks. And I didn't want this either.' I said thrusting the letter towards him.

'Who's it from?'

'The consultant at The Marsden. It's a complete bloody travesty! After all he said last time about the risk of donor sites, and harvesting tissue, he's now telling me that to try and make me look even half decent, he'll have to take tissue and muscle not just from my tummy but from both sides of my back! And even after that he'd still have to use implants to give me any kind of symmetry! Jesus! I give up.' I sat down heavily on the wooden step that separated the kitchen from the dining room and put my head in my hands. I saw Colin's feet before I felt his hand on my shoulder.

'Hey. Come here.' His voice was low. I stood up and leaned against him, feeling the rough bristle of his stubble against my cheek. He smelled of soap.

'Ali, I really don't want you to go ahead with this. I know it's your choice, but that's a huge amount of surgery, and you'd be left so badly scarred… He's already said there's a problem because of the radiotherapy, so what if it didn't heal? What if you went through all that, and it still didn't work? You're strong, you've proved that, but I still think this is risky.' He kissed the top of my head.

'I don't understand why he's gone against everything he originally said.'

'Perhaps it was the general consensus? He's had to talk it through with the other surgeons after the meeting and that may well have changed things.'

'So after all that humiliation, standing there virtually naked, looking like shit, nothing's changed?'

'Ali, you don't look like shit. You look gorgeous, and you've got beautiful skin. I don't want them to spoil that for you.' He moved his hands down to the small of my back and pulled me closer to him.

'If it was one thing or the other – tissue or implant – then that would be different. That's what I thought he would say. That's what I hoped he would say! I think you're right though. It's like robbing Peter to pay Paul.' I leaned up to kiss Colin and he put one hand gently on the side of my face.

'Talk to Roz. She probably knows what this kind of surgery involves.'

'I will, and I can run it by Mei Lin when I see her next week.'

'Sounds like a plan,' he said, smiling at me. 'Talking of which I don't have to leave for another hour or more, so I could check out those potential donor sites for you?'

'That sounds like an even better plan!' I said, reaching for the letter he was still holding in his hand, and putting it face down on the dresser. 'Walk this way!'

Sashaying up the step and into the dining room I turned to see him following me.

# CHAPTER THIRTY-FIVE

It's amazing what you can get used to when you have to, and over time I did get used to my rather odd appearance when I was unclothed. I didn't feel happy about it though. A friend of mine once said that if she'd have lost her boobs through breast cancer, it wouldn't have bothered her at all, as she'd never liked the size or shape of them. She said she would rather be cancer-free and flat-chested. I could understand that logic, but to me the loss wasn't just physical, it was deeply psychological, too.

It was only a month or so after my surgery that I was contacted by the charity Breast Cancer Care who asked me if I'd like to take part in their annual fashion show that October as one of the models. It was the same event at which I'd given my speech just the year before, only this time I'd be swapping the podium for the catwalk, along with twenty-one other women and two men who were living with a diagnosis of breast cancer. I was flattered to be asked, but more than a little apprehensive at the thought of being out there in my glad rags in front of two thousand people. It's not the same as working in front of a camera, where your audience is unseen, and I'd already conquered my nerves for that when I'd returned to work in November. Of course I'd done live broadcasts and appearances many times before, but things were different now. I remembered talking to some of the models in previous years, and how they had all described their day as uplifting and emotional, exhausting yet energising, but, above all, empowering. I said yes, and decided to worry about it nearer the time.


The physical scars healed relatively well, but the dent on the right side of my chest where the original tumours had been became more noticeable, and the skin felt incredibly tight and uncomfortable. Leaning forwards and looking at yourself in a mirror is never advisable once you pass the age of forty, as what was once firm has a tendency to sag. My tummy, although flat and pretty taut when standing or sitting, looked like an apple in a sock when I was leaning forwards or kneeling down! My breasts were equally unattractive. They were like two rectangular house bricks under the skin, the silicone implants having no natural shape to them. There was a distinct lumpiness across the top of my left breast, which, although I'd had it checked out and scanned, worried me. I found it impossible to lie on my tummy as the implants were so solid and immovable that I had to almost balance on them or shove a rolled up towel underneath them! It was also very uncomfortable for me to do any form of upper body exercise or to even swim. The muscle behind the implants felt as though it was adhered to them, and I couldn't do any stroke other than doggy paddle!

I'd discovered this while on holiday with Yo in Crete, in the autumn of 2012. We found ourselves in a beautiful little resort where the sea was as warm as bathwater, with fabulous frothy waves. It was like swimming in champagne. Not that I did a great deal of swimming, but it didn't stop us from jumping up and down in the sea like a couple of kids. On our last day the wind was up and the waves created a wall of water that we found irresistible. We were laughing like drains as the sea crashed over us, knocking us sideways.

'Christ on a bike!' Yo shouted, extricating herself from a mass of seaweed, and pulling me up from the depths.

'He wouldn't get far on a bike in this!' I shrieked at her, taking in a mouthful of seawater as the next wave hit. We were still weak with mirth when the waves subsided.

As we made our way back to the beach, I heard voices behind me. 'God! If a plastic surgeon had done that to me I'd have shot him!'

My bikini top had come untied, leaving my scarred, misshapen and nipple-less breasts for all to see. I started scrabbling at the fabric, losing my balance in the wet sand. Yo came to my rescue.

'Did you hear what she said?'

'It's bollocks Ali. Utter bollocks. How bloody dare she? She's got a face like a dog's arse anyway, cheeky mare!' she said, as she tied my bikini top up tightly. I grinned at her. She always made things better. 'Fancy an ouzo?' I said, hoping the strong spirit would dull my heightened sense of embarrassment.

'It would be rude not to!' she said, and so we picked our way over the stony beach and headed straight for the bar.


I'd barely arrived back in England before I was embroiled in the pre-show publicity tour for the Breast Cancer Care Fashion Show. I was relaxed following my week away with Yo, and had a lovely tan that made me feel more confident about my appearance. I was interviewed on *This Morning*, had countless chats with many radio show hosts, and some very lengthy telephone interviews with a number of journalists. I even appeared on the pages of *The Huffington Post* and the *Good Housekeeping* magazine!

The day before the event, I checked into my hotel and met up with the twenty-three other models who I'd be spending the following day with. We had a fabulous meal together, and found – not surprisingly – that we had a fair bit in common. There'd been several costume fittings prior to the day, but we'd been seen individually. On the day itself, with so many costume changes, we didn't have time to cover our scars or hide from those who were dressing us or indeed from each other, and it was then I realised just how fabulous some women's reconstructions had been.

There would be two shows; one in the afternoon, and then another evening performance. I wore a collection of clothes from a diverse range of designers including Stella McCartney, Biba and H&M. After hair and make-up, we had our one and only rehearsal, which was a hoot as we were all herded on to the stage together, and expected to move in time with the music. Our nerves didn't help us with the timings, but hanging on to that all-important phrase 'it'll be all right on the night' we waited in the wings for our cue. I don't know how I made it down the catwalk the first time, wearing killer heels, a pair of fishnet tights and not a lot else! My knees were like jelly, but the incredible roar from the crowd and deafening applause carried us all up and out there. Trying to remember what I'd been told to do, where to stand, and which part of the catwalk I was supposed to make my own, caused me more than a little consternation, but I did get through it and towards the end of the show began to really enjoy it. Some of the girls were like ducks to water, the guys too, yet others, like me, took a little longer. Waiting my turn and watching them from the wings, I felt quite humbled to be alongside such strong and brave individuals.

Nine months earlier, when I'd agreed to be a model, I'd invited my mum and my sister to join me on the day. I realised that for Mum it was an incredibly long way to travel and so had suggested she came to the afternoon show. I'd planned to book her into a hotel and then she could head home the following day. I thought my sister may be able to accompany her, but she was unable to take leave from her teaching job and Mum said that she really didn't think it was her kind of thing. Colin, Sam, Jack and Lucy however were all coming to the evening performance, along with Yo, Roz, Chris and a number of my closest friends from QVC. Edna had also been invited and was travelling by train to join us that afternoon; it was her first big night out since her husband Ian had died eight years earlier, and it meant so much to me that she'd made the effort. I felt completely cherished and supported. While the other models stayed at The Grosvenor to have lunch, I legged it back to the hotel for a much-needed cuddle from Colin, who was waiting there for me. Spending so much time with the other girls over the last 24 hours had been quite emotional because the only topic of conversation was the cancer; our lives before and after diagnosis, our treatment and the current state of play. There were at least four women who had secondary breast cancer, and knew that their time was limited. They were all incredibly brave and positive, and I found myself wondering if I'd be quite as courageous if I had the same diagnosis.

Before I headed back to The Grosvenor, I was able to briefly see the children and Edna, and I felt far more relaxed knowing they would be there in the audience. I saw my friends and QVC colleagues in the ballroom before I had to get changed, and their excitement was infectious. The families of all the models had been seated as close to the catwalk

as possible, and my gang were on the table at the
very end of the stage, so each time I walked out,
theirs were the first faces I saw. I had four costume
changes and with each appearance the applause
and my confidence grew, and I loved it! I forgot
my weird shape and scarring, and was lifted by the
enthusiasm of the crowd. I felt attractive – sexy
even – almost 'normal'. The final showstopper
saw us on the catwalk wearing the most incredible
evening dresses, and having been chaperoned
by a group of rather lovely male models, we all
stood in line as the audience rose to their feet
applauding, whistling and cheering. It was quite
simply unbelievable. We had five minutes for a
quick change into our own clothes before stepping
out once more on to the stage to receive a beautiful
bouquet.

As I made that final trip down the catwalk on my
own, the enormity of the occasion hit me. All these
people, so much incredible support, admiration
and love, and every one of us there for the same
reason: all our lives had been touched by breast
cancer. When I got to the bottom of the catwalk I
saw my children, my man and my friends. They
were all on their feet, in tears, clapping, cheering
and smiling, and as I turned slowly I could see the
entire audience also standing and applauding. I'd
done it! That feeling was one I will never forget,
and something I wish I could have bottled and kept
forever.

# CHAPTER THIRTY-SIX

We all deal with things differently, and it may well be that for you that having managed your surgery and subsequent treatment, you are more than happy to leave things as they are. I wish now that I'd been content with the status quo. Following the fashion show, I battled constantly with my emotions. I'd seen women who had lost both breasts and had perfect reconstructions. I'd shared a room the night before the show with a beautiful girl, far younger than me, whose surgeon had recreated her left breast to match her right exactly. I was jealous, but reminded myself that I was still here, and that was surely more important than how I looked. I knew I was lucky: many women don't make it, so I should be grateful for that. It was like a game of ping-pong in my head. At other times I thought, why should I have to accept it if there was an alternative? It had been well over a year since my second mastectomy and although I felt I was coping well with my lymphedema and the endless hot flushes brought on by the Tamoxifen, I was still dissatisfied. Every morning when I woke up, my misshapen chest was the first thing I saw, and I'd had to completely rethink my working wardrobe to accommodate it. I couldn't even wear a normal bra, as I now had two conflicting cup sizes! Shape-wear was my only option. Looking back, I know it wasn't that evident to anyone else, as once clothed and covered – I studiously avoided anything low necked – you'd be hard pushed to notice. Although there had been so many setbacks the last time I'd had surgery, I still thought it would be worth seeing my plastic surgeon and asking what, if anything, could be done.

'Are you really sure you want to do this? It was pretty awful last time,' Mum reminded me.

'That's true but I spend far too much time thinking about it. I just want to know what my options are.'

'You could just be flat like me? Far less hassle.'

'I know you're fine with it, Mum, but—'

'I'm not fine with it, but I am accepting of it,' she interrupted.

I sighed. 'Well, I guess I'm not. It's uncomfortable and a constant reminder of the cancer.'

'That's something we both have to live with, Alison.'

She was right, but I didn't want her to be.


Bearing in mind my previous experience when searching for an alternative consultant, and the incredibly invasive surgeries that had been suggested, I decided it was a case of better the devil

you know, and so I contacted the Spire Hospital.
The small consulting room was familiar to me, as
was my feeling of apprehension. This time it wasn't
the thought of being examined that troubled me, it
was the niggling doubt that perhaps what I wanted
was too tall an order. Having undressed behind the
blue paper curtain, I waited for my consultant to
join me.

When being examined for breast reconstruction,
the situation was the complete opposite to the
normal patient/doctor scenario. I would be the
one standing up while the surgeon sat on the bed.
My consultant was a very tall slim man in his
early thirties. He always wore a suit, and was well
groomed with an attractive but closed face. From
his position on the bed, his eyes were literally at
boob level!

'So remind me again what it is you want to
change?' he said.

The voice inside my head muttered 'You have to
ask?' but my response was more considered. 'Well,
firstly I would like them both to be the same size.
It seems as though the weight of this much larger
implant on the left has made it drop down. If we
could change that so it matched the one on the right
that would be great. Maybe through the same scar
underneath so we keep the marks to a minimum?
It also feels really lumpy across the top, which is a
bit of a worry, and very noticeable, so would you be
able to remove whatever that is, and have it checked
out? You don't think it would be anything sinister
do you?' I paused but when he didn't respond I

broke the silence. 'I don't think the implant on the right is a problem, but it's this big dent at the top that's really noticeable and uncomfortable.'

At this point he reached up and pressed my skin firmly with his thumbs, smoothing the dimpled surface.

'I am certain there won't be anything sinister there. I used strattice over the implants on both sides, and that could be what's caused the lumpiness on the left, so yes, I can sort that. The skin on the right though is very thin here,' he said, his fingers moving over and around the large indentation above my right breast.

Although I had no feeling there, it wasn't comfortable. I flinched.

'I was thinking that we could pad it out using a fat transfer from your thighs. Could you stand back a minute?' I did as I was told, and he knelt on the floor in front of me and started pinching the tops of my legs with his hands. I thought I was going to laugh! There I was in my knickers with this educated and attractive young man on his knees in front of me. I tried not to think of what Yo would say!

'Does this mean you'll have to take the skin as well as the fat to pad it out?' I tried hard to concentrate on something other than where his head and hands were.

'No, it's a fat transfer. Basically liposuction.'

I perked up instantly. 'So I'd have slimmer thighs?'

'Yes, it can have that effect, and there should be

enough here to fill this. We can always revisit in
a couple of months once it's settled.' I noticed his
knees didn't creak like mine when he straightened
up and sat down on the edge of the bed. 'You'll
have very small incisions on the inside of your
thighs where the tube goes in, but they'll heal
easily.'

'I like the sound of that!'

'It's pretty straightforward and doesn't take too
long either, so just a day or so in hospital.'

'Is there anything you could do about the
tightness and discomfort on the right? Or the scar
across the middle of the breast? It's quite uneven,
and hasn't healed as well as the other side.' I peered
down at myself. 'There's still a bit of areola there
too, which looks odd…'

His hands moved across my chest, pressing
gently. 'There's nothing much I can do about the
tightness, I'm afraid. It's capsulation, and often
happens following radiotherapy, even when the
implant is changed as yours was. I can tidy the scar
though at the same time as the fat transfer. Is that
it?' he asked, pulling himself upright so that he
towered over me in my bare feet.

'Apart from changing the implant on the left so
that it matches the one on right, yes. If we could do
that, it'd be great,' I said, feeling childishly pleased.

'If you call my secretary she'll give you a date,
but hopefully I'll be able to fit you in next week.
You can get dressed now.'

As he brushed past me and pulled the paper
curtain to one side, I saw myself smiling in the

mirror on the wall above the miniature sink. This time, I felt, it was all going to be okay.

A week later Colin and I arrived at the hospital where we were ushered into one of the private rooms. Unlike so many of my other planned procedures, I felt genuinely excited at the prospect of this one and its potential results. Colin had picked up on my mood, and although he was always a little concerned for me before any surgery, he agreed that this sounded a lot less complicated than the previous operations.

He watched me put on my hospital gown. 'Aren't you supposed to wear it the other way around, with the tapes at the back?'

'I think I have to wear it this way because they're working on my front. Ease of entry and all that.' I said.

'They might think you're a bit too easy if you don't put your paper pants on!' Colin said, handing them to me.

'Cheeky sod!' I retorted, snatching them from him and laughing.

'Make sure you keep them. I like the idea of tearing them off later.'

'You're on a promise.'

It wasn't long before my surgeon arrived, and while drawing on me with black marker, he told me that although I obviously wouldn't feel anything while under anaesthetic, some patients described the sensation following liposuction as comparable to being stamped on!

'God! That sounds awful!' said Colin

'No pain no gain!' I said cheerfully.

My surgeon looked over at Colin. 'It's quite an effective procedure, and straightforward too. So hopefully Alison will have none of the side effects she experienced last time.' He paused as if waiting for a reaction, but neither Colin nor I spoke. I didn't want to be reminded of last time. I wanted to stay focused on the positive return from this rather aggressive procedure: the hope of a pain-free and symmetrical chest.

'I think I'll take some from your tummy too – not that you have a lot – but we may need it. Is that okay?'

'Will that leave any scars?' Colin asked anxiously.

'No it's a tiny incision, barely noticeable,' my surgeon said, his black maker pen poised and pointing at my midsection.

'What do you think, Ali?' Colin looked over at me.

'I think it'd be fine. Go for it! I couldn't have the tummy tuck, so this is the payoff!' I smiled at Colin. 'Honestly, I'm fine with it. It's all good'


I do want to stress at this point, as I've tried to do throughout the book, that this is purely my experience of reconstructive surgery. The vast majority of women I've met over the years, who've had similar procedures, have had relatively few, if any, setbacks, and been completely satisfied with the results. But when I woke up after the operation I was shocked at how much pain I was in. I'd expected to feel uncomfortable, or maybe worst case scenario, as the surgeon had suggested, as though someone had walked over me in hobnailed boots. The truth was, I felt as though I'd been hit by a car! They gave me as much morphine as they could, bearing in mind I had only just had a general anaesthetic, but it didn't seem to be alleviating or controlling the pain, so I had to stay in the recovery area for quite a while until I was a little more comfortable. I felt every lump and bump as I was pushed on the trolley along the corridor from the theatre to my room, and was in tears by the time I got there. The pain wasn't centred in any one area, it was all over. I couldn't see where the fat had been taken from, because I had been zipped into an incredibly tight compression corset while I was under the anaesthetic. It went down to my knees, over my tummy, and up to my bandaged breasts. Any form of movement was excruciating, and when they lifted me from the trolley and on to the bed, I cried out.

'Ali what's happened?' Colin's concerned face looked into mine

'I don't know. It just hurts so much…'

'Is this normal?' Colin asked the nurse who was writing something on my drugs chart.

'Yes, I'm afraid it'll be uncomfortable for quite a while. There'll be a lot of bruising and the corset has to be tight to keep the swelling to a minimum and to help maintain her shape.'

'But she didn't have this done to change her shape, it was just meant to fill in a dent in her chest!'

'I am aware of that, but this type of compression will help her to heal more quickly.'

I tried to sit up a little, but it was agony 'For Christ's sake!' I almost shouted. Both Colin and the nurse looked at me.

'She wouldn't have had it done if we'd have known it would be this bad! Can't you give her something?' he said angrily.

'That's what I'm about to do,' the nurse replied through tight lips.

'Colin, it's okay. I'll be okay' I whispered as he moved towards me. Sitting down on the chair next to the bed he leant over and buried his face in my neck.

'I'm so sorry, Babygirl.' I couldn't even move my arm to stroke his hair, but my tears fell silently on to the top of his head.

The first few days passed in a drug-induced, pain-filled haze. Even lying flat hurt me, but to try and sit completely upright was impossible because the corset cut into me around my waist. I was told I was going to have wear it constantly for the next four weeks – night and day – and could only take it off to shower or bathe. There was an opening in the gusset to enable me to use the loo, but I found it impossible initially to bend sufficiently to do even

that! For the first few days I had to wee into a bowl
while standing up. Because of this, and the fact that
they didn't seem able to completely control my
pain, the promised two days in hospital stretched to
six. My constant hot flushes were purgatory because
of the corset, and the first time they unzipped it to
examine me, I saw that my stomach was completely
covered in bruises. No flesh tone at all, just black,
blue, purple and green bruises. My inner thighs
and the backs of my legs were the same: I looked
like a vividly coloured Monet painting. The dent
in the right side of my chest was now filled in but
extremely lumpy, although the scar across the centre
was very neat with the small amount of areola
removed as promised. The surgeon had removed all
the lumpy tissue on the left, so my breast was now
smooth, but sadly still far larger than the right. He'd
made the decision not to change the implant on the
left, explaining to me that he felt it would have been
too much trauma to my body at one time. 'Trauma'
was a good word, in fact, the only word to describe
accurately what I was going through. I knew that
even if the fat transfer hadn't taken as well as we
needed it to, I couldn't go through this procedure
again.

Apart from Roz, Yo and Colin, I didn't have any
visitors. I didn't even want the children to come and
see me. The potent mix of morphine and painkillers
were taking their toll, leaving me disorientated and
confused. After yet another disturbed night, I told
Colin I needed to come home. I didn't want to stay
in hospital any longer, and although the staff were

concerned about me, they conceded, plying me with boxes full of very strong painkillers. The journey home was hell, with every bump in the road sending shock waves through my body, and then trying to climb the stairs to get to my bed was purgatory. Added to my physical stress was my mental angst, as no one seemed able to tell me where the results were from the tissue that had supposedly been sent for analysis. I made a number of phone calls to the medical secretary, but she was none the wiser. Perhaps because I was drugged up to the eyeballs I wasn't making much sense.

Eventually she got the consultant to call me.

'I've been told that you've been chasing us for results from a tissue analysis?'

'Yes, the lumpy tissue you took away on the left side. You said you'd have it analysed to make sure there was no cancer there.'

There was a long silence.

'I didn't look remotely suspicious to me, so I didn't feel it necessary to send it to the lab,' he said eventually.

'But how can you tell just by looking?'

'As I said originally, it was due to the strattice I'd put in there last time. There is nothing to worry about. I'll see you next week for your follow-up appointment.'

He hung up and I closed my eyes. I needed to trust what he was telling me, but when you have a diagnosis of cancer, it takes a huge leap of faith to totally believe it won't ever come back.

It took a good few weeks before I felt even close to human again, and I was away from work for nearly two months. The only part of my body that didn't hurt was my chest, which made a change, the rest of my body was constricted by the bloody corset! I would have given anything to take it off, especially as that August was one of the hottest we'd had in years, but I did as instructed for the full four weeks. I was thrilled to be out of it, but I was dismayed to discover that where it had been cutting into my tummy something called 'dermal adhesion' or 'tethering' had occurred. My once smooth stomach now had a huge ridge across the centre of it, and a mass of rippled skin above it. Although the tiny scars had healed perfectly, there were small dents in the skin where the fat had been taken, and the overall appearance was similar to that of a large suet dumpling. The only improvement I could see was the size of my thighs, and they were indeed slimmer, although there was a fair bit of dimpling that hadn't been there before. Yet again, my quest to 'get back to normal' had gone against me, and it hurt me.

# Chapter Thirty-Seven

Work was my salvation in the months that followed the fat-transfer surgery. I threw myself into it, taking on extra shifts and spending additional time on my blog responding to Ali's Army. I felt dissatisfied and angry. This painful and seemingly pointless procedure made a mockery of my hopes for improvement. I'd also realised that I wasn't alone in thinking this way. People who cared about me were upset too, some making their feelings quite clear.

'I really think you need to leave things alone now. Just accept it.'

'Every time you've had something done, it's made things worse.'

'I bet you wish you'd left things as they were?'

And perhaps the hardest comment to contend with: 'This isn't about the cancer. This is purely aesthetics. You should just be glad you're still here.'

Harsh but true, and I understood why they felt it necessary to tell me, because this is the legacy of cancer. It affects not just the person with the diagnosis, but everyone around them. Because they care, they worry. If you call them and they don't pick up, but you don't leave a message, they worry. If you feel unwell, but aren't sure what's causing your pain, they worry. Every time you go for a scan and have to wait for the results, they worry. And even though time passes, and the cancer doesn't return, you still worry.

To be fair, the lumpiness had settled and my chest looked far smoother, but I still wasn't symmetrical and not only did I loathe the look of my stomach, the ridged area was very sore. I only attended one of my follow-up appointments with the plastic surgeon, whose reaction to my upset was purely to offer further liposuction! He made me feel as though I was searching for the Holy Grail, rather than some form of improvement, and before I'd even left the hospital I'd decided to look elsewhere for a solution. I had completely lost all confidence and trust in him. Colin was understandably concerned and tried to be as supportive as he could, but I didn't feel able to tell him initially when, before Christmas, I went to see a different consultant at a different hospital. Looking back I remember I'd based that decision on a conversation we'd had not long after the previous surgery. I was in bed, as I had been all week, and although it was early in the evening, Colin had come upstairs to be with me. All the windows were open, and the sunshine was still streaming in. I was zipped firmly into my compression corset, and was sweating in a very unladylike fashion.

'Where's your fan? Do you want me to find it for you?' he asked as he sensed my discomfort.

'No it'll wear off, just another one of these bloody hot flushes. Come and sit with me.' I patted the mattress next to me. He did as I asked, leaning back against the pillows.

'If I put a pair of stockings on with this, do you think you'd fancy me?' I smiled up at him. It had been weeks since we'd been able to even hold each other, and as with all the previous surgery, the lack of intimacy upset me, and made me feel insecure.

'I always fancy you, you daft mare' he said, brushing the hair off my damp forehead. I took his hand and kissed it, and then tried to manoeuvre myself so I could reach down towards the belt buckle on his jeans.

'Best not start what we can't finish' he said gently, putting his hand over mine.

'Who says we can't finish?' My question was punctuated with a deep breath in as I winced, the corset pulling tightly across my tummy.

'Sweetheart, you're lying there like a wounded animal, all bruised and sore. I really don't think this is a good idea.' I moved my hand from under his, and turned my face away from him.

'Ali, don't be like that. I know how much you're hurting, and I know it's going to take a while before you feel better, but this hurts me too. I hate seeing you like this. I hate watching you trying to move and seeing you in this much pain. I think that...'

'I know what you're thinking, and I know I'm not much use to you right now.' I interrupted, turning back to face him 'But I didn't have any idea it would be as bad as this.'

'I know. Neither of us did, and I get why you did it, but honestly? I wish I'd talked you out of it.'

'You wouldn't have been able to talk me out of it, and I'm sorry. Christ knows I never wanted any of it.' Tears trickled into my already damp hair, as Colin lay down gently next to me and kissed my face. Sometimes there are no words.

The surgeon I was seeing had been recommended to me by a personal friend, and although he mainly performed cosmetic surgery, he had started his career at the Royal Marsden working with their breast reconstruction team. I liked him on sight. He had a lovely smile, and relaxed demeanour, and his manner was gentle, his questions kind. I guessed he was much the same age as me, and indeed told me that his wife was just fifty. Having talked about my life, my job and the last two years, he examined me. He was sensitive to my situation and obvious upset, and once I was dressed he came and sat down next to me.

'You've mentioned your partner, and I'm very glad that he has been so supportive of you. How do you feel about your relationship, now that things are different for you physically?'

'I feel I'm very lucky that it really doesn't seem to bother Colin, he's never been any different with me ever since the diagnosis, and that side of our relationship is good.'

'But how do you feel about that side of your relationship?' he said softly.

No one had ever asked me that before, and I hesitated before replying.

'I feel sad. We've always been so good together, and Colin loved every bit of me. It wasn't just me that lost out, he lost out too. Parts of me hurt, the Tamoxifen is destroying my female hormones, and these blessed hot flushes always come along at the wrong time. My tummy looks gross, and I don't like him seeing me completely naked any more. I get undressed in the bathroom. I've lost my confidence, in fact, I feel less of a woman because of all this, and I guess I feel grateful that he still finds me attractive.' I felt tears pricking my eyes.

'I am sure he loves you very much, and I've no doubt he's very grateful that you are still here to enjoy life with him.' He patted my hand. 'I can help you. It will be quite straightforward to change the implant, and when I pop that in, I can cut a little skin from underneath each breast that will help with the rippling and also the ridging across your tummy.'

'Really? That would be amazing!'

'In time you may want to consider having nipples made. I've done this many time for breast cancer patients, and we just take skin from the inner thigh which can then be tattooed.'

'Gosh, that sounds good. I thought my only option was to have a 3D tattoo.'

'Well, this may be something for the future, and I always prefer to do a little at a time, rather than attempt everything at once. I'm sure you're aware that all surgery carries with it an element of risk, and bearing in mind your last procedure was only two months ago, I think we should wait until after Christmas to give your body its best chance to heal.'

'That's fine. How long will it take? And how long will I need to be in hospital for?'

Any negative thoughts or worries had disappeared. In spite of my previous misgivings following the liposuction, my mind was made up.

'Two to four hours in surgery, and a couple of nights in hospital. You have my secretary's number, so just call her and we'll fix a date in January. Do talk to your partner, though. I know you're the one having the surgery, but I suspect he'll be the one doing the worrying.'

When I told Colin that evening about my appointment, he listened without passing comment.

'What are you thinking?' I asked.

'I'm worried that you've not really thought it through.'

'I have. Trust me. This guy's different. I feel confident.'

'Are you absolutely sure, bearing in mind what happened before?'

'I'm doing it for you, for us.'

'Ali, please don't do it for me. I'm fine with things the way they are.'

'But I'm not. It not only looks shit, but it feels crap too.'

'I know, Baby. I know how you feel.' He sighed. 'If this will make you happy, then do it. But do it for you.'

'I just wish….' My shoulders drooped and I looked down.

'Hey.' His fingers tilted my chin back up. 'We all wish that Babygirl, we all wish that.'


In January 2014 I went in for my surgery. Having been through the form filling, test-taking and pen-markings, I donned my delightful gown and, by way of a change, net knickers rather than paper ones! This new hospital was only twenty minutes from Yo's house, and as I was the last patient of the day, and it was already five o'clock, Colin was planning to have supper with her while I was in theatre. The surgeon had suggested he'd need around four hours, so Colin had ample time. I was wheeled off to theatre to let the expert do his work.

All was well until I was in recovery and could feel pressure building up on the left side of my chest. It was exactly the same kind of sensation I'd had following previous surgeries, and it was incredibly uncomfortable. I couldn't believe it was happening again. I'd been in surgery for several hours and the surgeon and most of the staff had gone home.

The few nurses who were still on shift looked after me, and tried to ease my discomfort with morphine. My left breast was expanding at a rate of knots, and the tightness across my chest was making it difficult for me to breathe. I was beginning to panic, which didn't help, and was fighting the irrational fear that perhaps I had a tumour that hadn't been detected. The surgeon was back with me within the hour, and had me prepped and ready for theatre. I have never been so glad to have a general anaesthetic. I just wanted it all to stop.

It transpired that I had been bleeding internally. Over a litre and a half of blood, but no indication as to what had caused the bleed. I got back to my room at around 1:30 a.m., where Colin was waiting. He had thought I'd be back by nine, and was grey with worry, jumping up from the high-backed blue leather chair as soon as he saw me. I think it was the relief of seeing him that made me cry. He leaned over me, trying to avoid the various drips and wires.

'No one told me anything, I had a missed call from the hospital, but I didn't know what was going on. I really thought something awful had happened to you. Thank God you're okay.'

He kissed me and his tears were warm on my face. I felt incredibly weary and weak, and would have given anything for him to just scoop me up and take me home with him.

'I don't want to leave you tonight. I'll sleep here in the chair.' He said, stroking my hair.

'Sweetheart, I'll be fine. You need to sleep properly. You must be knackered.'

'I'll be with her tonight. Please don't worry.' The lovely night nurse came over to Colin, her smiling eyes looking kindly on us both. 'The morphine will help her sleep, and I'll make sure she's not in any pain.' She put her hand on his arm. 'You can come back as early as you like in the morning.'

Colin stayed while she organised my drip,

catheter, morphine dispenser – they had hooked me up to one in theatre – and my blood transfusion. The pain had stopped, and I felt myself drifting off.

'I thought I'd lost you,' were the last words I heard Colin whisper as I fell asleep

I couldn't have had better care, and was inordinately delighted when my bandages were removed, and a matching pair of breasts were revealed, complete with a cleavage. Most of the horrid hard ridges in my tummy had been broken down and smoothed out, and the surgeon had really improved the sagging and dimpled area too. Yo came to see me, and took a photo of his handiwork, which I planned to send to Kathy and Claire as a direct message on Twitter. I was still a little spaced out though, and had a mild panic believing that I'd actually posted the picture on the public feed rather than to their private accounts! Not quite my TV Babes material, but certainly not suitable for general viewing!

I stayed for five days in hospital, feeling happier and more settled than I had in a long time, but I couldn't shake the exhaustion. I hadn't intended troubling my local surgery with my symptoms, but once I was home I felt so ropey that Colin made an appointment for me. It was he who explained to the doctor what had happened, and once again, I was treated with kindness and understanding. Having carried out the required tests and a general examination, it transpired I had a chest infection and possible anaemia. The doctor prescribed antibiotics and bed rest, and within a few days I was feeling far better.

It had been three years since my diagnosis.
Five major operations and three minor procedures,
but now I felt that I was moving on with my life.
I was looking forward to being able to buy bras
again, and planned to treat myself, with a trip
to Rigby & Peller in London once I was back at
work. Breast cancer is a real slap in the face of
femininity, although I wondered for the umpteenth
time whether possibly, if I wasn't employed as a
TV presenter, with the all-seeing eye of the camera
peering into my very soul, I may have left things
as they were. The truth of course, was that I was
still the seven-year-old girl who had prayed to God
for breasts and loved everything that made me a
woman.

Colin proposed to me on Valentine's Day 2014,
in the Piano Lounge of the Grand Hotel in Brighton.
After a fabulous meal, and a fair few glasses of
champagne, he'd headed over to the talented
gentleman who was tinkling the ivories, and asked
him to play 'The Shadow of Your Smile', a firm
favourite of mine. As with all good performers, the
pianist had his own set list, but promised to play our
request in a couple of tunes' time. As Colin picked
his way among the romantic revellers, the guy
serenaded the packed room with 'Misty' – another
one of our favourites – and so Colin dropped to one
knee and presented me with a beautiful solitaire
diamond ring.

'Would you do me the honour of becoming my
wife?' he asked, as I took the ring from him and put

it on my finger. It was stunning! I burst into tears, my reply coming out in a rush. 'Oh God! Of course! I love you so much!'

I nearly knocked him over in my rather awkward attempt to hug him, which was a tad difficult with him kneeling and me sitting, but, as everyone in the room began cheering and clapping, we both stood up and held on to each other for what felt like forever. We'd come such a long way, and for the most part without a map, but I felt as though we finally knew where we were going, and the road ahead was clear.

# CHAPTER THIRTY-EIGHT

Following my engagement to Colin, the feeling of euphoria carried me through the whole of February. All our children were delighted, our families were thrilled, and everything seemed a little more secure. We decided on a June wedding the following year, to allow me time to get completely well.

Unfortunately I was still battling with the after-effects of my chest infection in January. I couldn't shake my cough, and my chest felt tight and uncomfortable. The hot flushes weren't helping either. I was having up to ten a day, and they were disturbing my sleep at night, which was making me struggle with my shifts at work. I'd also developed coccygeal pain in my tailbone, and sitting for any length of time wasn't easy – it was literally a pain in the bum! I was uneasy, knowing that breast cancer can metastasise in the bones, brain, lungs or liver, and I spent stupid amounts of time looking up information online, and worrying myself unnecessarily. Colin was the voice of reason, telling me to get it checked out properly, and so I arranged to see Mei Lin a couple of months earlier than planned.

As always she was incredibly receptive and understanding of my worries, and arranged for an urgent CT scan of my chest, abdomen and pelvis, and an MRI scan for my coccyx. I would have routine blood tests too, and she'd see me in clinic with the results the following week.

I think I've lost count of the number of scans I've had over the last five years, but there have been many. From the initial MRI scans and mammograms, to nuclear scans, CT scans, X-rays, and an echocardiogram. Lucy said she was surprised I didn't glow in the dark! I though MRI scans were my least favourite, as I always feel claustrophobic in the tunnel, but I was about to find out there was something worse when, in the summer of 2013, a few irregularities were found following my 360 Health Check. Due to shortness of breath I was treated to not just an endoscopy, which is where they feed a tiny camera through your nose, and down the back of your throat to check the oesophagus, but I was also booked in for a colonoscopy at the same time because of an issue with my bowels!

'Just make sure they do the endoscopy before the camera goes up your bum!' Colin said considerately.

Both tests were carried out in a consulting room not a theatre, and remembering Colin's comment, I was relieved to know that the endoscopy was to be first! As the doctor explained what was going to happen, my nerves got the better of me.

'Will you give me something to help me relax?' I asked, thinking of my gag reflex and worrying that I might be sick on his smart suit.

'I'll anaesthetise your throat with a pharyngeal anaesthetic, so that should be fine.'

'And for the other end?' I tried to make my tone light, but failed.

'Well, you might be fine. Many patients don't need any form of analgesic.'

'Um, I don't think I'm one of those.' I said with a nervous laugh. 'I'll have whatever you're offering!'

I was given a mix of Fentanyl and topped up with something called Midazolam, but I would have preferred a heavy blow to the head. Uncomfortable doesn't come close to describing how it felt, although I was told that my unnaturally elongated colon didn't help! The doctor wasn't able to complete the procedure, although he took a fair few photographs of my innards before abandoning it altogether.

The results of the endoscopy proved that I had Grade 1 GORD – Gastro-oesophageal reflux disease – but it was treatable with oral medication, and thanks to the anaesthetic, I don't remember much about it. I wish I could say the same about the colonoscopy! Mercifully the results were essentially normal, although on my notes it said that my 'sigmoid colon was tortuous'… I could have told him that myself!

On a serious note, it's not just the scans themselves that bring with them a sense of apprehension; it's waiting for the results that cause real fear. I have always been extraordinarily lucky and never had to wait more than a week for any of my results, but even those seven days are ones in which you, and those around you, count every hour.

Roz took me the scanner centre for the urgent CT and MRI scans that Mei Lin had organised. I'm sure it's her nursing background that makes her unflappable, and she did a magnificent job of distracting me by bringing with her a beautifully bound wedding planner. Having borrowed a biro from the receptionist, we filled it in, discussing wedding dress styles, and flowers. I felt incredibly excited, and the forty minutes or so it took for the rather disgusting contrast liquid I'd had to drink to get into my system passed in the blink of an eye. When the radiographer called me Roz squeezed my hand.

'I'll google the place in London that makes the 1950s style dresses, so we can make an appointment. Exciting!' She smiled at me. 'Don't worry, it's going to be fine, Ali.'

'It had better be. I will be *so* pissed off if there's something wrong.' I gave her a broad smile and followed the nurse to the scanner room.


Mei Lin rang me a few days later to tell me that there was no evidence of cancer spread in either of my scans, and my blood tests were also normal. She advised me to see my GP with regards the coccygeal discomfort, and talked with me about various strategies to manage the hot flushes. She planned to send me the Breast Cancer Care leaflet on dealing with menopausal symptoms, and also

a guide to ear acupuncture that had been known
to help women with severe hot flushes. They were
trialling it at the Mount Vernon Cancer Centre in
Watford, and I decided to give it a go. As always,
I was incredibly grateful to her for her wisdom,
kindness and complete understanding of how I was
feeling: not all cancer patients are as lucky.

Before embarking on the six-week trial that
would require diligent diary filling and regular
visits to the cancer centre in Watford, I made an
appointment at Rigby & Peller on the King's Road
to be fitted for my new bras. Roz had offered to
come with me, but it was something I wanted to do
alone. It was far too fragile a feeling to be examined
and something too personal to share, even with her.

The store is beautifully dressed with row upon
row of lovely lingerie, displayed as stunning
lace creations in all the colours of the rainbow.
With the exception of one large photograph of a
gorgeous girl, her breasts encased in black satin,
there were only mannequins modelling the various
designs. The fitting room was downstairs, subtly
lit, and furnished with rich purple fabrics and dark
mahogany furniture. I had been there before, many
years ago, and bought the Simone Perele collection
that had been hidden away in the back of my
chest of drawers since January 2011. There are no
tape measures involved in the fitting process. The
assistants understand the female form so well that
they can gauge your bra size purely by looking at
you.

'You are a 32F madam. Any particular style you

were thinking of?'

'Well before all this happened, I used to wear the underwired range from Simone Perele. Would it still work?' I looked in the full-length mirror at my nipple-less breasts, and then back at the perfectly formed and incredibly elegant sales assistant, her tight white blouse and black pencil skirt accentuating her figure.

'I can't imagine why not. You look fabulous,' she said with a kind smile. 'I am sorry for all you've been through though.' She paused. 'Shall I choose a couple of styles and bring them down? Any particular colour?'

She left me with three equally pretty options, and then excused herself, so I could try them on. The soft ivory lace and tiny satin ribbons sat beautifully on the perfectly moulded bra, and having slipped it over each shoulder, I fastened it at the back before looking up at my reflection.

You'd never know. No one would ever know. The soft fabric and beautiful lace edging covered my scars, and took away my sadness. I smiled at my softly rounded cleavage and was glad the sales assistant wasn't there to see my tears. I bought all three bras, and wore one of them when I went with Roz to have a look at wedding dresses in a fabulous boutique she'd found on the South Bank. I chose the first dress I tried on which was strapless, but had a complete lace overlay. With my new shape I didn't even need a bra! As the wedding was set for June, my first dress fitting was booked in for the beginning of April. I couldn't have been happier.

My new-found confidence led Colin and I to return to the plastic surgeon who'd given me symmetry, and enquire further about having my nipples reconstructed. This time he explained in detail how skin could be taken from the very top of my inner thighs and then grafted on to the centre of each breast to make the areola. He would then cut a key shape into the actual breast and using that skin with some very clever stitching, would create the nipple itself. There was always the option, at a later date, to have the nipple tattooed to give it colour, and make it even more realistic.

'Is there much risk involved with this kind of surgery, bearing in mind what happened before?' Colin asked warily.

'There's always a risk, but this is a relatively minor procedure and not overly invasive. Alison does have irradiated skin on the right, but judging by how well her other scars have healed that side, hopefully these would too.'

'What about the scars at the top of my legs? How long will they take to heal? I've had a fair bit of time off work already this year!' I said.

'All things being even, you should be back at work within a week, but you'll have to be careful with the dressings for a while. The scars in your groin shouldn't be noticeable after a few months.'

'I've started this ear acupuncture trial at Mount Vernon, and it's a six-week course, so after September would be best.' I turned to Colin. 'What do you think?'

'So you definitely want it done?'

'I think so. I thought we both did?'

'I'd like to think about a bit more, Ali. You're happy for the first time in a long time, and I don't want anything to change that.'

'But this would be the icing on the cake! It'd be done then. I'd be normal for the wedding – well, as near normal as I'll ever be!'

The surgeon spoke up. 'Please. Take your time, and let my secretary know once you've decided. '

Which is exactly what we did, and my surgery was booked for the second week in October.

The summer passed at speed. The ear acupuncture slightly alleviated my hot flushes, if only for a few weeks. We chose our wedding venue the day before my daughter announced that she was expecting our first grandchild! I was over the moon. The depth of emotion I felt at the news took me by surprise: a new life, when not that far back I had wondered if I would live long enough to meet my grandchildren.

Just before QVC's annual Breast Cancer Care fundraiser at the beginning of October, I had my six-month check up with Mei Lin. As she examined me I told her all about the wedding plans, Lucy's baby, and the scheduled nipple surgery. She told me how delighted she was for me, but then paused before saying, 'I think it would be wise for you to have another MRI scan before you go ahead with the nipple surgery. There's a small area of nodularity on the left side just above the central scar. Have you felt it?'

My skin prickled. 'No I haven't. Where is it?'

She guided my right hand on to my left breast and there it was. A small hard lump, in almost exactly the same position as the original tumour had been on the right side.

'I'm sure it'll be fine, but I'd rather you had it checked out before your surgery just to be certain.'

I felt as though all the colour had leached out of my life.

Two days later, I presented our fifteenth Breast Cancer Care show on QVC. I interviewed fellow cancer patients, and talked about my feelings following my diagnosis three years earlier. During the rehearsal, I'd spoken to my producer about Mei Lin's findings and my forthcoming MRI. His advice was sound. 'You do whatever feels right.'

I did mention it on air, although saying it out loud brought it home to me, and it was difficult for me to hold it together despite all the years I'd worked as a presenter. With my first grandchild due in May, and the wedding in June, I felt I had so much more to lose now. The support I received from my friends and colleagues was immense, as was the overwhelming response from Ali's Army on the blog.

Mei Lin called me a week later while I was at work.

It came up as an unknown number on my phone, but I recognised her voice instantly.

'Alison, it's good news. The report's back and the professor's told me there is no evidence of active disease on the left, and no local tumour recurrence on the right. They think it might just be the edge of the implant that's causing the ridged area.'

'Oh, thank God! That is such a relief! Thank you so much for letting me know.'

'I'm pleased for you too. It is good news. Great news. I'd like to catch up with you after your surgery, just to keep an eye on things.'

'Of course! Definitely. I'll be in touch. And thank you as always, for everything.'

I could breathe again.

# CHAPTER THIRTY-NINE

It was hard to believe it had been almost four years since my diagnosis, but as I checked into the hospital that October, I truly believed that this was the final part of my journey to find 'a new kind of normal'. Colin was with me, and Yo met us there, laughing out loud when I showed her that I'd finally mastered the art of tying the tapes on my hospital gown. There was an air of anticipation I think we all felt, and I carried it with me to the operating theatre, and held on to it as the anaesthetic crept coldly into my veins.

I don't know what it is about surgery and me. Other people seem to sail through it, and out the other side, with no side effects and enviable results. I woke up in recovery, shaking violently and in a great deal of pain. The pain wasn't in my chest but my legs, where the graft sites were. A score of one to ten is used when trying to ascertain how much discomfort you are in – ten being unbearable. My previous fat-transfer procedure had been pretty close to a ten, and this pain wasn't far off either!

I recognised the nurse from my previous surgery. 'Where is your pain?' she asked.

Struggling to speak coherently because my teeth were chattering so badly, I pointed to my lower half and stuttered 'Under there.'

The nurse checked under my sheet. 'I can't see anything unusual' she said, pulling it gently back over me. She patted my hand. 'I'll get you a blanket. It's probably the anaesthetic, but you may be a bit cold.'

The blanket didn't improve things, and my body continued to shudder and shake. The anaesthetist was called back in, and prescribed some Oramorph, which helped a little. I watched the hands on the clock creep round, and tried to focus on anything other than the stinging and burning at the top of my legs.

Considering it was supposed to be such a minor procedure I became paranoid, and thought that the nurse would think I was making a fuss. I knew that I would have to stay in recovery until the discomfort was controlled, and so I gritted my chattering teeth when they asked what my pain score was, and said 'five'.

'We'll get you something to help you to sleep once you're back in your room,' my nurse said, as she lifted up the sides of the bed, and locked them into place. I was wheeled back to my room, the bars on the bed shaking in time with my juddering body.

Yo and Colin were visibly shocked when they saw me, and as soon as Colin was close enough to comfort me, I gritted my teeth and tried to speak to him.

'It's my legs. They're so sore. And I think I've wet myself.' I was mortified to admit. 'Can you look?'

He pulled the covers to one side. 'Christ! Nurse! She's bleeding!' He shouted at the nurse, who was at the end of the bed. 'What the hell's happened? Where's she bleeding from?'

Within seconds the nurse was moving the blanket and sheet away from my body. 'I don't know. I'm going to call the surgeon.'

The horrible warm metallic smell of blood filled my nostrils and I felt sick.

Within the hour I was taken back to theatre and the wounds examined. There'd been a build-up of blood under the skin, like a giant bruise, and that's what had caused the problem. I was cleaned up, re-stitched and taken back to my room where I stayed for the following three days. The incisions at the top of my legs were not the tiny graft sites I had expected, but scars that were approximately four inches long, making it impossible for me to sit on a lavatory seat or anything other than a soft mattress. The bruising was on both buttocks, and went right the way down the inside of my legs and up to my tummy. As before when I'd had the compression corset, I had to wee standing up or hover over the loo for anything else, and walking was almost impossible.

Mum and my sister came to stay and were appalled to see me in such a state.

'I thought he told you this was a minor procedure? Weren't they meant to be skin grafts?'

Mum asked, shocked by the bruising and stitching.

'Yes, that's what he said, but it looks like a whole section of skin and tissue has been taken.' I had strategically placed a mirror on my bedside table so I could see my undercarriage!

'How long will it take to heal?'

That of course was the million-dollar question, and unfortunately the wounds continued to bleed, large clots squeezing their way out in between the stitches, so I had to go back into hospital. After a rather lengthy conversation with the surgeon, it transpired that I had misunderstood his description of the type of skin graft needed. A full circle of skin had been needed from the top of both legs, and with no local anaesthetic in the wound, it was the swelling, bruising and pulling sensation that had made it so incredibly sore. Obviously they needed to find out what was causing the bleeding, and so the wounds were once again opened, cleaned and re-stitched. Within three days I was home, and feeling far more positive.

Of course the payoff was the actual result of the reconstruction. When the bandages were removed, the nipples looked very realistic. Well, for the first week anyway. The left side continued to heal, but on the right, although the areola looked fine, the centre of the nipple, made from the breast itself, appeared blackened and heavily scabbed. When I went back to have them redressed, the surgeon told me that the blackened area was where the tissue hadn't taken because of the irradiated skin. It was possible that part of the nipple might survive, but

I was going to have to be diligent at keeping the area clean and changing the dressing regularly. We agreed that as the hospital was at least forty minutes' drive away, it would simpler for me to have assistance with this at my local surgery.

And so I did. For six weeks I visited the surgery every Monday, and changed the antiseptic gauze myself every other day. The left side was fine, the right a septic, swollen mess. I carried on working and didn't tell anyone what had happened. I knew what they would say, and it would be no different to what I'd told myself time and time again since the operation. Why hadn't I just left things alone?

On the 14th of December, I was at my local surgery, watching the nurse gently peel back the dressing with her tweezers. I smelled the familiar odour of festering skin.

'How long have you've been coming to us, sweetheart?' she asked me.

'Six weeks, I think.'

'You've done a brilliant job with these dressings, but that's a long time and it's not really getting any better. To be honest, I think the doctor should take a look. Is that okay with you?'

I nodded and watched her leave the room. My own doctor came to examine me. She was relatively new to the practice, and absolutely charming. In her soft Dublin accent she asked me what had happened since the surgery, listening and nodding when I replied.

'Alison, I know how much this means to you, and you've managed your dressings incredibly well, but I really think it's time to accept that it's not going to heal. The nipple needs to come off, and I'd like you see your surgeon as soon possible to get this done.'

I felt unbelievably weary. Worn down and defeated. The tears ran slowly down my cheeks and I shook my head. 'I don't know why I did it. I should have left it alone. You can't make a silk purse out of a pig's ear, can you?'

The doctor leaned forward and held my hand between both of hers. 'You did what you needed to do. And if I was in your situation, I am sure I would have done the same.' Her validation made me weep.

Two days later my surgeon, having examined me, agreed that he would have to remove the nipple. It was indeed necrotic and wouldn't heal.

'If I remove it, then the healthy skin around the areola will be fine and the whole thing should granulate over. I'm sorry. I know it's not what you wanted.'

'When do I need to come back in?'

'I can do it now. You don't have any feeling there, do you?'

'No I don't. None.' I said, a little nervously.

'Well at least this way, you'll be feeling much better by Christmas.'

I watched him gather together some surgical instruments and clean dressings, and as he sat came back to the bedside, I turned my face to the wall and closed my eyes. I heard the sharp scissors snip into the blackened flesh, and when he was done, I opened my eyes and saw it lying on a white gauze dressing. The detritus of my dreams.

I should have gone home, but I was due into work for a prep day. I wouldn't be going on air but had a whole raft of meetings in place. I tried to contact Colin but couldn't get through and so it was poor Charlie who got the fallout of my emotions when I saw him in the presenters' lounge. He couldn't have been kinder, and having told me that he would go and explain to our line manager that I'd had to go home and why, he gave me a hug.

'It doesn't get any easier for you, Ali, does it?' he said.

And for just a short while I'll admit, I allowed myself to think that.

My GP had contacted Mei Lin and so I saw her at the beginning of the New Year. The hole where the surgeon had removed the nipple was the size of a five pence piece, and showed no signs of granulating or healing over. Although the skin around the edge was healthy, Mei Lin was doubtful that it would close up of its own volition, and said she felt my only option was to remove the implant and stitch the hole together. The risk of infection was great, and potentially very serious. When I saw my consultant the following day, he was in agreement, and I was back in hospital at the end of the week. I had no choice in the matter, and although I knew it was the only way, it wasn't what I wanted.

It's difficult to put into words how I felt when I

woke up after the surgery. Reaching over with my left hand, I touched the flatness of my chest through the fabric of my gown, and once again remembered my mother's mastectomy scars. I thought of the beautiful bras I had bought last summer, and my wedding dress, the first fitting just three months away. I recalled the countless hours and days I'd spent in hospital over the previous four years. Of course I'd needed the initial surgery, but the reconstruction? Why had I been so driven? And for what?

Colin broke the silence, as if reading my mind. 'Ali, it doesn't matter, really it doesn't. We had all those years before, and we have all the years ahead of us. That's what matters. You're tired. Your body's had enough.'

I reached for his warm hand, bringing it up to my lips and kissing it. He smiled at me, and I noticed the way his eyes crinkled at the edges, and the shape of his jaw. There was just a hint of grey in his stubble that I hadn't seen before. He was right. I was tired. I'd had enough. No more. Somewhere along the line I'd lost sight of what was truly important. I was still here. I had a life; I had people in that life who loved me, and I had Colin.

'You still want to marry me then?' I asked with a small smile

'If you'll have me.'

'What, now?'

'I think we should wait until we get home, Ali,' he grinned at me, and I knew everything was going to be all right.

# CHAPTER FORTY

I first fell in love when I was six years old. His name was Stephen McKnight, and we both attended Sunnymede Infants School. He invited me to tea, and after our cheese sandwiches and fresh strawberries, he asked me to come upstairs and see the Airfix plane he'd made. I remember his bedroom was painted orange, and when he asked if he could kiss me, I said yes, but only if he got me some more strawberries.

When I was seven my cousin Geoff married his sweetheart Margaret, and Jenny and I were both bridesmaids. My aunty Eileen made the turquoise satin dresses, and we each had a ball of white carnations to carry. The smell of those flowers still takes me back to that day, the incredible excitement, and the memory of Jenny and I collecting as much confetti as we could and concealing it in our knickers! There were days when I would sneak into my mum's bedroom and rifle through her jewellery drawer until I found her engagement ring, tucked inside a blue velvet box. I would slip it over my finger and angle my hand until the light hit the solitaire, captivated by the way the colour filled the diamond like a kaleidoscope, creating beautiful and perfect patterns on the woodchip wallpaper. I would close my eyes and imagine the actor Adam West down on one knee – not in his tights as Batman of course - but suited and booted, as the more formal and fascinating Bruce Wayne. I was a hopeless romantic. Musicals like *High Society, Singing in the Rain, Young at Heart* and *South Pacific* were the stuff of my dreams,

I was really touched when just a few years ago my mum gave me her engagement ring... It fitted on my ring finger and as it caught the light, I felt the years fall away, and the magical memories return.


My marriage to Colin was to be my third, and if I had a pound for every time someone said 'third time lucky' it would have paid for the wedding! We had thought about having a quiet wedding abroad, or just sloping off and tying the knot, but on further reflection decided that it was the perfect opportunity to share our joy and make this a mighty celebration. We'd come a long way together, and had been supported and loved by so many of our family and friends, that this would be our way of saying thank you. We also wanted a church wedding, but as both of us had been married before, I wasn't terribly hopeful.

Our parish church was St Michael's in Bray. Colin and I met with the Reverend Richard Cowles to discuss our wedding wishes. We talked about our children, our lives, our previous marriages, and why

it was important to us to seal our love in a church –
his church. Reverend Cowles was wise, kind and,
above all, accepting, and the date was set for the
26th of June 2015. We couldn't have been happier.

The beautifully bound wedding planner that Roz
had bought for me was filling up, and there seemed
to be an inordinately large list of things that needed
to be done! Top of that list was my wedding dress,
and although we were now to be married in church,
a traditional full-length dress wasn't what I wanted.
The dress also needed to be something that Colin
would love, and after Roz's initial suggestion
earlier in the year, I'd picked out a 1950s dress
made by the designer Candy Anthony who had a
fabulous boutique on London's South Bank. Roz
and I had decided to make a day of it, and she came
and stayed with me overnight before we travelled
to London by train. The first dress I tried on was
in soft grey satin; strapless with a boned bodice
and incredibly full skirt with petticoats. It had a
removable lace overlay, complete with sleeves!
When I stepped out of the changing room to show
Roz, she wiped away a tear. 'Ali, it's perfect. Just
perfect.'

It was perfect to me too, and indeed was the only
dress I tried on, deciding on a pale blue satin rather
than the grey, as Colin's favourite colour is blue. I
hadn't needed to wear a bra, as my reconstructed
boobs were symmetrical and stayed in place, and I
was looking forward to buying something beautiful

to wear underneath my dress on the day. Of course just five months before the wedding, that all changed with the removal of my breast implant.

For the first few weeks after that final surgery, I'd worn a vest, but I knew that when I went back to work, I'd want something to disguise my flatness. Mum came to the rescue, having been initiated into the world of breast prostheses five years earlier. She'd been very stoical about the whole business then, and still was, and so it was a relief for me to temporarily let go of the reins. She took me to a stockist local to her that had a showroom. There were rows of different bras, and boxes full of the silicone prostheses and it struck me just how many women must have to live with breast cancer. One could choose between buying a bra with pockets stitched in to hold the prosthesis, or using the cover that comes with it, and popping that inside your normal bra. You'd be surprised how heavy these silicone boobs are, and how slippery, like eels! It was a world apart from the wonders of Rigby & Peller, but I did come away with a boob in a box, and a rather functional bra in which to put it.

As I fastened my seat belt, Mum put her hand gently on mine. 'I know it's not what you wanted, but you'll get used to it. I have, and it's not so bad really.'

'I know, Mum. You've done brilliantly. Perhaps if I give her a name, like I did for the expander?'

'I think that's a great idea! We all missed Dolly

once she'd gone.' She smiled and I laughed. 'How about Beryl? A boob called Beryl?'

'I think that would work well.'

And it did, and still does. As with all these things, it's very much a matter of personal choice, but if you do choose the same route as I have, then I'd like to mention a fabulous charity called Knitted Knockers. I discovered them later that year, and they actually knit breast prostheses. There is no charge, and you can choose your own colour and style. They arrive in a beautiful organza bag with a label that says 'Made with love, filled with hope.' I treasure mine.

I didn't find the customised bras that comfortable, so was delighted to discover that Rigby & Peller could stitch a pocket into the bras I'd bought from them, which would hold Beryl safely in place. I took delivery of them just before my first wedding dress fitting in April and on the same day Roz rang to confirm where and when we would meet.

'The appointment is at two o'clock and we could meet at Waterloo station and get some lunch on the Southbank first? Does that work for you?'

'Of course, that'd be fine.'

Roz paused. 'Ali, have you rung them and told them what's happened since the surgery?'

'Um, no. I haven't really thought about it.' That was a lie, as I'd thought about very little else all that week.

'Would you like me to ring them?'

'Would you mind? I don't really know what...'

'Of course I can sweetheart. Leave it with me. It's better they know beforehand, so they'll be prepared.'

I thanked her, knowing how lucky I was to have her there for me. She was always one step ahead of me, protecting me on my journey.

The seamstress was incredibly sensitive to my changed shape. A strapless bra wasn't an option, because the structure of it dug into my scars, so she suggested cutting the straps off the beautiful cream lace creation I was wearing and stitching that into the bodice. I could insert Beryl on the day, and it would be comfortable but, more importantly, it would be just the right shape for the 1950s-style dress.

I chose a pretty little net veil that was more like a fascinator, and could be pinned into my hair, and we agreed that the right sleeve of the lace overlay should be left unstitched, so we could adjust it in case my lymphedema played up on the day. Having removed my bra and handed it to the seamstress, I tucked Beryl safely away in my handbag, dressed and left the showroom, lopsided but happy.

I had been overwhelmed by the response on my blog when I announced my engagement, and so with Colin's blessing, I decided to share each stage of our wedding plans with these lovely and loyal viewers. We found a fabulous venue for our reception, and having confirmed the church, we then had to choose the music to be played, and the hymns to be sung. There's nothing worse than a half-hearted response from the congregation when they're not familiar with the songs! We also needed music to walk into and out of the church, and so I decided to ask my bloggers for their suggestions, and they responded in their droves. Literally hundreds of amazing ideas – songs I'd never heard of, and pieces of music that took me back to my childhood. Memories of my dad, sitting in his high-backed blue leather chair after Sunday lunch. Eyes closed, hands moving in time to the classical masterpieces he listened to on his gramophone, as though he was conducting the orchestra. He would remain in a trance-like state for as long as we'd let him, before Peter, Jenny and I took advantage of it, and climbed all over him, insisting that if he really loved us, he would take us to Bushy Park so we could ride on the swing boats.

Making a final decision wasn't easy, as each piece of music had its merits, but after much deliberation we decided on Elgar's 'Salut D'Amour' for Chris to walk me up the aisle, and 'Widor's Toccata in F Major' for Colin and I to leave the church to – I think my dad would have approved of our choices. There would be two hymns; 'Praise My Soul The King of Heaven' and 'Immortal, Invisible'. Both Jenny and Roz were to do a reading, and Jenny suggested Shakespeare's Sonnet 'How Do I Love Thee', with Roz opting for several verses from the Song of Solomon. We chose the Beatles classic 'Til There was You' to be played

while we signed the register, and were delighted to
be told that the organist would come and play this
for us on the grand piano that was next to the altar.
Result! Colin's three sons were going to be his best
men and Yo was to make a speech at the reception.
It was all going swimmingly.

Of course in the midst of all this excitement we
were counting down the weeks before the birth
of Lucy's baby due at the end of April. I was on
tenterhooks! My children always tease me as on
their birthdays I used to launch into a description
of where and when they were born, and how I
loved them on sight. 'Mum! We've heard it all
before!' they'd tell me, but I relished reliving those
moments.

Lucy was six days overdue when Simon called
to let us know that she'd finally been induced and
was in labour. I felt quite giddy. I just couldn't
settle, and so Colin and I decided that to keep
ourselves occupied we would tick another thing off
our list and go shopping for our wedding rings. I'd
already decided on a simple yellow gold band, but
we chanced upon a little boutique that had its own
collection of designs. I saw through the window
a brushed yellow gold ring with a row of tiny
diamonds along the top. It looked a little crown,
and went perfectly with my engagement ring. It
would need to be sized for me, but would be ready
in plenty of time for the wedding. Colin couldn't
make his mind up, and decided he'd like to check

out a few more places before making a decision.
I had my phone in and out of my bag every five
minutes, but it wasn't until later that afternoon we
had the call from Simon to say Lucy had given
birth by emergency C-section to a daughter, Honey
Beatrice. It had been pretty scary, but now mum
and baby were fine, although very tired. I will never
forget standing in the kitchen whooping like a little
girl before Colin joined me, and the enormity of it
hit me. I cried in his arms for quite a time. There is
something inexplicably wonderful about the child
you brought into the world bringing a new life
of her own to join the family. The overwhelming
feeling of love I felt when I first held Honey was on
a par with the emotion I'd experienced after giving
birth to Lucy all those years before. I felt she was
definitely a part of me.

'She's absolutely beautiful, Looma,' I said,
holding tiny Honey tightly in my arms. 'Well done,
sweetheart. You did brilliantly. She's perfect.'

My girly smiled at me. 'It's just like you said it
would be, Mum. I loved her the moment I saw her.'

'And one day you'll be telling her all about this
day, and how the sun shone, and how she made us
all so happy.' I closed my eyes and kissed the top of
Honey's head, thanking God for her life, and for my
own.


The next five weeks passed at break-neck speed,
what with work and fitting in weekly visits to see
Lucy and Honey, but with Roz and Chris's help

Colin and I got through everything on our wedding list. Although I'd asked my brother Peter to come to the wedding, sadly he and Sarah weren't able to make it, but my niece Clare was flying all the way from Sydney to join us. We were thrilled, and really touched that she was making such a monumental effort to be with us all on our special day. Her brother James was already living and working in the UK and so he would join us too which made it even more perfect.

My dress was ready for collection a week before the day, and as the lace overlay was removable, I didn't need to think about wearing anything different for the evening. I'd been struggling with finding the right pair of shoes, and in desperation had resorted to looking online. There was a moment of panic, when having ordered three different pairs of satin stilettos online, none of them fitted! I finally decided on a pair of Jimmy Choos. My first and only purchase from this fabulous brand, and mercifully my feet slipped comfortably inside the stunning cream satin, which was a mighty relief.

One thing I wasn't getting involved in was ordering the boy's suits, that was Colin's domain, but it was a tall order trying to get all five of our sons together at the one time for a fitting! With only four weeks to go he'd ordered the cravats, and two weeks later he'd found the waistcoats, but the actual suits didn't materialise until the week before the wedding!

With just two days to go, Roz and Chris arrived, having transported the wedding cake they'd made for us all the way from Dorset! It was a stunning creation, decorated in pale blue icing and with the most exquisite lace effect in white icing over the top. There were three tiers: one chocolate, one lemon and one fruit cake, and Roz had chosen the design to emulate my wedding dress. It was almost good enough to wear!

The church rehearsal was that night, and in place of my dad, I'd asked Chris to give me away. A constant tower of strength to me, Chris has the kindest soul, and I feel very lucky to have him in my life. The four of us have shared some fabulous times, but I think possibly the most memorable was the Three Peaks Challenge. Roz and Colin decided not to join us on the hike, but were there with dry clothes, food and encouragement at each of the three check points. Starting at 6:30 a.m. one very wet morning in May, we scaled three mountains, each well over two thousand feet high and completed the challenge at 7 p.m. It was physically and mentally one of the hardest things I'd ever done, and I know I wouldn't have made it without him by my side.

This journey would be a great deal easier, and with the reverend leading the way, we had to practise our walk up the aisle in time to Elgar's masterpiece. There was a sharp right turn and a very uneven floor tile at the bottom of the aisle, which nearly caused me to come a cropper, but Chris manfully steered me round it, and I got to the altar intact. We also had a bit of a moment when practising the kneeling bit, as my poor old knees weren't very flexible and I knew the plethora of petticoats would impede any movement. There was nothing other than the reverend in front of me, but I didn't think he'd thank me if I used his robes as a grab rail! Sensing my dilemma, the reverend suggested that on the day Colin held my arm so he could haul me up, but in a subtle way. We thanked him for his foresight, and having run through the final timings, left the church to celebrate over a delicious dinner in the local pub.

The day before the wedding had been busy. We had visits from most of the children, including Sam and Jack, and Aunty Edna had arrived in the afternoon. She was – in her own words – 'as excited as a schoolgirl', and I sneaked her into the back bedroom to show her my wedding dress... Moving the large sheet that covered it to one side, the soft blue satin and lace overlay was immediately visible.

'Alison it's absolutely beautiful.' She said touching the fabric.

'I thought it looked a little like the one you wore when you married Ian.'

'It does a bit, although mine was just satin. Funny to think that your mum and dad weren't with us on that day because you'd just been born, and now here I am with you for *your* wedding!' She smiled and I hugged her to me.

'I have something for you, something I carried

with me on my wedding day, that I thought you might like for yours.' Reaching into her pocket she brought a small blue organza handkerchief with two white lily of the valley embroidered on the corner. 'I thought you could pin it inside the dress for something old, borrowed and blue.' I took the fine and exquisite square of fabric and looked at her.

'Thank you. It means so much to me that you're here; that you're always here for me.'

'I wouldn't have missed it for the world' she said.

Colin spent a great deal of time putting together a medley of my favourite songs to be played while we had the wedding breakfast. He always tends to leave things until the last minute, and out of choice will do all his Christmas shopping on Christmas Eve! He was to be spending that night at the wedding venue, along with most of our children.

'I'd better be off guys,' he said, having gathered together most of the things he needed. 'You've been the best.' He hugged Edna first, and then Roz and Chris. Leaving them in the kitchen, I followed him out into the hall.

'I'll miss you tonight, Mr Elsworth,' I said, winding my arms around his neck and leaning into him.

'We'll have some making up to do tomorrow night then, Mrs Elsworth.'

'I'll look forward to it.' I kissed his warm mouth and then traced the line of his jaw with my finger. 'I love you. More than you know.'

I lay alone in our large bed and watched the clouds move across the moon. I felt excitement and anticipation, wanting the night to be over and the day to begin. Closing my eyes I remembered that very same feeling when I was child on Christmas Eve, unable to sleep and desperate to see what Father Christmas had left me. 'All good things come to those who wait,' my grandmother had told me when I went into her room for the umpteenth time, and she'd sent me back to bed. And she was always right. After five years of waiting, I was ready.

# CHAPTER FORTY-ONE

'Marmite or marmalade on your toast?' Roz poked her head around my bedroom door at around seven o'clock, looking as though she'd been up for hours.

'Hello love. Marmite please. Did you sleep okay?'

She came into the room, carrying a cup of Earl Grey for me. 'Not really, I was far too excited!' she said, placing it on my bedside table. 'How about you?' I grinned.

'Me too! Is it sunny?'

'Not yet, but it's still early.' She plonked down on the bed next to me. 'I can't believe it's finally here! Woo-hoo!'

I couldn't quite believe it either, after all the months of planning and sorting – the lion's share of it done by Roz and Chris – it was finally my wedding day.

I sat up and hugged her. 'Thank you so much for everything... and I mean everything!'

'My pleasure sweetheart. We're so happy for you and Colin. It's going be brilliant. Do you want your toast up here or downstairs?'

'I think I'd better shower first and wash my hair before June gets here. Is Chris up yet?'

'Yup, but I think Edna beat the pair of us! Chris has already showered and I've got him on toast duty. The pair of them are in the kitchen.'

'Bless him. I'll have mine when I'm done. I suggest you leave now, before I put you off your breakfast!' I said, pulling the covers back.


June Kelly Bain is an absolute sweetheart. A professional make-up artist who runs her own business, freelancing regularly at QVC, she'd transformed my face on many occasions, most notably for promotional filming, and my Breast Cancer Care appearances. Today she had very kindly offered to do my wedding make-up. She was also going to put my hair up for me and coiffure Colin's girls' too, which they were very excited about. I was still wrapped in my towel when my mobile rang, and I heard her lovely Irish lilt.

'Ali, how're you? '

'Fine June. And you? How's it going?'

'Grand! Well, actually not. I've had a bit of mishap. Not me, the taxi driver has. He was trying to turn the car around because he thought we'd come too far, and now he's reversed off the edge of a small bridge into a ditch.'

'Oh God! Are you okay?'

'Yes, I'm fine.'

'And where are you?'

'Well, that's the thing. I don't know. I think it's

the entrance to a farm. Do you know where that'd be?'

'I haven't got a clue.' I said unhelpfully. Undaunted, June continued.

'I'm pretty sure I can't be far away, so I'll just grab my bag and start walking.'

'Whoa! June! Let me get some clothes on, and I'll come out and find you.' I said, dropping my towel and grabbing my pyjamas. I saw her as soon as I stepped out on to the road. She was only a hundred metres away, and mercifully heading in my direction.

'June!! Over here!' A vision in pink jeans, pulling a large suitcase, my saviour made her way over to me.

'Geez, Ali, you put the heart across me! Did you not know there was a farm? How long have you lived here?' she questioned, hugging me.

'Nearly three years!' I laughed. 'I am sorry, June, you've probably been up since the crack of dawn! We're just here.' I led her on to the gravel drive. 'Let's get you some toast.'

We left the poor taxi driver to extricate his car from the ditch.

June already had my rollers in place and foundation on when Colin's girls arrived, all three of them carrying their own make-up collections. Aunty Edna was beside herself. I don't think she'd ever seen that much make-up, and to be fair it looked more like the beauty hall in Selfridges than our dining room, by the time Vicky, Rae and Lily had decanted all they'd brought with them. There was barely space on the table for the toast and tea that Chris had prepared! It was like watching artists at work, and even June was impressed. It certainly gave the photographer, who was the next to arrive, plenty of photo opportunities! Although I've being doing my own make-up for years, I have never been able to create the same kind of look that June did that day. I was thrilled. She started working on my hair, moving the mirror slightly so that I could see what she was doing, just as the sun broke through the clouds creating its own reflection in the glass.

'Yay!' I shouted to no one in particular. 'The sun's out!'

'The sun always shines on the righteous.' said June reverently.

'Which is probably why I'm in the shade!'

'Shift over a bit then' she said.

Roz brought more toast, my sister Jenny and her partner Linda arrived, and then Chris left to pick up my bouquet and the buttonholes. Time was ticking on, but June was working flat out, and created the most the most fabulous up-do for me. She had the three girls to attend to next, but promised that if she had time, she'd help Edna with her make-up and she'd sort Jenny's hair out too, God love her. Jenny looked every inch the lady in a cream lace creation, and I took her upstairs to show her my dress. I spotted my shoes, placed somewhat bizarrely on the dressing table!

'It was probably the photographer. He may well have taken a picture of your stockings as well!' she said, admiring the lingerie laid out on the bed.

'Thank God I wasn't wearing it, eh?'

'I love the shoes! And the dress is stunning, just perfect.' She turned to me 'You're going to look beautiful, like you always do.'

'Well, I've got a lot of competition!' I said, hugging her to me.

We were still upstairs when we heard someone burst through the front door. It was Colin.

'Did I leave a jacket here last night?' He sounded rattled. 'Jack had Richard's suit by mistake, but they swapped, and now he can't find his jacket. I could have sworn it was in the suit bag.' His footsteps bounded up the stairs as Roz shouted after him.

'Ali's up there! You mustn't see her; it's bad luck! Let me look!'

'I won't see her, it's in the spare bedroom.'

I didn't hear Roz's reply as she was drowned out by our friends Martin and Jean's greeting. They'd just arrived, driving their fabulous old London black cab in which Martin was going to chauffeur me to church. Before Roz could even close the front door, we heard Chris coming in with the flowers, and then Colin heading back down the stairs.

'Like Piccadilly Circus down here! Ah Chris I'll take those buttonholes with me.'

'Hello mate, everything okay?' Martin asked

'Yup fine thanks, just a bit of a rush! The car looks beautiful. Thank you so much. Hello Jean! Thanks for all those flowers in the cab – Ali's going to love them. See you both at the church!' The door slammed, and I suddenly felt nervous, giving an involuntary shiver.

My sister put her hand on my arm and told me not to worry. 'They'll find the jacket. It's probably still in the suit bag! You know what men are like when it comes to looking properly!'

'But Jack and Sam are ushers. Perhaps I'd better go and have a look myself.'

'No, I think you ought to get dressed. You don't want to be late. Linda and I are going to have to head off. I promised Mum I'd get her into the church early. Are you happy?' she asked me.

'Very.'

'Then everything's going to be okay' she told me.

It seemed as though everyone was leaving at the same time. The girls all looked beautiful. 'See you at the church, Step Mummy Ali!' they chorused, air-kissing me so as not to spoil their lippy. I just had time to say hello to Jean before Jenny and Linda left, taking her with them.

'I've put your bouquet in a little water, and you can have it once you're dressed.' said Chris. 'I'll be waiting down here for you.' I thanked him, grabbing the opportunity to smell the fabulous fragrance of the fresh freesias, roses and lily of the valley.

As a nod to my wedding dress, Colin's girls, Jenny and Roz had all chosen lace outfits. Roz followed me upstairs, so elegant, and pretty as a picture in a mix of soft pink and cream florals. She unhooked my mighty petticoat from the curtain pole, standing it next to the sky-blue satin dress so that it looked like a giant cloud.

'God! You could get lost in there!'

'Luckily Colin's got a great sense of direction.'

We heard Chris call up the stairs. 'Yo's here!'

Roz turned to me 'Have you got everything you need?'

'Thanks to you I have.' There were so many other things I could have said, but I didn't trust myself not to cry, so I put my arms around her instead.

'I know how long you've waited for this, sweetheart,' Roz said. 'It's going to be the best day ever.'

Yo appeared in the doorway, beautiful in a blue-and-white polka-dot dress and they swapped pleasantries before Roz disappeared along the landing. Yo reached up to get my dress off the hanger.

'We've got about fifteen minutes, Ali.' I climbed into my huge petticoats, the small hanky Edna had given me pinned to the netting, and then she zipped me into the blue satin, carefully pulling the lace overlay on over my head. Chris had stitched the sleeve together earlier in the morning, and my arm was possibly the least swollen it had been in months – the gods were definitely smiling on me!

Having buttoned the lace up at the back for me she grinned. 'That is so you, Colin's going to love it!'

'I do hope so.'

'Ali, he'd love you if you wore a paper bag! I hope you don't need a wee tho! You'll never get *into* the loo, never mind onto the seat!'

'I'll have you know I've got my Tena Lady in

place!'

We were still laughing as June came into the room, and Yo stood aside to let her fix the small veil to my hair. It ended up being pinned to the elaborate up do on the back of my head as it flattened my fringe at the front, and we all agreed it looked a lot better there anyway. Grabbing her bag, Yo said she'd be waiting for me at the church so she could check my dress and make sure I'd not got my petticoats tucked into my knickers.

'Christ, they'll have to be big knickers to get that lot in 'em!' said June, accepting Yo's offer of a lift, and following her out of the room. I was alone.


I slipped my feet into my Jimmy Choos and looked up at my reflection in the full-length mirror. I couldn't have been happier. The dress fitted perfectly, cinched in at the waist, and billowing out from underneath the blue satin. The soft curve where my breasts used to be was intact. You'd never guess. The woman smiling back at me was someone I hadn't seen for years, and hadn't believed I'd ever see again. I knew now she'd never really gone away, I'd just lost sight of her.


Martin timed the drive perfectly, and I was relieved that there was plenty of room for my huge skirt, although it was a bit of balancing act whenever we went round a corner. I couldn't get my feet on the newly carpeted floor of the cab, so I was very glad that Chris held my hand for the entire journey, and not just to keep my balance – metaphorically it's something he's always done alongside Roz, and something for which I will always be grateful.

'Thank you for taking Dad's place today' I said as Martin negotiated one of the many speed bumps in the high street.

'Sweetheart, thank you for asking me. Your dad would be so proud of you. We're all so proud of you.'

I would have answered, if I'd have known how to answer, but I squeezed Chris's hand instead.


Martin stopped outside the church. Trying to extricate myself from the back of the taxi in a ladylike fashion was a little like getting out of a car with an open umbrella, but Yo was on hand to take my bouquet and save my dignity, and then she and I walked together out of the sunshine and into the stone porch way of the church. She pulled my petticoats straight, and smoothed the satin and lace over them.

'Are you ready?' she asked me.

I nodded. 'Yup. I'm definitely ready.'

She touched my face gently with her hand.

'You've come such a long way, Ali, and look at you now.' And of course she'd been there with me through all of it. Always watching my back, encouraging me, defending me and loving me. Through the good and bad times, whether I was right or wrong.

'I couldn't have done it without you. None of it.'

Following the reverend into the church, and holding
tightly on to Chris's arm, we successfully avoided
the raised flagstones and mastered the Tattenham
Corner curve of the aisle with ease. Everyone was
smiling. Our friends, our families; Roz beaming
from ear to ear, Mum leaning out of the pew, her
eyes bright with tears, Sam and Jack looking so
smart in their suits and my gorgeous girl Lucy, her
smile wide, holding baby Honey.

Colin, his broad shoulders obscuring my view
of the altar, turned and smiled at me; my big strong
man. 'You look beautiful, Babygirl,' he whispered. I
stood alongside him and reached for his hand.

The reverend spoke, the entire congregation sang
our first hymn with gusto, and the service began.
Jenny and Roz read beautifully, and I even managed
to get up off my knees without pitching forwards
on to my petticoats. Every word of the service
struck a chord and the reverend did a marvellous
job of involving everyone. When he pronounced us
husband and wife, the cheering and applause nearly
took the roof off! 'Till There Was You' isn't the
longest song, and so the organist played an entire
Beatles medley while we signed the register. We
knew all the songs!

My husband and I stood at the altar, and then
turned to face everyone. The sun shone through the

stained-glass window at the back of the church and created a confetti-like pattern of colours over the congregation. I felt a huge wave of happiness and gratitude looking at all those smiling faces, and an incredible sense of peace. It was as if the tide had finally turned and would carry us to an easier future. Colin looked at me in the strong steady way he always has done and we walked forwards and out into the sunshine.

# ABOUT ALISON KEENAN

Alison Keenan was born in Buckinghamshire, educated in Surrey and now lives in Berkshire. She started her career at Shell Centre on the Southbank in London; from their public affairs department she moved into book publishing, then advertising. A chance meeting led to work as a voice-over artist, then a more regular commitment, presenting a daily chat show for BBC Radio Shropshire. Alison moved into television in the '90's, working on ITV's flagship show 'This Morning' for four years as a stand-in host for Richard & Judy. Alison also worked for BBC's Watchdog Value for Money Show and The Holiday Programme, before embarking on her current career at QVC, the shopping channel.

Alison's interest in writing brought about opportunities for her to write for the BBC TV series Doctors, and to work on Channel 4's documentary Dispatches.

In 2011, Alison was diagnosed with breast cancer. Some years later she decided to write this, her first book: A New Kind of Normal. The book was inspired by the popularity of the blogs she wrote throughout her cancer treatment and those followers who supported her.

Alison is married with three children, five step-children and a granddaughter.

You can follow Alison Keenan on twitter @alikqvc, or find her on Facebook. For more information, please visit: Alison Keenan – Official Website.

Lightning Source UK Ltd.
Milton Keynes UK
UKHW012144301018
331481UK00003B/456/P